Three Dogs and a Dancer

by

Stephen Ward

Three Dogs and a Dancer by Stephen Ward

All rights reserved
Copyright, The Estate of Stephen Ward © 2014

The moral right of the author has been asserted

Stephen Ward is hereby identified as author of this
work in accordance with Section 77 of the
Copyright, Design and Patents Act 1988

Book Cover Design by Nick Buchanan © 2014
Book Cover Photograph by Chris Ward © 1994

This book is sold subject to the condition that it shall not, by way of trade or otherwise, be lent, re-sold, hired out or otherwise circulated without the author's prior consent in any form of binding or cover other than that in which it is published and without a similar condition including this condition being imposed on the subsequent purchaser

A CIP record of this book is available from the British Library

ISBN 978-1-326-04475-6

This is the First Edition of this book © 2014

This book is dedicated to:

My parents, John and Joanna Ward
for giving me the opportunity.

Min Stewart
for giving me the encouragement.

My God
for the wondrous gift .... to dance.

Three Dogs and a Dancer by Stephen Ward

About Stephen Ward

Stephen Ward was born in October 1950 at Newcastle General Hospital, and spent his childhood years with his mother, father and two brothers in the family home at Newcastle-upon-Tyne. Educated first at Wingrove Junior School and then at Rutherford Grammar School, he commenced dancing classes when he was nine years old with The Elsa Wilkinsin School of Dancing in Jesmond, Newcastle Upon Tyne. When he was twelve years old, Stephen won a Royal Academy of Dancing Scholarship that enabled him to take extra weekly ballet classes with Louise Brown in York. At sixteen years of age, he was accepted as a student at the Royal Ballet School in London, where he completed a three year professional dance course culminating in his student's performance at the Royal Opera House in Covent Garden, London.

Stephen's first professional contract was in 1970 with the Ballet Gulbenkian in Lisbon, Portugal. Continuing his career, he moved to the Royal Swedish Ballet Company, Stockholm in 1972, and again to the Cullberg Ballet Company at Stockholm in 1973. He became a principal dancer and soloist in 1975 with the Lucerne Opera Ballet Company in Switzerland, and in this role returned to the Gulbenkian Ballet Company in 1977 before going to the Ballet Rambert, London in 1979.

In 1982, Stephen founded his own 'Focus on Dance' company, a performing and educational contemporary dance company based in Bournemouth, England. He directed and danced in this company, which toured the south and south-west of England during the period 1982 - 1986. His company was disbanded in 1986, and Stephen took his dance to the streets of Europe. He has subsequently performed to street audiences in the major cities and towns of Switzerland, Germany, Austria, Holland, France and Italy.

Stephen bought an abandoned wood-store and vineyard in 1989, in the village of Fiano, ten miles north of Lucca in the Apuanian Alps, northern Tuscany. Between his street dance tours, he converted the wood-store into a modest house, grew grapes, and worked towards self-sufficiency. With cameraman, David Ball, he made a dance video ' A Street Dancer's Journey' in 1994, in which he danced on location in places of outstanding natural beauty in Switzerland and Italy. The dance video was completed and edited in Cologne, Germany in 1996.

The book 'Three Dogs and a Dancer' was written by Stephen between June 1995 and April 1996. Stephen Ward died in 2013.

Stephen and Puppy – Photograph © Chris Ward 1994

A Tribute

To a dear Brother and Friend

Stephen was a special person who contributed so much to the people he came into contact with. His life style was one of self sacrifice and dedication to his art of dancing. His love of life gave him the strength to carry his convictions until the day he died. The title of this book is significant. Stephen had a deep love of nature, animals and - especially dogs. The 'three dogs' of the title are the three dogs in the cover photograph with him: Mossy, Puppy and Hector. He adored them, as he did a later arrival, Migie.

I feel proud to have known Stephen for what he did in this life. It is such a shame that Stephen could not see the fruits of his writing talents in print. All through his life he wrote from the heart, enabling his feelings to come to light through the written word. It was his greatest wish that his book should be printed. He did try to achieve this with great effort, but I am afraid his cruel cancer took him away from us all before his life's dream could be realised. As Stephen's book is finally published, I would like to record my thanks to those who have made it possible: to Nannerl Wenger, and also to Nick Buchanan, Seán Street and John Ward for their editorial help and expertise.

I sincerely hope, you the reader, will realise what this man meant to me and to all his friends.

Chris Ward, March, 2014

Three Dogs and a Dancer by Stephen Ward

Three Dogs and a Dancer

by

Stephen Ward

Copyright: Stephen Ward
© 2004

Three Dogs and a Dancer by Stephen Ward

CONTENTS

1. The Overture, July 1995.   *13*

2. Street Dancer' Incognito, 1985 - 1995.   *21*

3. The Three Dogs.   *35*

4. The Purchase of my First Home, 1988 - 1989.   *53*

5. New Stage, New Debut, New Beginning, 1986   *63*

6. Out of the Light and into the Darkness, 1970 - 1974.   *83*

7. Out of the Darkness and into the Light. Scotland, Part 1, 1975.   *93*

8. Out of the Darkness and into the Light. Scotland, Part 2, 1975.   *125*

9. A New Partner on Tour. Switzerland 1989.   *161*

10. A Television Show in Cottbus. Winter 1990.   *177*

11. Journey from a Vineyard in Tuscany to Amsterdam and the Kelly Family. Spring 1990.   *217*

12. 'Giamboree'. My Neighbours, Chris and Karen Redsell, Summer 1990.   *251*

13. Puppy's Litter, Spring 1994.   *283*

14. An Introduction to a Journey, Summer 1994.   *333*

15. 'A Dancer's Journey,' August - September 1994.   *351*

16. A Letter. "Dear Reader ………"   *409*

17. Conclusion, or the Next Rung of the Ladder.   *419*

Three Dogs and a Dancer by Stephen Ward

Chapter 1

The Overture
July 1995

"Hector's disappeared again. He hasn't passed by here has he," I gasped to Karen, my English friend and neighbour. I was somewhat out of breath, having walked rather quickly from my house up the steep road that passes beneath the house and winds up the hill. Halfway up the hill a narrow track cuts-off and meanders to a delightful cottage set into the hillside, and quite hidden by embankments on either side until one reaches its vicinity. "I've not seen him, Stephen. How long's he been gone?" "Just a couple of hours, but you know how he is. It could turn into a couple of days and, well, he may not come back this time."

I was worried about an earlier incident in February 1995, and fearfully anticipated a sequel. While away on a three week trip to England, from my home in the foothills of the Apuanian Alps in northern Tuscany, my three dogs, Hector, Puppy and Mossy, remained behind in an enclosure on my land. Hector, who was Puppy's mate and the father of Mossy, had disappeared three days after my return. This was not unusual. In fact it was a comparatively common occurrence and, prior to January, was not cause for too much concern.

Three Dogs and a Dancer by Stephen Ward

Hector, a large sized mongrel with black and brown markings, had been rescued seven years previously from the streets of Lucca, a nearby town. I gave him a home before the dog-catchers found him and put him down as an abandoned dog, lacking any form of identification. He was a young dog of around a year old when this change in his fortunes occurred. Previously he had wandered Lucca's streets fending for himself, living off scraps lying around the dustbins and alleyways, endearing himself through his amazing charm to the various restaurant owners and cooks. Even now, at nine years of age, he had lost neither the art of independence nor the ability to attract the attention of a sympathetic crowd of people, meandering fearlessly and non-aggressively in their midst. His early introduction to life had taught him survival and this instinct never left him although, from a dog's point of view, he had lived the life of a king since the moment I discovered him.

Hector had no social hang-ups, either with people, or with other dogs and bitches. He would never instigate a fight, even in competition with other dogs over a bitch in heat. Sadly, this happy-go-lucky trait in his character, coupled with his endearing instinct, led to the second and quite dramatic change in his fortunes in January.

While I was in England, my neighbours, Karen and her Canadian husband Chris Redsell, together with Italian friends Piera and Marcello Barzanti, who owned a week-end house between my own home and the Redsell's cottage, provided the dogs with nourishment and exercise. On my return, I was told that the three dogs had spent most of the last week outside the supposedly foolproof enclosure that I had constructed prior to leaving. Hector had found a way of escape. Subsequently, it proved impossible to keep them confined, a new escape being discovered every day by either the Redsells or the Barzantis. Puppy and Mossy did not wander far from home and always returned at might. However, Hector's keen sense of smell had detected a bitch in season somewhere in my mountain village of Fiano, and had not been seen for three days.

When I arrived at La Cassetta, the name of my home, Mossy was the first to see and greet me. He was lying on the steps of the village church, just below where my house and land are situated. His raucous exuberance at my appearance immediately roused Puppy from her daytime slumber, and she rushed through the open gate of the enclosure to jump on me – twenty-five kilos of delighted, writhing animal. Both dogs then proceeded to display their pleasure in their usual rough and noisy play together. They were mother and son, with only twenty months difference in age between them. Mossy was not quite a year old.

As their activity gradually subsided I looked around and called for Hector. There was no response. Talking to Chris and Karen half an hour later, I heard Hector panting as he approached up the track to the Redsell's cottage. He had heard the greeting given me by the other two dogs. Suddenly there was Hector, no exuberant greeting, just a quiet look of trust and welcome, of calm contact. He put a paw in my hand, his chin on my bended knee, and a gave a barely audible moan - perhaps of reproach at my going away. Traits that were Hector's and his alone. Traits that endeared Hector to me when I first got to know him at the Redsell's cottage, for it was they who rescued him from his homeless plight in Lucca. He was then desperately thin, with a broken foreleg, and a tatty, filthy plaster that was more of a hindrance than a help for his leg. They had had his badly damaged leg reset by a veterinary surgeon in Lucca, paid the expensive bill and brought him back to their home in the hills. There he slowly began to walk again, albeit with a pronounced limp, and seven years later he still has this limp. His leg was susceptible to pain from any knocks and strains, but it never hindered him in the way that was to become evident in the days following my return.

Hector was given his name by the Redsell's young daughter, Emily. He lived with the Redsell family for a year after his rescue, in secure freedom on the hills around Fiano. Initially, he was in enforced confinement until the joints set in his broken leg. The injury was compound and complex, and no weight could be put on the leg for several weeks. But gradually he regained the strength in the wasted tissues around the bones, his youth and vitality helping him on a rapid path to recovery.

My first introduction to Hector was during a visit to Chris and Karen, whom I knew previously when we all lived in the South of England, prior to their moving to Italy. I was touring around Europe in a camper van, dancing on the street as a busker, having disbanded my own professional performing and educational dance group in England. After a difficult period in my life, I had ventured into Europe free and independent, without any of the normal responsibilities of children, houses or employment. The experience with my dance group; Focus On Dance, had been invaluable. It gave me the confidence that anything is possible, if one sets out to achieve it with a positive attitude despite all drawbacks and setbacks – which had been a feature of my dance group during later years.

When you build something from nothing one has to believe in oneself. You have to believe that the obstacles are there to help increase confidence in overcoming them. That the people you come into contact with, and the way you react with them, are to help one see and understand oneself all the better. The four years experience of running my own dance group taught me to have a positive attitude, not to be afraid of people, and gave me an insight into the path I wanted to travel in life.

I began to see, as many have before me that, instead of growth and success leading to truth and honesty in one's dance expression, the complexities of leading a dance group created greater stress.

Coupled with an increasingly difficult financial climate in the arts world, where grants were becoming very difficult to obtain, I found myself unable to cope. I also discovered a side of me that I grew to dislike intensely, namely allowing myself consciously to be manipulated by the people who control the purse strings. The people who offer the work and venues for work, the people who assess and decide the status of one's dance group, and ultimately the trend-setters - those that decide what the public wants to see or should be seeing.

I found that when one has a message to give that costs money, to give it, and the working project must be financed from outside, one risks having the message distorted, misinterpreted and sometimes completely changed. Dance, and the creative process of the dance, had been my passion for many years. I had all of my life danced before I even knew how to, or indeed what dance was. In my career, I had danced in theatres around the world with a number of companies. I had danced-out my emotions, everything I could not say in words I found expression through my dance. With this instinctive knowledge, I started 'Focus On Dance' and saw it grow quickly into an established and respected dance group in the south of England. The group was soon touring the south and west of England, with powerful names in industry on our list of financial sponsors, and appeared to be established with a secure future.

I was enjoying the challenge of building the dance group, and the satisfaction in seeing it grow, but I also became aware that the business side of the group was becoming increasingly complex and involved. The demands of management and creative dance were frequently in opposition. Outside influences crept in to change the direction of the dance group, which were not to my liking, however it was funding problems that resulted eventually in my disbanding the group. I came away from the experience with two things, my confidence, which was intact and much boosted, and the company vehicle - a mini-bus converted into a high-roofed camper van. With Focus On Dance I had become a prisoner, now I had freedom with the ability to travel and having insight from four years of experience with my Group. This was one thing I was certain of. Although only thirty-six years of age, I baulked at being tied-up in any situation where I was not free to dance according to my instincts. These same instincts told me to travel, to simply get on the road and find myself.

At this point a lady enters my story, who was a great influence on me in my life during this period of change. Her name is Marguerite but known by many, including myself, as Min. When I reflect on the ten years since she first introduced herself to me, Min has unconsciously been the instigator of every major step and decision that I made and which has taken me to where I am at the moment. Without Min, I doubt I would have had the courage to take my dance to the streets of Europe and see it bloom. Without Min, I would not have known Chris and Karen Redsell, to whom she introduced me in Bournemouth, and so would not have visited them in Italy.

I would become their neighbours in Italy eventually, and without them I would not have discovered the new lifestyle that has revolutionised my attitude to life. Without Min I would not know Hector. It was she that he singled out that evening in September 1988, on the steps of the Giglio Theatre in Lucca, when he hobbled up to her with his broken leg. He offered it to her as she knelt down to stroke him while others looked-on in amazement. It was her heart that he stole as he laid his chin on her knee, and looked up with his deep brown eyes and into her own, tear stained and red. As she sat there knowing that next morning, she and her husband, John, must take a flight back to England, Hector had left her and limped off into the gloom of the square in front of the theatre. Min was so deeply touched by the experience, how a mere street dog had chosen her from the other theatre-goers, had succeeded in charming her, that she knew immediately she must find him and secure a home and help for his leg - in the short time before her departure. But he was gone, his black body melting into the evening darkness, into the alleyways, dustbins, the backdoors of restaurants - a beggar with the heart and soul of a prince.

But this is just the beginning, the preface and overture to a fairytale, albeit a true one. That evening back at the Redsell's cottage, where Min and John were staying, Min was so overcome by the experience that she convinced Chris and Karen that they must, after taking them to Pisa airport the following morning, return to the area around the theatre and search for the animal. Of course, he was found. Otherwise this story would not continue - a story without an end. The true story of a simple dog, whose life had become woven intricately into the life of a performing artist. Of the adventures and situations in which both dog and man found themselves, and of the bond that tied them together, leading eventually to a family of dogs and their dancer-master.

Three Dogs and a Dancer by Stephen Ward

Chapter 2

Street Dancer Incognito
1985 - 1996

Hector was not the only animal in residence at the Redsell's abode. The menagerie included six hens, a vociferous rooster, two cats, a goat, two geese and a hive of bees. Nor was he the only dog. A year earlier the family were given a young puppy of sheep-dog origin; a bitch and full of energy. She was neutered prior to Hector's arrival, though he was obviously not aware of this initially. Ginger, as she was called, was completely black, a little smaller than Hector but very strong. They became inseparable once Hector was back on four legs again, although Ginger showed her frustration at his inability to keep up with her breath-taking speed.

Ginger was a typical bitch, a home-bird who rarely ventured outside of the Redsell's territory - which did not extend very far. Hector's influence was to change all that, and the two dogs were often found down at the lower village of Loppeglia, playing with the village children. Hector quickly became known and loved by the village folk for his gentle nature, and adored by the young boys who played with him for endless hours. However, there was concern when two sheep were found dead from a flock that normally grazed in the field above the Redsell's house. The blame was pinned on Ginger and Hector, apparently by a witness. Chris was faced with a hefty fine in compensation that put an end to dog-wanderings for a while. Hector was put on a long, permanent lead where he could exercise but not escape. Without him, Ginger had no incentive to go far. Instead, she took to stealing the eggs from the hen house until Chris coated a home-made cement egg with chilli pepper. The stealing stopped after that.

On my first visit to the Redsells, neither dog had yet arrived. On my second visit, eighteen months later, both dogs were in residence and had been for some time. I took great pleasure in going for long walks with them, through the superb sweet chestnut forests. These forests start just yards from the top of the village, and extend northwards over a vast area encompassing the Apuanian National Park - a protected area of high alpine mountains from which the famous Carrara marble is mined. By now, I had been a street dancer for two years and found that I could make a reasonably living from my performances on the streets and squares of Europe's cities. I had no regrets whatsoever about terminating the activities of Focus On Dance, which became a millstone around my neck during its final year. No one offered to take on the company, and so it went out of existence and all the valuable educational work with it.

In the meantime I had gone from one extreme to another. Choreographer, principal dancer and company director who talked to major sponsors, local politicians and the media representatives of newspapers and television. To a travelling busker incognito, who wandered from city to city as the fancy took him, sometimes remaining for weeks in the mountains or by sun-drenched Mediterranean beaches. I danced when I wanted to and did not take life too seriously. My dance was about entertaining, showing-off my performance and enjoying myself - it did not go much further than that initially.

It was very simple and uncomplicated. On the back of my camper van I welded a small extension which housed a bicycle and accessory bag, a section of vinyl dance flooring, a self-constructed bicycle trailer made out of metal water-tubing, and an old pram axle onto which attached the heavy dance floor. This odd-looking contraption, often described as a cannon by bemused passers-by, hooked onto a coupling at the rear of the bicycle. There was also a powerful, battery-operated music cassette player, a wooden collecting box for donations, a pair of ballet shoes, towels, a bottle of water, and a roll of brown parcel tape to tape the dance floor to the ground. It could not be simpler. With these few items, that have changed little over ten years, and my home on wheels, I toured the cities in Europe and enacted a good quality, visual dance show. I earned sufficient from the donations to live tolerably well, and keep my body in good physical shape. No publicity to arrange, no sponsors to hassle, no administration overheads, no venues to pre-book and pay for, no people to employ, and definitely no worries. How could it be so simple. And yet it was, and is still.

There were three factors that influenced my decision to disband my dance group and expose my dancing to an audience on the street. First, a few months before terminating Focus On Dance, I was contacted in May 1986 by the organising body of a national dance festival. They proposed that Focus on Dance participate in a week of dance activities where, throughout Britain, dance was to be promoted by performances, demonstrations and workshops - not in theatres, studios or sports halls, but in the streets, car parks, fields and beaches. In fact anywhere where the non-dance public could be exposed to the art of the dance. No profit was to be made and no financial help was offered. However, as a participant, the dance group could advertise its own activities under the auspices of this national event that, the organisers assured us, would receive national and local media coverage.

I saw this as an opportunity for publicity, participating in something original, and being involved in a national dance-promoted event. But my dancers thought otherwise and flatly refused to participate unless they were paid. As I was unable to use sponsors' money for the event, and there was no other funding, I decided to present a one-man show to represent Focus On Dance and our participation in the National Dance Week. I organised three locations in Dorset and arranged for two amateur dance groups to work with me. Together, with freely given help from the group's technician who provided the sound, we made the event into a special attraction and attracting good publicity in the local newspapers. My contribution was two choreographed solos from the group's repertoire, and three improvised solos for which I was totally unprepared. I tackled each performance with confidence, professional ability and panache, as befitted my sixteen years experience. Two of the three events attracted enormous crowds, and I thoroughly enjoyed the experience of performing before an audience who had not paid to stop and watch, but were there of their own free will. The feeling of dancing on an improvised stage, out in the open with fresh air and sunlight, was so extraordinarily satisfying that I wondered why one so rarely saw dance of any sort outside the theatre environment - at least in Britain.

The second factor arose while I was on a visit with friends to Florence in Italy, a few days after the outdoor experience of National Dance Week. The beautiful Piazza della Signoria, in which are housed the outstanding works of famous renaissance sculptors, is a place of unique inspiration. The Town Hall is of medieval origin, and overlooks the square to give it an overwhelming sense of history, art and expression – standing alone in the centre, one can feel the voices of harmonic unity speaking to the senses. In the years following this first visit, I danced many times in the square. Each time I felt the same voices saying to me that, one day soon I would use my dance to speak of it for others to share.

Extraordinarily, during one of my later dance visits, I found the entire square fenced-off and being excavated two metres below the present surface. Ruins of an early Roman site had been found, an important discovery revealing some of Florence's early foundations. Around the excavations were notices stating the intention was to record the findings, remove and preserve articles of a non-permanent nature, and then cover the remaining ruins with cement - preserving them and restoring the square to its former purpose. The work is long completed, but subsequently the City Council decided to discontinue its tolerance of street activities in the square and, indeed, throughout the city in general. The police are now very quick to put a stop to anyone contravening this new law. But, on my first visit to Florence and to this square in particular, I was quite over-awed by a wealth of street activity that I had not seen elsewhere.

The piazza was crowded with tourists from every corner of our world. Many were admiring the square's rich profusion of classical art, but many had also formed large circles – there were perhaps twenty of them throughout the square. At first I thought there was some political or other special celebration in progress, but the centre of each circle was empty apart from one or two people. Occasionally, there was spontaneous or mediocre applause from one of the circles. From some circles flowed music, from others shouting was heard, and others there was silence. On closer inspection I found that each circle was an improvised theatre, and that within each one was an artist - painter, acrobat, fire-eater, comedian, mime, musician, singer, statue - and a collecting box for donations to show appreciation. I looked at them and my mind and imagination took off. Not one dancer anywhere to be seen. No one mesmerising the public with the wonderful grace, movement and aesthetic pose that only trained dancers can deliver.

Three Dogs and a Dancer by Stephen Ward

In ten years of street dancing throughout Europe, I have only once seen another dancer outside the theatre environment. This was at Bern in Switzerland, where I saw a Flamenco dancer accompanied by a Flamenco guitarist. They were excellent, and had the undivided attention of myself and many others, who were not slow to show their appreciation. It was interesting to witness another dancer performing on the street, as it made me realise how people might react to seeing my own performance. While I do not have the monopoly on street dancing in Europe, the public's reaction to seeing me is nevertheless one of surprise initially.

For years the cities' streets have been echoing with sounds of would-be Bob Dylan and Donovan performers, to say nothing of the South American Indian music groups - some brilliant, others less than mediocre - who play the Peruvian and Bolivian folk music. I have often seen the disillusionment of excellent musicians at the non-reaction of passers-by, simply caused by too many so-called artists jumping on the bandwagon to make easy money. People become indifferent, thinking every street artist to be unemployed and their music as maudlin. "They didn't make it and had to go on the street, poor things." Often I am met with similar reactions. "Are you studying dance." "Are you too old to secure a contract."

"Times are hard in the theatre, huh." I now have set replies to these comments, although at first I took these comments seriously, wondering whether the quality of my dance warranted such reactions. Generally though, most people are astounded to see professional dance on the street, and are attracted to spend a few moments away from shop windows simply because it is novel, original and very visual.

Inevitably, I came into contact with many other street artists over the years. Anyone who is a true busker, and knows what it is to be a busker, will say their art finds true expression on the street. Most were previously employed in a professional environment, but found their art had a more expressive outlet when performing in front of passers-by with no obligation to stop, watch or listen. Many street performers make a good living playing long hours, when this is permitted by the police, because they are good, have personality and can play-off with their audience. Often their prime motivation is to make money, but usually they do not last long, burning themselves out. The 'soul' disappears from their music and their performances become work rather than expression. Others do well because they have real talent, and this comes across no matter how ignorant the public. For these street performers, the primary motivation is to express their artistic 'soul.' The donations they receive may be fewer but are invariably of a larger denomination.

Every true busker has his story. He is an inveterate traveller, rarely remaining in any one place for long, bearing his soul to everyone in his art, and meeting all manner of situations. In large industrial cities, he will find usually that he attracts others living on the street - alcoholics, beggars, drug addicts. They are frequently lonely people who find it simpler to approach a busker and engage in conversation. Later in my street dancing experiences, as the expression in my dance changed to a more profound communication, I found myself in the position of ministering to desperate people. Because of their intense and often delicate state of mind, they were in the right place mentally to understand the deeper meaning behind my dance. Being desperate and therefore lacking timidity, they would ask me to talk to them over a drink after my performance. I found myself being prudent and careful about where these encounters might lead me. But gradually I adopted the attitude that, if I were bearing my soul uncompromisingly in my performance for all to see, I must react in a positive and helpful way for those who sensed the real meaning behind my dance - and for whom a door had been opened, allowing in the light.

A busker will always have encounters with city police, usually because he is not performing in the stipulated place or at the correct time, pre-supposing that the local council has drawn up any regulations concerning street acts and artists. Or maybe his act is too loud or, as is often in my case, it occupies too much space. In most cities I have found the police to be initially polite and helpful, although not always. I understand well that part of the policeman's role is to prevent public nuisance on the street. From my own experience, I know that most street artists do not deliberately set out to be an annoyance to anyone, choosing a 'pitch' that is not an encumbrance, and changing 'pitches' regularly to avoid any prolonged disturbance to office workers or shop owners. But on rare occasions I have experienced a lack of respect and sensitivity by police in certain countries, being made to feel more like a criminal than an artist giving freely of his talents to everyone.

Buskers attract other buskers, and it is always pleasant to arrive in a town and find someone you already know performing there. Generally, there is a camaraderie between street performers and one is assured of a good laugh and a wealth of stories. Perhaps the most popular story is the 'gold mine' city where someone earned 'this much' in a day. All buskers exaggerate their income in conversation with each other, as though it was unacceptable not to be earning a small fortune, all of the time. Yet we all know hard times, when no-one wants to watch you, when the police prohibit you from performing in a place, or when it pours with rain for days and days and a good, sheltered spot for your performance seems impossible to find. When your guitar is stolen and you do not have the money to replace it. Or, in my case, when a dance floor is removed from where I left it for a short while, having to be retrieved three days later from the local rubbish dump.

No two days are the same. Each day is unique and, in essence, this is one of the main attractions of street performing. Initially, every busker goes through a great deal, psychologically, in gaining the courage to take his act to the street. He is usually a person who thrives on adventure and adapting to situations, who needs the challenge of controlling his own destiny, and being independent of any system that seeks to strangle him with security.

Having successfully experienced being a street performer, he finds difficulty in returning to a normal existence, with its nine-to-five job, mortgage and 'responsibilities.' He finds he no longer fits into this pattern of life, and yearns for the freedom, the road ahead and the 'show.' In my own life over the past ten years, I have contrived to avoid 'normality' concluding that what is normal is only relevant to the individual, since we are all different. By asking that each person in our society conform to a norm, because it enables the society itself to run more smoothly, we contribute nothing to the evolution of our human species - or to its life alongside the other forms of life that inhabit our planet.

Most people appear quite content with their existence, and do not search beyond the limits of their five senses. But a few seek something they have difficulty in defining or explaining. It pulls at them until they either erase it from their lives, risking frustration to themselves and those around them, or look deeper within themselves. In so doing, they discover the inaudible voice that puts them on the road to a different life, a path leading to fulfillment and greater wisdom, which discovers joy and never-ending creation and inspiration. I believe that when you discover this new direction, you never look back. Suddenly, all the doors are open, and you become amazed at situations put before you that encourage and stimulate you to the next level - the next chapter in your experience. This is my story since I took my life in both hands, and plunged head first into my controversial way of life.

On returning to England from Florence, I was not at peace with myself. In my mind I saw the image of the Piazza della Signoria, with myself in its centre. Nor could I forget the wonderful feeling of dancing spontaneously in the open air at Bournemouth, during National Dance Week, with only a dance floor rolled out on the flat, cemented surface. Whatever the future held for me, I arrived swiftly at the conclusion that Focus On Dance was not part of it, and that I must regretfully let it go. Yes, I was frustrated and angry that four years of richly creative work were to be discarded arbitrarily, through my inability to convince local authorities to fund a project of such immense value to young people in our dance-educational programme. But I was also conscious I had given the project everything that I had to give. That it had become a means to an end and not the end in itself, and as an individual it was time for me to move on. I knew not to what. But, with my decision made, I neither wanted to look back or did so. My decision most decidedly proved to be the right one.

The third influence behind street dancing becoming an alternative means of my making a living, was Min, the rescuer of Hector - the dog who in later years was to become mine, or perhaps more correctly, I was to become his. My first visit to Italy was made in the company of Min and her husband John, and we stayed at the

Redsell's cottage - Chris, Karen and their daughter, Emily, were not to occupy the cottage permanently for another year. At that time, Hector had not entered the story and perhaps had not been born. While staying at the cottage, we made the acquaintance of a unique couple who were friends of Chris and Karen, Maria Gloria and Carlos Grippo. Chris had originally met Maria Gloria when she worked in the Regional Council offices at Pescaglia (Southern Apuanian mountain area) where both she and her husband also lived.

Their friendship was made some years earlier when Chris and Karen, married only a year and previously living in Rome, had come to this part of northern Tuscany one summer and fell in love with the area. They found an old sheep barn for sale with about a quarter of an acre of land and, not being Italian, were enquiring at the Council offices for permission to reside in the area, among other things. Maria Gloria responded to their enquiries in a very helpful and understanding manner, a trait not always evident in people who live in isolated areas, when dealing with foreigners. But although Maria Gloria was born in Italy of Italian parents, she had lived most of her life in Argentina where she met and married her husband, Carlos of Uruguayan origin and an artist by profession. Maria Gloria returned with Carlos to her own country, but with an attitude and mentality stemming from much broader origins, which is immediately perceptible when conversing with her.

During the first months that Chris and Karen were working to convert their barn into a home, with their first child on its way a friendship developed with the Grippos, rapidly developing into a close bond as both couples found themselves strangers within their own, respective social environments. The Redsells found that Carlos was not only a very talented painter, but that he also possessed an original sense of humour, which I too had pleasure in later discovering. It was therefore natural that a friendship emerged between people who were refined, and shared such a sensitive and artistic temperament. Min, John and I had been 'briefed' in England prior to out departure for Italy, that Maria Gloria and Carlos would call during our stay so as to be of service, should we require it. We found them to be every bit as warm and hospitable as we had been lead to believe. Within a short time of our meeting, we were invited to dinner in their tiny house spread over four floors in the heart of Pescaglia, which like many mountain villages is built on a steep gradient. It was a memorable evening during which we were also showed some of Carlos' paintings.

Later, in October of that year, I set off from England to experiment with street dancing on the continent. The camper van having been transferred to my name from Focus On Dance, with all its modifications, I set myself a time limit of six weeks, by which time it would be too cold in northern Europe to continue dancing outside. By that time, however, I would know whether I should start to look for work, or continue with my new concept.

Shortly before this, Karen left England for Italy with Emily who was now four years old. She was accompanied by Andrew, a good friend of the family, who was scheduled to finish the building work on the nearly completed five room cottage. The intention was that Karen and Emily should precede Chris, who was still under contract as co-leader of the viola section of the Bournemouth Symphony Orchestra, in an experimental return to live permanently in Italy. Emily would begin pre-school education on arrival in September, and Chris would join them for Christmas together with members of Karen's family. At that point they would assess if the move to Italy was feasible for the longer term. Min offered to join Karen and Andrew in October, stay until Christmas, and give moral support. John would travel out with Chris in December, to join his wife and stay for Christmas.

I was not part of this plan, having decided of my own accord to become a wayfarer - a dancer without direction, a rebel without responsibilities. However, I did agree to take Min as far as Lausanne on Lac Leman in Switzerland. There she would first visit friends before travelling by train to Lucca, whereupon Karen would meet and bring her to the cottage that was now named 'Croce.' Prior to these arrangements, we became aware that Maria Gloria and Carlos would also be near Lausanne in October, so our travel plans were coordinated to allow us to visit them while they were there. Carlos was exhibiting a collection of his work at an exclusive private gallery for modern art, in a village thirty miles north of Lausanne. He and Gloria would be there at the end of the exhibition, to meet the purchasers of his paintings and pack up the remainder of exhibition for return to Italy.

My agreement to take Min to Lausanne had one important proviso, which she readily accepted. This was that she would help me, with moral support, in making the transition from professional dancer, choreographer and director, to street artist, busker, and free entertainer. It was no mean feat, as I was soon to find out.

Three Dogs and a Dancer by Stephen Ward

Chapter 3

The Three Dogs

My planned sojourn in England for three weeks in January 1995 would have been shorter, but I thought that I had secured a good dog-minder for the period. However, my initial plan went wrong when, three days before my departure, I received a letter bearing disappointing news. The fellow busker who was coming to La Casetta (my new home in Italy) to stay with the dogs while I was away, wrote to say he regretted he was now unable to come as intended. A major disagreement with his wife precluded his bringing her, his two children and their dog to Italy at that time. He begged forgiveness and stated that he would try to bring them in the Spring.

I had gone to England the previous year, partly to visit my family, and partly to discuss the feasibility of making a professional video film of my dance. On that occasion I was away for only eight days, thinking it unwise to leave Hector and Puppy for any longer in the enclosure I made for them below my house, where my old caravan was permanently parked. Notwithstanding the fact that they lived very comfortably in both the caravan and the enclosure outside, Hector would always attempt to escape during my absence in his desire for freedom. Arrangements for their feeding and exercising were made with Chris and Karen Pedsell, and with Piera and

Marcello Barzanti, prior to my departure. However, on my return, I was told that Hector was never around when they visited the dogs, as each day he always found some means of escaping from the enclosure.

I was keen to avoid a similar situation this year, knowing that I would not be at peace while I was away. Therefore, during an earlier surprise visit from my friend, Gary, I secured a promise that he would return in January with either his family or alone. I was pleased and relieved to plan an extended three week visit to England, based on this agreement. Now, at very short notice, I was forced into adopting the same strategy as last year, but for a longer period. After explaining the change in plan to my friends and neighbours, I found them ready to repeat the favours of last year. But a proviso was introduced, and this was that I reinforce the enclosure to prevent any escape by the troupe of dogs, now augmented by the recent arrival of Mossy. This I did, double-checking every corner of the outer barrier for stability, and every space for a potential hole through which a large dog might be able to squeeze. Finally, convinced that I had made the enclosure dog-proof, I departed for England with encouragement from my dog-minders that all would be well and I should concentrate on the next three weeks of my busy schedule

On my return, I was enormously relieved to find Hector, Puppy and Mossy all well and seemingly none the worse for their three week separation from me. My concern convinced me of their increasing importance in my life and lifestyle. This importance extended beyond the times when I was at La Casetta, to the many street-dancing tours when each of us became a member of a team, and respected each others roles within the team. For instance, my new camper van had smaller proportions than the original, and everyone had their own space for travelling or sleeping. It was important for each of us not to abuse these silent understandings if friction was to be avoided. The three dogs also knew instinctively whether my departure from the vehicle would include them. On the occasions when they were to be excluded, there would be a 'huffed' silence as they sensed they were to be left in confinement, sometimes for long periods. Six brown eyes would look up at me, from heads laid on the floor, as though to say, "We know, you don't need to tell us."

In the days following my return from England, however, Hector underwent a crisis that caused him great physical distress, and mental agony for myself. It also threatened to jeapardise our system of co-habitation at home and abroad. For three days all was very well as we gradually returned to our normal routine. Puppy would always be the first to announce the arrival of the dawn as, at the first stirrings from my bed, she would gently push her muzzle into my neck. If I didn't react to this with a warm hand reaching out to caress her, she would return to the covered settee, where the other two dogs had not yet woken and wait until my next stirrings. On the other hand, if I announced that I was also awake, then the nuzzlings were no longer gentle but gleefully frantic. Her forepaws would ascend to the height of my pillow, while her bushy, blonde tail battered the legs of the table at the side of the bed. On hearing this commotion, Mossy would yawn, stretch his fore-legs and rear-legs, and then leap from the settee to the bed barely touching on the floor - a jump of three metres. Inevitably he alighted on that part of me which is the most sensitive, causing me to scream in anguish, and complain at my rude awakening. He and Puppy would then play boisterous games on my narrow single bed until stopped, while I allowed myself to wake-up in the more civilised fashion befitting a human being and artist.

Hector, having always been aloof from Puppy and now from Mossy too, accepted their games with mature disdain, much as a long-suffering father looked on the antics of a younger son. He was always a loner, which is perhaps why I took to him so much, since I am of a similar character. He was always separate from the other two dogs, preferring the company of humans, and the only time I saw him react intimately with the dogs was when Puppy came into her second season at the age of eighteen months. Then, for five days and five nights, they were very definitely together. In fact, they were literally quite inseparable for most of the time. In my human and emotional way, I believed this to be a show of affection as Hector was very gentle with Puppy, and her response was one of acceptance and willingness. However, when the euphoria was over and Puppy's enticement receded, Hector became aloof once more. He appeared to tolerate begrudgingly the co-habitation with his mate, never showing her any aggressiveness, but neither desiring her company particularly.

When Puppy's eight puppies arrived, three months after her five day honeymoon with Hector, his behaviour surprised me whenever he came anywhere near his offspring. Hector was probably eight years old yet he reacted like a dog out of control, dancing on his paws to avoid the puppies, and making tremendous leaps to escape from them. He refused absolutely to be in the same space as them that, at the time, happened to be the caravan. I asked myself whether this behaviour was due to Puppy's warning growls as he wandered inadvertently into their vicinity, or was it from terror of eight rodent-like creatures that had suddenly invaded his territory. Certainly his first response to Puppy, when I brought her home at five weeks old, was cool if not ice-cold. However, it was not as bizarre as this comical and frustrating behaviour. But it was definitely a cause for concern, considering the overcrowding we would experience shortly as the puppies, their mother, father, and myself left in the camper van for a busking tour of Switzerland and Germany. While on tour, seven of the seven weeks old puppies would be found homes – as told later in my story.

Hector's first movements of a morning, would therefore be towards the door rather than towards my bed, knowing that after master had eventually roused himself, had a cup of tea, done his toiletry and generally got himself together, then a gambol through the chestnut forest above the house was on the cards. On very rare occasions, a walk down through the village of Fiano might take place – this route used to be our regular circuit before the arrival of Puppy or Mossy at La Cassetta. Now though, it is a route not often taken due to the many hazards which experience had taught me to avoid. One practically never sees dogs in the streets and steep alley-ways of Fiano, simply because the dogs that inhabit this area are tethered guard dogs who never get to investigate any territory beyond their two metre chains which form an extension of themselves. Or they are hunting dogs, in which imprisonment in huts and sheds with little light or space is their lot. One hears these animals constantly and sorrowfully at night, when their vociferous pleas fall, for the most part, on deaf ears. One never sees them between the months of February and September when they are shut away from all their instinctive activities - an all-male contingent waiting for winter and the hunt.

Inevitably the local people have grown up without the canine contact that we favour so particularly in England. It is therefore perhaps not surprising that the older faction of the village community should unite in their fear when the two younger of my three dogs exuberantly rush in and out of the entrances and premises that comprise the village. My shouts and explanations that the dogs are not wild, dangerous or aggressive, but merely high-spirited, go unheard as I am accused of a crime worthy of punishment, and told that I must lock away my dogs, as many of theirs are, or at least hold them on leads, be-muzzled. I have therefore learnt that to have a peaceful existence in Fiano, it is important to try and prevent my dogs from coming into contact with the village population. In the forest I rarely meet anyone, and never any other dogs. So when we depart from my land onto the tiny road that leads from the church, past my house, to the village cemetery, and then on as a track into the forest, we inevitably follow it. That is to say Puppy, Mossy and myself turn initially in this direction. However, Hector without fail, always dashes from the gate and down the road towards the church, in the never-ending hope that we will all follow him. Alas, it is now only very occasionally that I take my dogs that way now, and never unleashed.

When Hector first came to live with me I never concerned myself with where he was. He was allowed to have a free spirit such as my own. For most of the time he honoured me with his presence, not allowing me out of his sight, always by my side in work and in leisure. He was emotionally indemonstrable as an animal, in contrast to his two later co-inhabitants, but he had a very individual and, at times, quite spiritual quality of amicability - with his paw in my hand, and head on my knee. With such a gentle nature, when he did wander from the confines of my land, which was unfenced, it was not cause for any worry although I would feel concern when his subtle disappearance extended overnight. Initially this could be quite often, but in latter years was less so. Never did I receive complaints over his behaviour from the local people, and indeed the children from the lower village of Loppeglia, where he could often be found in the Piazza, had really taken to him. Twice I received requests to collect him from outside of houses where a bitch on heat could be found.

Depending on the season of the year and the particular weather of that moment, most of the day for the dogs would be spent in inactivity. They were mainly inside the house during mid-summer, mid-winter or during wet spells, and outside at less extreme times of the year. Each had their preferred places to lie and only rarely would they be found altogether. Because of the generation gap between Hector and Mossy (some eight years), there was little or no desire on Hector's behalf to accompany the latter in his boisterous games, however enticing Mossy made them appear.

Puppy, however, was always keen to join in his playful nonsense, though most of the time she preferred to bring me a stick or a pine cone to throw for her prompt retrieval. She has endless patience to wait and acutely observe, until I made a move for whatever she had brought. At that instant she pounced on her possession with a speed that inevitably secures the object between her jaws long before my dexterous fingers even approached its vicinity. If I then hurl the object for her repeated collection, I must first prise it from her teeth, and she possesses the remarkable ability to avoid my grasp with her head. Eventually, more often than not, I will absent myself from this game in exasperated frustration, muttering that should she wish to include me then she must willingly drop the object and withdraw to a distance where it will be safe for me to pick it up without fear of collision. This, on occasions, she would do, though not because I asked her. During her puppyhood her preferred objects of play were always stones which I, in my ignorance, allowed until I discovered one of her canine teeth to be chipped. Since then I have discouraged stones in favour of sticks or cones and the education is slowly bearing fruit.

Mossy is naturally strongly influenced in his activity by his mother, although his passion in similar instinctive pastimes is considerably less. His great pleasure would seem to lie in energetic play with Puppy that very rapidly can build to a crescendo. One is absolutely convinced that they must be tearing each other's eyes out. Just how their teeth and skulls manage to avoid the more susceptible parts in each other's anatomy, particularly around their heads, is a mystery to me although I must say that both the audio and visual performances are very entertaining. Mossy has, in vain, attempted to enact this game with Hector. The latter's reaction to these efforts is to ignore his offspring, avoiding his playful tactics equally expertly until such a point is arrived at where his irritation overcomes his patience and a gentle, guttural growl is issued as a warning. If this warning goes unheeded (which is rarely the case now, for Mossy is rapidly learning from experience) and the potentially delicate situation is exacerbated, then it might well result in a harmless, un-aggressive snap with accompanying sound effects - at which Mossy turns, once again, his attention to Puppy.

Hector has not always been so unconcerned with playful antics, as has been earlier described during his sojourn with Ginger and the Redsells. His games as a young dog were, however, restricted by his damaged leg that, I believe, has always given him pain although one would never conclude this from his behaviour. During the three years before his mate arrived on the scene, and he and I were inseparable buddies, his main passion in play-life was a good game of 'hide and seek'. He changed the standard rules a little to suit his abilities, but in essence the object was the same. During our walks together, normally in the woodland where he was free and left to his own devices, he would remain but a short time by my side, preferring the scents and sounds that are part of forest life. I had little fear that he would ever catch any wild animal, the scent of which he may discover and follow, for his foreleg prevented him from obtaining the running speed that another dog of the same build might achieve. Though at times, when his intent was strong enough, he could surprise me with his energy.

His rule then to this game of 'hide and seek' would be to wander off, seeming engrossed in his own pleasures, giving me the opportunity to abscond from the main forest track. Sometimes he would be out of my sight for a few minutes, but sometimes for an hour or more, so I never knew how long I had to 'hide.' I was as equally motivated in this game as Hector. However, I was well aware that his power of smell as well as his speed at running were assets that could at any moment, bring that particular phase of our game to a close. The advantage that I had over him was that I could hear both his bull-like thundering through the forest bed undergrowth, and his very heavy hoarse panting as he drew near, following accurately the traces of scent that I had left behind me.

Once I heard him, I knew that the game was either immediately up if no deceptive maneuver could be made, or even if it could, then Hector would not be fooled for long. Adrenaline flowing, I would urgently seek for streams that I could follow to throw his scent, or large moraine rocks that I could climb and hide among where access for dogs was difficult, or holes into which I could scramble but which in fact would delay the conclusion only for a few moments. I would make massive leaps over dykes, backtrack and change direction perhaps twenty times in each round of our game. The inevitable conclusion was always a wonderfully joyful moment when man and dog would roll about among the twigs and leaves in abandoned activity: man trying to grab dog, and dog leaping about in all directions to avoid the grasp, and yet playfully attempting his own grasping with his strong jaws.

Only once was the conclusion not quite as expected, or as anticipated, and this was due entirely to my unwitting attempts to throw Hector off my scent. I was at that time a guest teaching at a dance academy in Neuchatel, in the French-speaking part of Switzerland, and staying with the director of the Academy, Marcel Veillard, a friend and colleague from former years. As my daily teaching commitments did not begin until early afternoon, my mornings were unalterably spent with Hector in the beautiful beech forests that line the hills above the town. As usual, Hector had kindly given me the time and space to disappear deeply into the obscurity of this wonderful natural hiding place, before deciding that time was up and he must actively seek me out. I had adopted the usual tactics of expertly finding ways to throw him off the scent.

Unfortunately though, and little realizing the consequences, during my wanderings I made a large circle through the woods and arrived back close to the point where we had earlier entered the forest together. Here was an enormous morainic rock that I had used in our game earlier in the week. I knew that I could climb up and be completely hidden from Hector who would discover my scent but be unable to follow. I had only been there for some ten minutes before, as expected, I heard Hector's bulldozer sounds as he came tearing past the rock. The problem was that he didn't stop, but disappeared shortly afterwards into the maize of trees beyond me. After a moment when all trace of his rushed passage was gone, I reflected from the top of my fortress; either he had picked up the scent of another animal and would be gone for some time, or in a moment he would realise his mistake and backtrack to find me - whereupon I would descend to open ground and meet him.

I waited. Half an hour passed and I began to be a little concerned that shortly I should be heading back to the town to commence my afternoon teaching, which would extend late into the evening. I left my viewpoint and followed the direction that Hector had taken, calling all the while and wondering what would be my best course of action should Hector fail to appear before I must descended into the town. I retraced the steps I had taken earlier while playing our game, meeting en route other dogs and dog-owners who had no recollection of seeing a black dog on his own in the forest. Eventually, by this time quite worried, and thinking that it would be eight hours before I was free to return and look for him, by which time it would be well into night, I descended unwillingly to the house where I was staying to prepare for my afternoon teaching.

On opening the front door to me, not only Marcel but also Hector greeted me, the latter quite exuberant in his joy at finding the wanderer returned, like a prodigal son. The tide had really been turned on me this time, as Hector had already been back over an hour having apparently followed my scent, after passing the rock, on to the previous scent from our earlier entry into the forest. This, of course, had led him right back to the house, our original point of departure. I reproached myself for my previous unkind thoughts towards him back in the woods. He clearly would have felt it undeserved should I have scolded him, as was my initial intention, no doubt feeling strongly that he had played the game according to the rules.

These were magic moments that will remain with me always. Other games with the two newcomers, and just as equally entertaining, have taken their place. It is impossible to play 'hide and seek' with Puppy as she never lets me out of her sight and, in the light of what happened to Hector after my return from England in the January of 1995, I will not allow Mossy to wander far from home, or from myself and the camper van when we are away on tour. Meal times for the dogs used to be provided in the late evening after our final walk at dusk. I changed this later for two reasons, the first being the addition of Mossy to the family who, as a young puppy, was understandably unable to pass the nighttime without needing to defecate. I found that by feeding Mossy early in the morning following our first walk, he was more likely to get rid of his waste matter during the day, outside of the house, or more particularly during the evening's outing. The second reason was that the two male dogs also had less incentive to disappear suddenly during our morning walk, when they were fresh, active and energetic, if they knew that feeding was to follow immediately upon our return. In the evening it appeared easier to control their urge to wander; with a strong voice and a quick eye.

Of course, during my recent absence while in England, such attempts at discipline would seem to have been useless. A way of escape had been found, undoubtedly by Hector, from out of my dog-proof enclosure. Reports from my frustrated dog-minders, as well as those from the four wood-cutters operating a local concern below my house, were as follows:

In the first week of my absence all three dogs had remained unhappily in the enclosure.

In the second week all three dogs had remained with the woodcutters during the day, and returned to the enclosure at night - the gate having been left open by Chris to allow their entry as attempts to maintain their imprisonment proved useless.

In the third week Puppy and Mossy spent the day with the woodcutters, Hector opting for total freedom and only periodically making an appearance.

It was clear in the investigations that were undertaken on his behalf, the week after my return, that Hector had found something worthy of missing a meal or two, distracting his attention, and enticing him away from home territory. For what had happened during that following week would appear to have taken place some distance from La Casetta, and possibly even from Fiano. My conclusion, with practically a total lack of evidence, was that he had picked up the scent during that third week of a bitch in heat and may even have had access to her later when, shortly after our reunion, he disappeared for three days.

Initially I took umbrage that Hector, only seventy-two hours after my return, should decide that my company was not required. Perhaps he was justified in going away considering the length of time that I had abandoned him. In the traumatic days that followed, I could not help feeling that had I not left the dogs for three weeks, the situation that was about to present itself could have been avoided. After twenty four hours had elapsed, I came to the conclusion that his disappearance was the result of a secret 'amour' tucked away somewhere, that he had met or at least scented during that final fated week before I returned. Previous occurrences of a similar nature had always concluded well; he had always returned eventually, or been discovered still intact and in one piece before being extracted from the situation. This time was to prove the exception.

Forty-eight hours later I was beginning, clairvoyantly, to sense doom. At that time I was extremely busy and pre-occupied with work about my land that had been considerably delayed due to my recent absence. Towards the end of Hector's third day of disappearance, I instinctively dropped everything, and became determined to seek him out. I would call at his usual haunts, including houses where he had been found before, where he would create a vociferous nuisance from the other side of the fence with an odorous bitch. I was determined to question everyone I found in the village to discover his recent movements, but I did not even get beyond my own front gate.

Although Hector was only a dog for the majority of people, when any human lives in close intimacy with other animals, and particularly when that person finds that he or she can relate instinctively much better to animals than other humans, (which is not rare), then something special happens. Something that people who have not found themselves in that situation have difficulty in comprehending. A mutual respect occurs, beyond our understanding of normal methods of communication, an ability from the human angle to consider such animals as equals, as friends, as entities from whom one can equally learn as well as teach. The God-given gift of compassion, which in essence defies analysis, and which in our world of ego and stress to succeed is ever being thrust aside, I believe is not only particular to humans. I have often sensed such a feeling in my dogs when I have needed tenderness during a moment of stretched emotions.

As the law stands in Italy, all domestic dogs including hunting and guard dogs, must have an identification number tattooed somewhere on the surface skin of their bodies. Hector possesses such a number, as does Mossy and Puppy. Therefore, should a dog stray from its home for any length of time, or become a nuisance to other people through no fault of its own, a simple call to the local police can solve the problem harmlessly in a matter of hours. If blame is warranted, then it can be assigned to the owner. However, should a dog not possess an identification number, it may be put down immediately. Hector was not only suitably tattooed, but he also wore a very prominent collar attached to which was a metal address and name-plate. He was therefore immediately identifiable as a pet, and not a stray or vicious animal.

One may be able to communicate on certain levels with animals, and I believe this is done through mental imagery and sensation, but unless we can perhaps tune into the different frequency on which animals may operate, we cannot get from them what we as humans base ninety percent of our communication on, namely facts, events and situations. Not often do our conversations with each other extend beyond these three readily accessible subjects. We do think very often far beyond these on the-surface topics to more spiritual matters such as feelings, sensations and revelations. These equally communicative topics mostly manifest themselves to us through mental imagery and it is not everyone who seeks to explain their meaning or from whence they came, much less talk about them with anyone other than the most intimate of friends or family.

In the hours following my arrival at the front gate in search of Hector, I was exposed to and confronted with such a multitude of contrasting feelings. I felt bombarded from all angles with emotions, with accusations, with challenges, and with solutions. Within myself, I was in turmoil as I demanded facts, and needed to know the events and the situations surrounding the last sixty hours of Hector's activities. I spent endless time trying mentally to communicate with him, to force my mind into his, to get a mental picture of where he had been, and how he had been able to return to La Casetta in the condition in which I discovered him lying in a heap outside my front gate. Eventually, as the turmoil subsided, I stopped allowing my mind to be filled with pointless accusations, with suppositions, and with solutions to what seemed a new problem. I searched deeper and was left with the peace that acceptance brings. I felt that I understood better the meaning of compassion, and turned my thoughts towards Hector and away from myself and the angry pain I was suffering. Then I gave way to myself and cried, and knew instinctively that this emotion was compassion, and that my crying was the true result of a lesson that I had been confronted with and that I had learnt.

During my life I have been challenged, as I believe everyone is, with certain situations - many of which were wonderfully joyful. At the same time, I have experienced the sadder, sometimes traumatic occasions, but each one equally poignant and worthy of deep thought, that have helped me onto a more profound level of understanding and a more sincere communication with myself, and therefore with others. Some of these situations will unfold in this account. This present series of events was one such situation, and it not only affected my approach to life but had quite an astounding effect on my dancing, which found a new richness due to my better understanding of what constitutes compassion.

The veterinary surgeon at Lucca, to whom I had rushed once, I had discovered that the wounds around the face and neck of Hector, together with the dried, matted, blood-stained hair over most of his body, more serious than anything I had seen on him due to a scrap or a fall so I was immediately very concerned. Normally Paulo Faldini, a younger man than myself, would have a joke and a laugh with me while practicing his broken, heavily accented English on the several occasions during the year when I needed to present my dogs for their various annual vaccinations. Being a busker and international traveller with three dogs, necessitated not only a passport for me, but also required for each of them a valid proof of inoculation, particularly against rabies, that needed to be verified by border police between countries. Rarely did I need to occupy Paolo's time for any other reason. My dogs were healthy, happy, well fed and well exercised.

On arriving at the surgery I was relieved to find the waiting room empty. Normally, no matter what time of day or evening I would arrive, I would inevitably have had to wait at least an hour before being able to enter the surgery itself. During the half hour drive, normally forty five minutes for me in my van, down the hazardous, narrow and winding Italian mountain road from my house in Fiano to the village of San Martino in the valley below, and then onto the faster main road to Lucca, my mind sympathetically and instinctively switched-off to everything except the road ahead, and to Paolo's waiting room. I was profoundly praying for an empty road and an empty surgery. All other thought was already obsolete, having been discarded the moment I turned the ignition key to my van. Hector, when I had discovered his limp body in the grass opposite the entrance to my home, had not responded to my call. My initial relief at seeing him had caused me to scoff myself for my supposed psychic feelings of concern. When a harsh shout at him still produced no reaction, I approached him and, with immediate horror, saw his distorted face, swollen lips, ears full of strange lumps, and tightly closed eyes oozing dark blood. Closer observance found two large wounds on his chest, around the shoulders. The blood was dry, the hair thickly matted, and must have happened not the day before, but the day he had disappeared some sixty hours ago.

My shock at his condition was yet to reach a further stage when, on lifting him to his feet and encouraging him on his extremely unsteady legs to go in through the gate, he appeared to have no sense of direction. I called him a final time, whereupon his face suddenly turned towards me, eyes staring wide-open, and swimming in blood. "He doesn't see me, he does not see me" I remember shouting at an invisible entity, my own eyes filling, not with blood, but with tears. "Hector, lovely Hector, what on earth has happened to you"

Three Dogs and a Dancer by Stephen Ward

Chapter 4

The Purchase of my First Home

1988 - 1989

The discovery that Hector was totally blind, following the diagnosis and explanation of his condition by Paolo Faldini, the veterinary surgeon, brought with it a state of partial shock in me. Paolo's immediate investigation of the wounds around the chest area disclosed pitted skin with innumerable tiny dry scabs from which, earlier, blood had obviously flowed. The eyes were so tightly closed that scrutiny seemed impossible. Although in removing the dog from the diagnostic table and setting him on his weak legs, and my calling to him causing him to open them, Paulo was quickly able to assess their condition. He stated simply and clearly that in his opinion the left eye was beyond redemption. It had already become opaque through the internal bleeding. Paulo said that it would be impossible to know the condition of the right eye, which was totally red, until the blood had cleared away naturally.

Hector had been shot twice at close range, with a lead shot pistol. That first consultation was brief and to the point. Medication was administered and prescribed. The questions came later, at a second consultation after few days, when I was in better control of my emotions. The journey home to La Casetta that dark, cold evening, the first in February, with my friend and companion lying motionless on the floor of the van, was but a blur. I could hardly see through the windscreen, though the night was dry, so fast and relentless were my falling tears. It seemed then to me that the wonderful magic which had surrounded La Casetta, my unique home, and which I had proudly claimed as my own the moment I had bought the property six years ago, must now surely cease to be. I could not, at that moment, nor in the days that followed, envisage continuing with my lifestyle, idyllic as it had become to me, with the same enthusiasm and verve that I had maintained up to that time.

Perhaps this crisis would not appear, in the eyes of many, to be very profound or challenging. And yet, as I helped Hector out of the van, through the gate and up the twelve stone steps to the entrance of my home, watching him stumble into everything, confused and totally dependent, I thought if his sight never recovered I would always be reminded of this awful incident. I would forever be comparing the 'befores' and 'afters', and be deeply saddened, remembering constantly the romps, the games of Hide-and-Seek, and the chases through the fields and forests. My heart really went out to him as I could not help but see myself in a similar predicament.

For many years now I had enjoyed and appreciated the enriching sense of freedom in my life. Most people would perhaps tend to conclude that I had also shunned responsibility, which was not altogether true. However, there are certain responsibilities that people seem to take on automatically, such as mortgages, loans for unnecessary luxuries, and also the problems of certain other people who are very content to pass them on, and of which I have tended to stay clear considering them chains around the neck. My life so far had been a challengingly simple one, and the lack of complications had left me free to store up knowledge from my own experiences. In deciding to take on a dog, and then eventually three dogs, my desire to allow them a free life was really an extension of my own desires and beliefs. I certainly had the perfect lifestyle, both at La Casetta and 'out on the road' which allowed them this freedom and, bar the occasional dilemma, had seen them revel in the type of activities and antics that only freedom in a natural and suitable environment would release. In observing their instinctive play, and particularly in Mossy and Puppy, I too reveled in the fun and, in my contentment, I pronounced my life at La Casetta to be complete.

It was against this background that I wondered whether life would be diminished by both Hector's physical handicap, and my own new mental handicap in trying to come to terms with the fact that he had been shot, seemingly deliberately and with intent perhaps to kill. Who but me could know how much I valued my companion. Who but me would search his inner soul to seek to know why this had happened. Hector had had such an enormous part to play in developing my initial enthusiasm with La Casetta. Together we had made a massive move into a new life. He had just as rapidly made the four stone walls and roof of my home, his home, and when those stone walls eventually developed into a tiny, one room dwelling, he moved into his palace and knew that that was where he belonged - despite the necessity to wander from time to time.

La Casetta was acquired by me in November 1989 for the sum of Italian Lire 22,000,000, which then had the value of £10,000. The building comprised four stonewalls, one of which was built into the side of a hill. The walls and terra cotta tiled roof were in very good condition, considering that the building had never been inhabited during the sixty odd years of its history. There were two tiny rooms on two levels, each room measuring four by four metres. The lower room, whose foundations were built on rock, had an earth floor, one very small window, and a large door that was by the side of the main entrance to the property from the road.

Access to the upper floor was not via the lower room but up twelve stone steps built into the side of the hill, at the base of which stood the building. These steps led to a two metre-wide space at the back of the house at the first floor level. A breeze-block retaining wall separated the continuing hillside from this space, which also led to the entrance of the upper room at the rear of the house. From inside this room, which had a terra cotta tiled floor built on chestnut wood beams, one had the choice of two splendid views from two windows. One view was towards the south east, through the leaves of a large chestnut tree on the opposite side of the tiny road at the base of the house, and beyond to acacia forest and olive groves. No other dwelling came into sight through this window. The other window faced south west towards the full expanse of this beautiful valley, at the top of which the village of Fiano lies, drawing the eye further on to the distant forested hills and open sky. Looking down through the valley, one saw the red roofs of the quaint mediaeval village of Loppeglia, just below Fiano.

That first panoramic view, one morning in late October 1988, from this room which stored fifty bales of hay and evidenced the presence of rats, was breathtaking to say the least. I cast my eyes around the space as Chris Redsell and Bruno, the proprietor from Loppeglia, chatted in Italian - of which at that time I had no knowledge. Apart from the hay, a few archaic and simple farm utensils, and copious rat droppings, there was nothing in the room. The three enormous chestnut beams holding the roof structure showed little evidence of worm or deterioration. The limestone mortar haphazardly cast against the stonewalling had an appealingly warm look. The large and simple wooden door, with an enormous lock and bolt, beckoned me through to an inner door within myself. In my own eyes I had already moved in and settled, something that I never imagined would be applicable to me. Within my heart I felt that this tiny barn and quarter of an acre of attached hillside had been reserved just for me. That, for the first time in my life, and at the age of nearly forty, I was being given the gift of my own first home.

Hector and Ginger, both at this time still resident at the Redsell's cottage, had accompanied Chris and myself on the guided tour of the property, and were to all intents and purposes as curious as myself. Investigating the bales of hay with disdain, presumably rife with rat urine, they had opted to romp up and down the overgrown terraces in the heart of which lay the house. Following their example, Bruno, Chris and myself exited the house and continued up the steps, which were by now no longer stone but simple indentations in the earth, and barely visible underfoot because of thick, unruly couch grass and dead vegetation. We found ourselves in the midst of a vineyard. The grapes had long since been gathered and the long, protruding stems from the year's new growth claimed little foliage. As we ascended, and the two dogs merrily chased each other in and out of our legs, the panorama broadened as we reached the upper confines of the land and the vines gave way to olive trees. My heart missed a beat. A very clear image came to my mind's eye of myself, a dancer, amidst these olives, on my own stage, performing for no mortal soul, but nevertheless to a huge public. I could not but take this as a sign that the property would one day become mine, and here I would dance and know that I had come home.

"Lena and I had wanted to build a small house up here at the top of this land when we were younger," Chris translated for me Bruno's statement. A look of sadness was apparent in his eyes. He continued: "The vineyard and olive grove belonged to my wife's side of the family. When she married me she left her family's home in Fiano to come and live with me in Loppeglia. Eventually she inherited the property and we always said that we would make a little summer residence right on this spot, with the magnificent view spread before us. Our only son loved the place as a child and took an interest in the work on the vineyard at various times of the year. We always talked about our little house-to-be and how we would set about constructing it.

"But our son died some years ago at an early age and we have no other family who want the property" he said, his eyes moist, his face resisting emotion. "Its too much for us now at our ages". He paused, gave me a searching look and demanded of Chris, "who will look after the vineyard if Stephen buys the property." My response via Chris was that I would certainly take on the responsibility of the work on the vineyard. Bruno thrust aside this reply, looked even deeper into my eyes, and asked if I had ever worked a vineyard. "No, but I can learn." A smile came to his lips and he clapped me on the back. I took this to be an encouraging gesture as we descended once again to the cottage, which was now closed up again and given back to the rats and insects that squatted in the crevices of the walls, and behind the thick, solid beams.

I could not be still during the days that followed, sensing an urgency and a restlessness that often precedes a major upheaval in one's life. This was not accompanied by any indecisiveness on my behalf. Indeed my decision had already been made the moment I had stepped out of the gate and back onto the road, during that first introduction to La Casetta with Chris and Bruno. I knew I would buy 'The Little House,' for such is its English translation. The question was how soon. Two years earlier I had invested £8.000, the remaining amount of a considerably larger legacy left me by a deceased aunt, in an English business offering an excellent return on capital left for a minimum of three years. However, my bond would not mature before October 1989 in the following year.

Apart from the £10,000 purchase fee for La Casetta, I was warned that I would also have to meet the costs of the notary at the signing of the contract, a transaction tax payable to the government and local council, a fee for the legal representative who would secure planning permission for the transformation of the barn into a habitation - a condition of my purchase, and a further tax ultimately to the council for the privilege of modifying an existing building. All told, a sum of at least a further £3.000 was mentioned. Never before having found myself in the complex involvement of the property market, much less with the intention of buying a house and vineyard in rural Italy, where I had not even the simplest knowledge of the spoken language, I wondered if I would not find myself out of my depth in deep water.

Chris and Karen, at this time, were amazingly encouraging. Evenings were spent talking about undertaking, such a seemingly major operation, without back-up capital. Obviously the primary importance was to secure planning permission to develop the building, and certainly the purchase would not go ahead without this. Italian law states that, only under exceptional circumstances, will permission be given to transform any building into a habitable dwelling that had not been previously constructed for this purpose. In fact, ultimately, because the location of La Casetta was in such close proximity to the village church, and therefore within the confines of the village itself, permission was granted on the grounds that its development would be an asset to the community.

We also talked about the property as a lasting and secure investment. This certainly rang true when, some months later, after planning permission had been secured and contracts signed, I was notified that my newly acquired estate had quadrupled in value. I hasten to add, for the benefit of would-be foreign property buyers, that I acquired my modest house and vineyard by chance at the tail-end of a booming trade in cheap rural mountain dwellings. Prices have since escalated considerably as English and German visitors have snapped up dilapidated premises for development into summer homes. Subsequent stringent new laws are now a considerable dissuasion to potential buyers.

Chris and Karen had discussed with me the practicalities of being able to buy the property outright without involving loans and mortgages. Certainly, considering my status as street dancer incognito, it seemed unlikely, if not impossible, unless the truth were to be grossly distorted, that any bank or building society would deem me a respectable or reliable enough client to be worthy of a loan of thousands of pounds to buy a property in England. It was even less likely that a similar loan could be secured in Italy. With my £10.000 investment, I would not of course be acquiring a mansion or villa, or even a modest 'one up, one down' into which I could move directly. But, as Karen explained, I would also have no problem with having to meet monthly payments. As well as my camper and a caravan in England, which could be brought out to Italy, I would at least have a roof over my head. In addition, since I was still comparatively young and very healthy, most of the building work could be executed by myself under Chriss' guidance. He had built his own home from scratch, single-handed. And finally, Karen observed, I would be under no financial pressure to complete the house before the set a three year time limit for such completion, once payment of the tax for modification had been made to the council.

In fact, at the date of writing, some six years after I purchased La Casetta, work of a permanent nature had not yet commenced because of circumstances outside of my control, and about which I was only informed after I handed over the money and signed the contract of purchase. These circumstances comprised a complete ban by the local council of all construction or building work on premises in the Fiano area, except in cases where the lack of such work would result in potential danger to local residents. This ban had, I believe, been stipulated in 1986, following considerable damage that year to the structure and foundations of a number of residences due to land subsidence. Unknown to its founders, Fiano had been built on land which had a tendency to move as a result of the pressure of natural underground watercourses. After heavy rain, the watercourses quickly became torrents of strong current that bore with it rock or earth that had been loosened due to weathering.

In 1986, the situation became so serious that many residents had to abandon their homes. Temporary mobile homes, which still remain today, albeit empty, were provided and sited throughout the village by the council. Many residents made justifiable claims for compensation. These were legally accepted, since no action had been taken by the council to remedy the problem, even though obvious signs of impending damage had been observed and reported for a number of years. A state of bankruptcy was declared by the council and, in order to protect itself from further new claims, a 'hold' was announced on all existing and new applications for construction and development work.

When I was informed of this state of affairs, the information was accompanied by a follow-up letter informing me that work was about to commence on an attempt to divert the water flowing under the village into other courses outside of the habitable area. Upon remedying the problem, residents would be informed that new applications for construction would again be considered. Work on diverting the watercourses finally got under way in May 1995, nine years later, and as far as I am aware, no headway has yet been made towards resolving this dilemma. All this appeared to be a major stumbling block in the future plans for my exciting new acquisition. In fact it now appears that, very much to the contrary, the delay in sorting out the problems of the watercourses has greatly worked to my advantage, and contributed considerably to my having discovered a new, very challenging, but immensely satisfying style of living. I will however wait until later in this story to tell about these discoveries.

Three days after first viewing La Casetta and the adjoining land, I descended to Loppeglia again with Chris Pedsell, to the residence of Bruno and Lena. It was explained to them that I was very keen to buy the property at the suggested price, but was unable to gain access to my capital until October 1989. Would they be prepared to accept a deposit of ten per cent on the value of the property, the rest to be paid one year later pending planning permission? Lena, a fair-complexioned lady, with silvering hair and a warm, smiling face, confronting me for the first time and stated on behalf of her husband and herself that they would accept these terms. Within a month, a loan of 2,000,000 lire was forthcoming from my parents in Newcastle-upon-Tyne, England, a written receipt received, and a strong handshake given that declared the house and vineyard mine in one year's time - provided that I could meet the remaining payment of 20,000,000 and associated legal costs.

Three Dogs and a Dancer by Stephen Ward

Chapter 5

New Stage, New Debut, New Beginning

1986

With a major new direction, purpose, and challenging year ahead, at the end of which I was determined to possess sufficient funds to complete the contract for La Casetta and cover the legal costs, I set my mind to the task of dancing. On dancing as perhaps I had never danced before. On dancing with such conviction that I could prove to myself that the art of the dance had a rightful place, as much on a bright, sunlit street corner as in the artificially-lit enclosed theatre or studio. That I could, with this conviction, bewitch my public into giving generously into my little wooden collecting box that sat on the ground, at the foot of my dance floor

At this stage, with two years of street dancing experience already behind me, my performance had been somewhat modified since I first started out in Lausanne in October 1986. This was partly due to necessity, since experience was teaching me that if I was to make enough money to survive, then I needed to span out my dancing to enable me to dance for a longer time. Initially the show was so energetic, such was my desire to attract attention, that within a short time I was exhausted and unable to dance until the following day. I very soon also discovered that besides eliminating jumping of any sort, any dancing on tarmac, paving stones and even rough cobbles soon took its toll on my leg and back muscles. Therefore, in those early weeks, initially in Lausanne and later in Switzerland and Italy, I became aware that if my performances continued at the same throw away energy levels as I had enthusiastically started out, it was debatable if I would be able to complete the target of six weeks that I had set myself for the experiment. These realizations, coupled with a much deeper awareness that I had touched the surface of something that had unlocked a door within myself, hitherto unopened, prompted me to think more carefully about what I was doing and where I was going with it.

Enter Min once again. The journey from Portsmouth, our port of embarkation on the south coast of England, the journey through France to Lausanne, and a week in that city before Min's departure by rail further south to Italy, was full of adventure and discovery. I had come away from England with the disciplined attitude that I must put aside thoughts of a holiday or entertainment. This was to be a re-adjustment to a totally new direction in my life and a time when I intended to learn a great deal. I set out with very little in the form of financial security, but with a great deal in enthusiasm, and a determination that somehow I would survive from what I earned on the street. I was certainly equipped with the knowledge of how to make ends meet. In fact, since leaving secure work in a professional theatre atmosphere some four years earlier, and embarking on Focus On Dance with two out-of-work dancers in Bournemouth, I had learned quickly how to play the rope between the two ends. Without the benefit of back-up capital, or initial financial support of any kind, I and my two employees had discovered innumerable ways of living and building a company on practically nothing,

Since adolescence, I had always maintained an interest in gathering wild foods. My parents had initiated this curiosity in me when, every autumn, we would go looking for blackberries in the woodlands of County Durham, around Newcastle - the city in which I was born and grew up. Undoubtedly it was an excuse for my father to relive the days of his youth, growing up in a small mining community, on the edge of a magical and mystical forest that appeared to stretch forever - or at least in the eyes of a child. "They were the days, son, when we did not have a lot as children, but we made the most of what we did have: space, and plenty of it," he would tell me. "You could get lost in those woods, and never worry about it. The games we used to invent, the lads from the village and me. We were always in for a hiding when we got back home, clothes muddy and hair all over the place. But it was worth it every time."

Although having never put it to the test, I had a certain panache and confidence that, faced with the necessity, I could survive for a period on what I could find in the forests and waysides of the country. The fact that, some eighteen months later, I would be confronted with this very predicament and could prove to myself after ten weeks of concern and hardship that it was possible, was an important lesson. So, setting off from England into a very hazy future, I at least had some experience of self-survival tactics. Min's knowledge of edible food was about equal to my own, as was her enthusiasm. However, the sharing of a common interest produced many a fascinating find and the desire to look a little closer at what we normally took for granted. Armed with three illustrated books encompassing just about every plant, edible or poisonous, in a Northern European climate, we boldly plucked and ate with hesitancy, a number of herbs, fruit and fungi that we had never heard of before. Nearer Switzerland, from trees apparently abandoned at the edges of woods, we collected apples, pears, walnuts, and hazelnuts. The first sweet chestnuts had also fallen from their spiny shells and although, in Switzerland, they do not mature to the enormous size of their counterparts in Italy, or as I discovered later to my delight around La Casetta, they were nevertheless a much better proposition than those in England - which, during my ventures, have not been worth the effort of collecting.

On arrival in Switzerland we headed straight for Lausanne town centre and parked the camper van near the Cathedral, above the shopping precincts. I was already nervous about my debut the following day as street dancer incognito, a strange sensation considering my sixteen years experience of performing in a theatre. Min was profoundly understanding, sensing my unease and yet, at the same time, giving me the confidence to go forward. I felt too, that I could not go back, having come this far. In the cool morning light, after a good sleep, I investigated the town centre very much in the same way that I still now investigate a new city and a potential site for my dance. Preferably a place without traffic noise, flat and horizontal, enough space for people to stop and watch without inconveniencing those that wish to pass on by, and not too close to a shop or store entrance.

I found a space in the commercial centre of Lausanne, after I had nervously exhausted practically every other possibility, and had seen, as the morning advanced, the crowds that were frequenting the site. But I talked myself out of a debut in such a revealing place, and returned to the van disconsolate with the thought that perhaps I had lost my nerve. Min proposed that I attempt my 'baptism' in a quiet spot to begin with, and suggested the Cathedral Square just above us. She had been sitting there quietly and had watched a few children playing with their mothers close by, an occasional visitor to the Cathedral, and the odd passer-by. However, as the morning had by now slipped away, we postponed my inauguration until the afternoon.

By two o'clock, life was starting to return to the streets, and; gathering up my courage I set off with my one-man dance-company, stage and orchestra, whilst Min offered moral support from the rear. There were not more than half a dozen people in the square. The children had gone. As I set-up, an elderly couple approached and curiously enquired of me what I was doing. Were they going to complain, I thought to myself, or go away as soon as I commenced? Perhaps no one would want to see a dancer on the street. Maybe I would feel useless and rejected, and be unable to continue the experiment at all. What on earth did I think I was doing there anyway! Was this all a big mistake?

Min watched me calmly, her smile reassuring. The couple had not gone. Others were drawing near. Suddenly, the half dozen people had increased to ten and the square seemed, in my mind's eye, to be overcrowded. I commenced. Was the music too loud? My movements were not flowing, and I felt stiff and encumbered. Was someone turning to leave? At the end of the dance, just three minutes long, there was applause. Intrigued smiles adorned all the faces around me. No one left. Someone brought me a coin, then another and another. I realized then that I had forgotten to put out my collection box. With a dumb expression on my face, I bashfully produced the box and waited for the interim music between dance pieces to finish before starting my next dance. But it was too long, I had miscalculated how much time I would need to recuperate before re-commencing my dancing. People would surely lose interest and leave. Had sixteen years of professional performing prepared me for this?

No one left. I danced again, and once more there was applause followed by coins. After my third dance I felt I needed to stop, to disappear, to hide from everyone, from myself. I rolled up the floor and picked up the box which at first sight appeared to be full. The 'huge' crowd of ten people dissipated leaving only Min and the elderly couple, who came to enquire where I was from and then left themselves. Min and I looked at each other and suppressed peals of laughter. At the van, I counted ten Swiss francs - just over three pounds sterling. I was elated. I could barely believe I had done it. Later I would dance again, and then also in the space that I had discovered that morning in the busy commercial centre.

Reflecting now on that very modest start at the age of 36, in a new direction with dance, after many years of successful performing, first of all as a member of the corps de ballet, then as soloist, and finally as a principal dancer, I cannot but be amused that I should have been so terrified of doing something that, simply in a different environment, had become a way of life. Nevertheless, when I also consider the very particular language and form of communication that I have adopted using the dance, during its ten years of development on the streets, somehow it seems right and proper to me that the old should be cast aside and the new given a different life, in much the same way that a baby starts with nothing other than the love of its parents. Although I was not then aware of the invisible love that had taken my dance, and molded it into something way beyond my understanding, it was not very long before I began to sense a big and wonderful change in my life, and my attitude to life as expressed through my dance.

Later that afternoon, outside of one of Lausanne's major shopping stores, I again nervously set out my floor which this time seemed to occupy the entire pedestrian precinct. Blinkered shoppers, with maybe only one thing on their minds, walked over the floor even as I rolled it out. Crossly, others made a diversion from their straight-line objective to avoid the obstruction. Some stopped and watched, bicycles zoomed hither and thither, and over and above all this movement was the hum of busy street life. A very different atmosphere to two hours ago by the Cathedral. Would my dance be lost amidst the competing 'shoppers' dance? Would the music be simply absorbed into the distorted music of daily city sounds reverberating between concrete walls? Could I concentrate on my intricate movements without being distracted by so much mass movement? If I could master this situation, I felt, then surely I could master the experiment generally and learn to overcome the obstacles. In the background Min caught my eye, pouring confidence into me telepathically and urging me on.

"I am afraid that you can't do this here," stated a sympathetic policewoman, at the end of my seventh dance. I had been aware of her, waiting until my dance had terminated, and who was now confronting not only me but a crowd of perhaps sixty people. I quickly and politely apologised, enquiring where it would be possible to continue my show. "Street artists using amplified sound are not allowed in the central shopping area of Lausanne at any time, but the police will probably tolerate your show at Ouchy, down by the lake". One or two people approached closer to eavesdrop on the conversation, and enquired why such an activity was not allowed in this place. "There has been a telephone complaint about the music from a resident. In such cases the police are obliged to intervene," she calmly explained. The crowd merged back into the rest of the movement of the precinct. Only a few individuals remained to stare consolingly at me. Min approached and asked me the problem, which I explained to her feeling foolish and exposed. I quickly packed away my equipment and disappeared into the safe confines of my van.

Three Dogs and a Dancer by Stephen Ward

Once there, my rapidly deteriorating mood quickly changed as I counted the donations in my wooden box. Over twenty pounds in Swiss francs and this in just over forty minutes. While I had been dancing, with the numbers gathering around me increasing, and the applause consistent at the end of each dance, I had found myself relaxing and responding, becoming oblivious to exterior sounds and movements. Indeed the crowd on all sides of me seemed to contain the magic to block the influences from outside. On that initial day, despite being the first of many subsequent confrontations with city police, I had been badly bitten with the bug that was to change my whole direction in life. It was the beginning of a ten year revelation. Min and I celebrated that evening in the van at Ouchy, by the Lac Leman, with the French Alps in the distance over the water.

The euphoria of the previous day quickly subsided the following morning when I realised, on trying to remove myself from the bed in the roof of the camper, a headroom of about fifteen inches, that it was going to be a major task just to get up and get dressed. Min in the lower bed responded with concern to my groans and complaints as I attempted to wriggle from my space, a complicated process at the best of times. My camper van was a testament to the ingenious creation of a garage mechanic, who had made the original and unique conversion from a ten year old mini-bus. From the outset I called it my 'Royal Box' because of its theatricality in interior design. It was fitted out from roof to floor in padded red velvet, with varnished wood paneling and fittings. There was no wardrobe or refrigerator but it did have a complete kitchen with oven. The driver and passenger seats revolved so that one could sit in any direction. The original rear end doors that are normally standard on a mini bus had been sealed. A seating arrangement had been installed around the rear of the vehicle with a round table that could be lowered from the roof to convert the area into a large double bed for two children or, for my benefit, a single bed that was only long enough if one slept diagonally, with head and feet tucked into corners.

The other extendable bed in the raised roof was much larger and longer, and therefore more comfortable, except that with so little headroom it demanded a certain athletic prowess to get either into or out of it. But the great practical advantage to my van was that, unlike any other camper I have seen, it had a very large vacant space directly inside the side entrance. This vacant space enabled me to carry out my essential daily training and stretching prior to dancing. With the extendable bed pushed back into the confines at the rear of the roof there was more than enough headroom to move about without the necessity of stooping. All in all, the camper van served my needs perfectly for ten years until, sadly, it had to be taken off the road. Now it lies on the driveway beneath La Casetta, awaiting the day it will be taken down the valley and into a scrap yard. A wealth of memories repose in its rusting, corroding 'carrosserie.'

To return to the morning after the night before, my body simply denied me its normal cooperating agility, a gross stiffness and pain having taken up quarters in every joint and every muscle. I could not get out of the bed, neither could I lift my head the five inches that the space afforded without help from Min who had quickly risen from below to find the cause for my oaths. The feeling that one's body had completely seized up was not new to me. I must presume that all dancers of all ages experience muscular stiffness in the same way that I have from time to time. This is often at its most exaggerated state when the body is worked in a way to which it is not normally accustomed. A non-dancer may claim that a dancer's body is specifically trained for grueling work and therefore accustomed to any type of movement. This is true perhaps in classical ballet companies, where most of the movements done in regular daily training are virtually identical to those performed on stage. However, it is not the case in contemporary dance where the interpretation of the word contemporary is very loose, and expression is a matter for the individual dancer.

The majority of my sixteen years career in the professional theatre has been spent with contemporary dance companies, culminating in three years with the Ballet Rambert - now Rambert Dance Company - before moving on to found Focus On Dance. The Rambert Dance Company is based in London and is Britain's oldest dance company dating from the 1920's, long before the Sadlers Wells, and subsequently the Royal Ballet, came into being. It took its name from its founder, Marie Rambert, one of the great Ballet Dames of this century's English dance scene. It remained essentially a ballet company, offering a stage to some of the world's budding great choreographers over the years until, in 1966, a newly appointed associate director alongside Marie Rambert, persuaded her to change the company's direction. Norman Morrice, who had been through the ranks of Rambert's school and company, and who had also spent time observing the fascinating emerging contemporary dance scene in America, brought a fresh, almost brand-new statement to British dance. Ballet Rambert continued to offer a stage to new choreographers, each of whom had their own statements to make, and most of which had never before been voiced in the world of British dance.

By the time I arrived at the door of the Ballet Rambert in 1979, to commence rehearsing a daring, full evening, contemporary work by the American Glen Tetley based on Shakespeare's play, The Tempest, the company of only twenty dancers had found its own identity, and convinced a hard-headed British theatre public that contemporary dance was indeed going places - not only in America or Britain, but elsewhere too. Ballet Rambert found itself considered as one of Europe's leading contemporary dance companies. Such was its recognition that it was often invited to perform at international events where previously contemporary dance had no foothold. Nearly all the leading contemporary choreographers on both sides of the Atlantic had already worked for Ballet Rambert, or were booked for forthcoming seasons. From the start, the company also adopted a policy of encouraging creative talent within its own ranks and, as a result, had given birth to names that already were becoming internationally known.

I stepped into this charged and vibrant atmosphere one cold January morning, having arrived in England from Lisbon in Portugal, where I had previously been working with the Ballet Gulbenkian. Here, two months earlier, I had worked with a guest choreographer, Christopher Bruce. He was the associate director, choreographer and principal dancer in the Ballet Rambert and a man who, the moment I began working with him, gained my absolute respect. It was really the greatest of good fortune, - or perhaps, as I now look at it, a further step in my mapped out future - that I happened to work with Christopher at that time in Lisbon, in a company where I was beginning to feel disillusion on a personal level as a dancer.

Working with him on a dance entitled 'Wings', originally created for the Ballet Rambert dancers, gave me an enormous lift in confidence as well as an insight of how powerfully dramatic and expressive dance at this level could be. During that physically demanding and invigorating period of rehearsal and subsequent performance, I enquired about the possibility of my being able to work with him as a dancer in the Ballet Rambert. He told me, then and there, that Glen Tetley was shortly commencing rehearsals for his Tempest and that the company would need extra dancers. The company of eighteen was to be augmented to twenty four, and four of these newcomers would be male. As he was not the director in charge, he suggested that I telephone London and speak to John Chesworth, the artistic director of the company. When I did so, I was informed that I was to be accepted as a result of a personal recommendation from Christopher.

My curriculum vitae up to that date made reasonably impressive reading, and I certainly had no complaint having chosen a career in dance. Already, at the age of twenty nine, I had toured the world, lived and worked in six different countries, had a great deal of experience in the techniques of both classical ballet and contemporary dance, as well as in teaching and choreographing. I also found myself to be very much at home performing on a stage, no matter where it was. Nothing, however, could have prepared me for the new world that was about to open up before me when I entered the Ballet Rambert studios that chilly morning in January 1979.

I had arrived in London by car from Portugal, towing behind me a small touring caravan. The car I had bought three years earlier whilst working at Lucerne in Switzerland, where I had earlier bought my first caravan. This second caravan had become my home while I was with the Gulbenkian Ballet Company, and been purchased second-hand in Portugal. I parked it temporarily on a commercial site in East London before I was able to find a more permanent location from which to commute to the West London studio, during the three month rehearsal period with Glen. Whilst being a touring caravan it had not to date, during its six year lifetime, toured a great deal. In fact it had not toured at all, having remained static for those six years on a camping park at Monsanto in Lisbon, from whence it had been bought. Its journey from Lisbon to London was indeed its first tour, and apart from being static for a further three months in London during rehearsals, it then did not cease to tour for a further ten years until it eventually went on its last journey - to be finally parked on the driveway specially created for it at La Casetta,

Three Dogs and a Dancer by Stephen Ward

The caravan, which in Lisbon had provided a small but cosy respite during my two year contract with the Ballet Gulbenkian, was - during the next three years with Ballet Rambert - to cover thousands of miles of British roads while touring for almost forty weeks of each year, and reach every conceivable corner of the land. Indeed, my experience with Ballet Rambert was a revelation in artistic satisfaction. I found myself endlessly performing the works of great choreographers, nearly all of whom I respected and trusted totally, and notably among these were Christopher Bruce and Glen Tetley. It was a very busy three years which could have taken a dreadful toll on my body had I not, primarily, been totally engrossed and involved in my work, and been privileged with excellent opportunities for daily dance training with first class teachers. During this time I learnt what it was to push one's stamina to its limits and survive to say that I would do it again and again, at any time, and at any cost.

My caravan proved the ideal home to which, by now, I had become well accustomed. Quite simply, I by-passed the expensive and, for the most part, depressing London apartments and provincial 'theatrical digs', and carried my home everywhere with me. The company schedule was such that we worked Tuesday to Saturday each week. While, after the final performance on Saturday, all the other artists were either rushing to catch last trains to London or preparing themselves for an often long drive, I simply hopped on my bicycle and calmly rode back to my caravan, with two free days to quietly travel to next week's destination. It seemed such an ideal arrangement that I could not imagine why others were not doing something similar. But then I have always preferred the serenity and spiritual peace of open spaces and natural surroundings, which life in a caravan enabled me to enjoy. Also, being something of a loner, meant that I was not always comfortable in company and, while enjoying the theatre and theatre life, I was usually quite happy to put a cap on it all at the end of a performance. In any case, I found myself often mentally stretched and spent, as well as physically shattered, after a performance with the Ballet Rambert. My own familiar space with all its peace and tranquility was a heaven-sent blessing to me.

As the artists in Ballet Rambert were, for the most part, on tour and only resident in London for two or three weeks of rehearsal in the year when adding a new work to its repertoire, it did not prove difficult to persuade the warden of the Camping Club site at Chertsey to extend my permitted stay there for the odd occasion. This very attractive camping site was located beyond Richmond, by the River Thames, about three quarters of an hour's drive from the studio. The move from Portugal to England necessitated some rapid modifications to my caravan. The first two weeks were somewhat uncomfortable before a gas heater was installed and the walls lined with insulating cork. But as the fast and breath-taking schedule for the Tempest got under way, I was more than encouraged with the new professional world of Ballet Rambert and prepared myself to put up with anything just to be part of it.

I quickly settled into the company's working routine, finding myself in demand as a dancer and also, because of my teaching experience, called upon to give introductory workshops to schools while on tour. For me, these workshops would be a real complement to the later evening performances, and I often returned to London at the end of a tour to find a string of letters awaiting me from teachers and pupils alike, expressing how the introductory workshop had greatly increased their comprehension and appreciation of a performance. My own creative abilities, which later had an outlet in choreographing the work for Focus On Dance, were given a voice with Ballet Rambert. Each year, a period was set aside in London for rehearsals and the performances of choreographic work that any member of the company could prepare, using colleagues from within the company. This was a time of wonderful creativity for me, and an invaluable experience in mounting dance on a professional stage with professional dancers and live musicians. In short, I was living as a dancer. Living dance as it should be lived; every moment of every day, and not just once in a while as I had done with other companies. The inspiration was endless, the experience of unfathomable value. It was the beginning of the good times, the beginning of a more mature approach to dance and to the values in life.

This diversion from the dilemma in not being unable to remove myself from the upper bed in the camper van, serves as a reminder to the reader that my present predicament was by no means a new one, and therefore not a particular cause for concern. I knew that in a matter of hours most of the aches and pains would have subsided, provided I could get up and move about. However, it caused me to think about the new type of stamina I would need to build in order to maintain my energy output during dance, and that I must be wary of solid stone stages from now on and react accordingly. Notwithstanding this, my elation from the day before remained with me, and in all honesty I can say that it has never left me since. Neither has the influence that I value so much of my dear friend, Min.

That afternoon at Ouchy, with my aches and pains almost subsided, a good crowd of walkers gathered on the lakeside promenade. I once again prepared to dance, this time against the superb theatrical backdrop of a turbulent Lac Leman, with the impressive French Alps towering in the distance. When one has for all of one's performing life, danced in limited spaces, artificially lit and mostly with other dancers on stage, well aware of barriers and limitations, one is taken mentally unawares by the tremendous exhilaration of the experience when suddenly the barriers are removed. Such was my response to the realization that I was here, dancing alone in an enormous space, behind me an empty expanse of water broken only at a distance by mountain and sky. Before me was a gathering crowd, who began to take second place in importance to the grand environment in which I was about to express myself.

The performance at Ouchy, only the third of thousands of similar subsequent experiences, allowed me a first insight into the world of freedom into which I was about to step. My dance however still had a long way to go before I knew clearly where I was going with it. However, I now felt secure in the knowledge that I could continue this experiment alone. Also aware that Min's time was limited, and that we still had an invitation to attend the final evening four days hence of an exhibition of art by Carlos Grippo at a gallery at Ballens, near Lausanne, we opted to leave the lake for the mountains.

Le Lac de Joux, at an altitude of 1400 metres, lies in the Jura range that forms the northern frontier of Switzerland, and extends from Geneva in the west, to Constance on the Bodensee in Bavaria. The majority of habitable land in Switzerland lies in a plateau between these mountains and the grandiose barrier of the Alps to the south and east. On a clear day, from high up in the Jura mountains, the extraordinary wall of the Alpine Range - snow-covered at any time of year - distinctly demonstrates its prowess as a mighty barrier, appearing to stop the world at that point. Such is its success as a wall of separation, that two distinct climates adorn its northern and southern slopes, and with them the development over centuries of two diverse cultures.

The two hour journey from Lausanne to the base of the Jura, was delightful with heightening leafy colours from autumn's influence. As we gradually ascended the Jura, these colours became more intense until the deciduous woodland eventually gave way to mountain conifers. The idyllic spot where we camped for three nights by the side of a tranquil, trapped lake, has become a milestone in my memory of those first days of new and poignant discovery. I was tremendously motivated by my three contrasting performances in Lausanne and immensely excited with the prospect of being able to travel onwards into the future, earning my living as I went, with nothing other than a camper van, a bicycle and a dance floor.

Important though each of these settings has been in preparing me for what I was about to embark upon, it was somehow the magical feeling that I was permitted to capture, just for an instant, while dancing at Ouchy that pierced the deepest into my soul. To be able to build a bridge between what I enjoyed doing the most and the environment in which I most enjoyed being seemed an impossibility until this moment. Up at the lake in the heart of the Jura, the magnificent natural splendour seemed to cry out to me to take it, and incorporate it into the amazing gift of my dance. Everywhere that I wandered, by the pebbly shore of the lake, deep into the heart of the pine forest, high on the rocky peaks, everywhere became a stage on which I saw myself dancing. My heart pounded at the thought of what my future might behold. How could I know then, where I was being led? And yet I knew. Insight is a wonderful privilege.

Although many times in following years I was to re-capture this extraordinary sensation of dancing as a free and unencumbered spirit, as an integral part of nature, somehow I could never retain it and make it the reason for my dancing. Until, that is, eight years later, when a series of mind-boggling events happened while making a professional video film of my dance. Not on the streets and squares of Europe's cities, but in the majestic natural settings that I had envisaged at the outset of my new adventure. From that time onward the revelation has never left me and, provided I respect its source and set my mind on that course, it never deserts or fails me. This, however, is not the right moment in this account to expound on that event and the energies surrounding it. Suffice to say, for the time being, that in my opinion when something major is about to happen in our lives, we do not enter into the experience without spiritual preparation, no matter how unconscious we may be of this.

Maria Gloria and Carlos welcomed us with warm and open arms, amidst a throng of obviously wealthy and influential guests who were mostly purchasers of the paintings on exhibition. The art gallery, a fish out of water amidst the cow bells and odorous smells of manure which describe Swiss rural life, would be more likely to be found amidst a setting of surrealistic, spatial edifices, say in Brazilia or New York. This was Ballens, a tiny dairy-farming community about thirty miles from Lausanne near the base of the Jura mountains. Apparently the gallery enjoyed considerable success among the elite art connoisseurs of the French-speaking region of Switzerland and, to a lesser degree, from further afield. This was immediately apparent, not only from the guests in attendance, but also by the number of red spots attached to many of the paintings - each signifying that painting to be sold. Carlos was not the only painter to be exhibiting, and shared the exhibition with one other artist. The work of both exhibitors was sufficiently avant-garde to suggest immediately that purchasers of the sold paintings were definitely not, in the main, of local origin.

Carlos and Maria Gloria introduced us charmingly to our hosts, Edward and Elizabeth, who promptly asked what we were doing in Switzerland. We demurred. "Well, we are actually just passing through on our way to Italy, to in fact where Maria Gloria and Carlos live," I hurriedly explained in French, conveniently bypassing the whole truth. Some polite conversation continued, during which we were invited as friends of Carlos to a private party that was to follow on from this somewhat formal, final evening. We accepted with alacrity and having spent what seemed to be the right amount of time carefully observing and inspecting the works on exhibition, we politely removed ourselves and exited into the 'perfumed' air of the farming community. The contrast between the interior of the gallery and its human as well as artistic contents with the exterior environs could not have been more dramatic. Our ability to adapt quickly to these extremes showed itself immediately as, once outside the village, out came plastic bags into which went windfall apples and pears that lay by the side of the road, walnuts that were everywhere, and the few wild mushrooms that had survived the ravages of the cattle in the vicinity.

Suddenly, in a dip in the field, and therefore not visible until we were right on top of them, lay four football-size, white objects which, upon seeing them for the first time in my life, were not immediately identifiable or recognizable. Min however, being astute, was of the opinion that they must be giant puffballs, a species of excellent edible fungus. Giant puffballs they were, all at the perfect stage of picking and eating. Neither of us had ever been confronted by such a sight before. That mushrooms can grow to this size was almost beyond my comprehension.

I wanted immediately to break one to see what was inside. Min stopped me and intelligently offered the suggestion that, as we had nothing to take to the evening party at the gallery, should we not present ourselves each bearing a giant puffball as a rather novel offering. We took two and left the other two, either to mature and reproduce, or as a further discovery for other enthusiasts. When the door of the gallery was opened to us by Edward, later that evening, we found the social atmosphere a little lighter. Inside, we were among a dozen or so other guests and presented our gifts, much as the Three Kings might have done two thousand years ago. The atmosphere grew even lighter as all the guests crowded round us, amazement showing in their faces.

We had stolen the limelight for a moment, stepped up onto the stage and acknowledged the applause. Everyone was thus relieved of the formality of boring small talk, and the party got off to a good start. People, whose lives revolve around such formalities, let their hair down as they bundled into a tiny kitchen to watch Elizabeth cut up the puffballs that, to my astonishment, contained pure white firm flesh, and fried them without ceremony in shallow oil. Discourse flowed as Edward brought up from the depths of his private wine cellar, some dusty bottles with aging labels and delectable contents. I think, during the course of the evening, Edward must have made about ten descents to his cellar, each subsequent ascent disclosing ever dustier bottles with labels barely legible, until his final unsteady ascent produced 'The Piece de Resistence', the finest bottle in his very fine collection. The puffball was a very novel hit with everyone present and both specimens were consumed with relish.

Some weeks later, at a reunion with Maria Gloria and Carlos at their home in Pescaglia, the four of us recalled the episode of two wayfarers bearing gifts from the land to present before the court of kings and queens. After relishing the moment, Carlos recounted what Edward had said to him the following day while packing-up the remaining unsold paintings. "It was probably the most expensive party I have over thrown, considering the wine we consumed, but when I remember the look on the faces of all those wealthy people at the sight of your two friends, and what they held before them, it was worth every Swiss franc." The evening after the re-union, Min left by train for Italy. It was an emotional departure since we both knew that the days preceding our parting had been a special gift to each of us, full of laughter, full of light, full of life. I watched the train leave, wondering what my future held in store.

Three Dogs and a Dancer by Stephen Ward

Chapter 6

Out of the Light and into Darkness

1970 - 1974

In order for the reader to understand how and why my lifestyle in recent years had become intricately involved with wheels, and tiny homes that moved about on top of them, it is necessary to backtrack well over twenty years to explain a whole series of happenings. Each of these happenings connected to the other, and each seemingly as much a preparation as the other for the last ten years that form the basis of this book.

I had, at the age of twenty-four, been living and partly working for two years as a dancer in Sweden. The first year I was contracted with the Royal Swedish Ballet Company at the Royal Opera House in Stockholm. It was a depressingly unhappy period because, after dancing for three years with the Gulbenkian Ballet in Lisbon, who had offered me my first professional engagement while still a student at the Royal Ballet School in London, and to whom I later returned before joining the Ballet Rambert, I found myself in such a very contrasting situation in Stockholm: work-wise, life-wise and environment-wise. I suffered a mental crisis that ultimately affected my health very badly and my dance.

While under contract in Lisbon, initially in a classical ballet company to which I had gone at the age of twenty, the artistic directorship changed. With the arrival of the new and powerful director, Milko Sparemblek, there also arrived the emergence of contemporary dance in Portugal. Milko Sparemblek was of Yugoslav origin, and had come into the limelight while working at the Metropolitan Opera House in New York, at a time when many new and innovative choreographers were emerging from companies such as The Martha Graham Dance Company, The Joffrey Ballet and Jose Limon Dance Company. The Gulbenkian Foundation, a worldwide organisation providing funding for art, culture, creativity and education from investments made originally by oil tycoon, Calouste Gulbenkian in the 1950's and 1960's, was the perfect environment for Sparemblek.

The extraordinary edifice spread over two acres of land in the heart of Lisbon's commercial quarter, comprising a unique concert auditorium which could adapt perfectly to a proscenium-arched theatre, two studio theatres/conference halls and an outside amphitheatre, was the world headquarters of the Foundation. From this building, of which perhaps eighty percent was given over to luxurious offices overlooking exotic gardens, millions of dollars were spent in commerce, and even greater sums invested in futuristic projects in every corner of the world.

Needless to say, the ballet company, choir and orchestra were housed in the Foundation amidst tremendous luxury, contrasting sharply with the poverty and suppression that in the early 1970s were evidence of the latter years of the Salazar Dictatorship. The Foundation was seen as acting in an ambassadorial capacity. In the three years of my first engagement with the company, I worked with no less than thirty choreographers, many of who were from the United States. Much of the work was experimental as the company was searching for an identity, and was not of tremendous value to myself. However certain choreographers struck a much deeper note within me, sufficient to convince me that contemporary dance was perhaps worth considering in my future career, and was a legitimate alternative to classical ballet. Milko took a shine to me and, although in age and experience I was limited, my naivety of the theatre gave way to a tremendous energy and enthusiasm as I found myself in practically every ballet that was mounted.

Within five months of my joining the company, and immediately prior to the official change in directorship - although Sparemblek had by this time virtually taken over - the Gulbenkian Ballet, together with an entourage of famous Portuguese performing artists, was sent to Osaka in Japan to represent Portugal in the Expo '70 World Fair. Here Milko, having partly organised our programme, enjoyed a great success and as a result, endearing himself to the company and in particular to me. I was not sorry to see the last of the boring, back line corps-de-ballet steps of the classical ballet productions, with endless performances of the same classical dances, as our company moved into a frantically exciting period of new and, to me, daring contemporary work. My vocabulary of dance movement was being augmented weekly and, although much of it was eventually discarded, it showed me that expression through the body in modern ballet had a far greater outlet and impact than that of classical ballet.

A year after our visit to Expo '70, thanks to Gulbenkian's largesse and Sparembeck's success as company director, the Ballet Gulbenkian embarked on a two month tour to four African countries: Mozambique and Angola were still politically under Portuguese control, Rhodesia had not yet become Zimbabwe, and President Banda was still trying to re-create Oxford and Cambridge in Malawi. For myself, at the tender age of twenty-one, my eyes were opened wide during this tour. The dances I was given for the performances on tour were more than enough to satisfy and fulfill me, especially being only eighteen months into my profession. But for myself, in my youthful energy, it did not stop there. I knew of course that this would undoubtedly be a once-in-a-lifetime experience, as had the previous year's visit to Japan. I wanted to know, I wanted to learn, I wanted to see and to sense everything about Africa, as much as I possibly could. I wanted to capture everything that my senses could contain, and from every angle, so that I could reach my own conclusions on such controversial subjects as the repressive regime in Rhodesia, or the blood-sucking tactics that Portugal was using on its colonies.

Every moment of the day was filled. I took risks that no one knew about and which, if they had become known, measures could have been taken to discipline me - or even sack me from my job. During days when rehearsals prior to the performances were not held, I skipped the daily class routine and headed in search of discovery, armed with a little money and a fully loaded camera. I took buses, sometimes containing more animals and birds than black-skinned humans, to places about which I had no idea and where I never saw other white-skinned people. I gesticulated with fishermen casting nets into the ocean, sometimes miles from the nearest habitation. I ventured into wilderness alone, without experiencing the fear that perhaps I ought to have had. I took tiny ferries to palm-tree islands and walked for hours through banana groves, not knowing whether I would make it back in time for the evening performance.

Once, in an African hillside village in Malawi, I was attacked by a very hefty woman who took umbrage at my insensitivity in photographing her humble dwelling, and the even humbler sources of nourishment drying on simple mats on the baked ground before me. I was followed for miles along a dusty track inland in Angola by a young boy of perhaps nine or ten, and who eventually came alongside and allowed himself to be photographed. The ice having been broken, although verbal communication was out of the question, he made my day by showing me the sights along the way that for him were common, but which up to that time I had only observed in documentary films of the natural world. In Salisbury, Rhodesia, I deliberately wandered alone into an area of the city that I was told to avoid. There, in an all black bar, I had an exhilarating conversation - once it was ascertained that I was English and not a white Rhodesian or a South African – with half a dozen people and the barman about heart-felt topics of human rights, apartheid and inequality.

Apart from these risky adventures during the tour, which were not discovered, possibly because I never missed a performance, I enjoyed organised trips with company members to coral and tropical islands, game reserves and splendid lavish meals provided by Embassies. In eight short weeks, visiting eight cities and travelling by every means of transport that existed, I felt I had good grounds for the conclusions that I drew, and still draw, about Africa and human life there. Perhaps, to avoid controversy, I will say only this: I returned to Europe gob-smacked at my previous audacity in feeling that I was in any way superior to anyone else on this earth, simply due to the environment or country into which I was born. That superiority, in its truest sense, is given solely as a gift to a person through humbling, deeply searched understanding, and the wisdom to see that all men are created equal.

Such was Africa for me. But perhaps an equally poignant education awaited me when, in the summer of 1972, and one year after its African tour, the Gulbenkian Ballet was invited to dance in six cities of a very different continent: South America. This tour did not stretch beyond Brazil, although the country is large enough to extend not only into different climatic areas, but also into different time zones. The six cities ranged from Sao Paolo, an enormous, sprawling industrial and commercial city in the south of the country, to Recife in the north which is practically on the equator. In between were Rio de Janeiro, a veritable playground for the internationally rich; Bello Horizorite, a city of commerce made rich by the fabulous wealth of precious and semi-precious stones to be found in the region of Minas Gerais; Brasilia, the then comparatively new and controversial capital of Brazil, created from nothing in the centre of the country; and Salvador Bahia, a city of contrast between the very rich and miserably poor, built on two distinct levels on the coast of the western Atlantic Ocean.

For me each city had something very different and fed my hunger for experience, whether it was the exotic magic of Rio de Janeiro and its splendid natural location, or the extra-ordinary friendships that developed between a group of our dancers including myself, and a few young dance enthusiasts from Sao Paolo. Or perhaps the surrealistic effect on the mind of Brazilia's spacious city design, with its symbolically magnificent parliament and diplomatic areas. But my overall impression of Brasilia was quite different to that of the previous year's tour of the four African countries. I was in a different place within myself. To start with, at the end of the Brazilian tour, I had decided to move on from Portugal to Stockholm where I would join the Royal Swedish Ballet Company. I had already secured a contract there following an audition a few months previously.

This third and final year with the Ballet Gulbenkian, under Milko Sparemblek, had been an important transition time for me with the dance. A time when I began to take the dance and what could be learnt from it, a great deal more seriously. In the final year I had gained a lot more responsibility with my solo roles. In Africa I had been, and wanted to be, alone to be free to experience without restriction. In Brazil I found myself desiring less solitude, in favour of the warm and friendly social atmosphere that was everywhere in evidence. This, coupled with a greater discipline towards my work, and the discovery that - unlike those areas in Africa to which I had access - the Brazilian cities were not so very different from those of Europe, and in particular Portugal. All this resulted in less of desire to go gallivanting around a country with which I was unfamiliar, and more towards the necessity of experiencing the unique blending of three very different human races: namely European, African and the South American Indian.

With perhaps my naive and uneducated knowledge of deep social problems, I tried to work out how Brazil managed to survive harmonically with rampant racial inequality, and three breeds of the human race rather than two. Perhaps I was simply blinded by the wonderful time I was having socially, but my conclusions were of a more positive nature than was probably warranted as I observed around me physical inter-breeding of a most exhilarating beauty, and the apparent harmony of social behaviour between everyone with whom I came into contact, no matter their colour or lineage. This was the image left with me, as I sadly departed from Brazil and returned to Europe and on to a new environment with, yet again, the distancing problem of a new language to master. In the months that followed I desperately tried to recall my mental strength and security, with which I had journeyed through three years of euphoria in Portugal, as I was swept into an acutely alienating atmosphere of the Theatre Royal, Stockholm.

With a deepening mental crisis creeping over me, I struggled to analyse how my personality could so dramatically change from place to place. Allowing myself to wallow completely in my own misery, I went down and further down until it seemed I could not go any further without something drastic happening. At that point I found myself desperate and in need of help, and yet unable to make the effort to reach out to anyone. The moment when it seemed that surely I must now start to go up, a motor accident occurred and I sank even further into the hell that I was creating for myself. While I was not seriously injured, a curious condition resulted that defied medical analysis and forced me to give up temporarily my career in dance. After eighteen months of a deteriorating back condition I concluded, falsely, that I would need to consider a new line of work.

When my annual contract with the Royal Swedish Ballet came to an end, I was unable to renew it - even if I had the faintest desire to do so. Left in a total quandary, without the physical or mental strength to help myself or even to seek the company of colleagues, I went into total seclusion fearing even to leave my apartment and confront other people on the street. Eventually help came from an unsought source. Birgit Cullberg, the founder, director and choreographer of the Cullberg Ballet Company also in Stockholm, whom I had got to know while at the Royal Opera House, came to know of my condition and came quickly to the rescue. This rescue was in the form of an offer. A contract providing me with a full salary for up to three months, during which time I would be found medical help for my back injury. After this time, I could either take-up full time work with the company as a dancer, or be free to terminate the contract if I was still unable to dance.

With this new hope, which initially dragged me out of my despair, I went into my second Swedish winter. The atmosphere in this smaller, more intimate, contemporary dance group was a welcome contrast to that of its larger counterpart. However, because of my disadvantage and disability, and my still fragile state of mind, I could not raise myself sufficiently from my dilemma to appreciate it and regain my desperately needed self-confidence. My back did not improve sufficiently to take up full time work and so, as agreed, my contract was terminated after three months and I signed on for the Swedish Social Security. The long Swedish nights of that second winter seemed endless. Yet again, I made little effort to help myself and I sank into an even deeper into a state of despair, often having vociferous arguments with myself convinced that the whole episode could have only one eventual and morbid outcome. I was told by the Swedish authorities that I would be unable to claim social benefit for longer than six months due to the number of my previous contributions. Now with a dread of leaving Stockholm, I tried to hang on to what little courage and sanity I had left.

Three Dogs and a Dancer by Stephen Ward

Chapter 7

Out of the Darkness and into Light

Scotland - Part 1, 1975

Slowly, as the lakes and rivers around Stockholm began to thaw and the sun started to show a little strength, so did my deep depression begin to thaw and my hope strengthen. I tried to make my thoughts turn towards leaving Sweden and returning, as a prodigal son, to my parents' home in north-east England. Three months later I was on the train from Stockholm to Bergen in Norway, where I would stay for a couple of days before taking a ferry across the North Sea to Newcastle upon Tyne. The eventual outcome that I had imagined deep in the middle of winter in my cold apartment, alone and feeling mentally sick, had not materialised. With the advent of Spring had come a major advent in my own life. A tiny seed of hope had been sown in my heart that germinated first into the renewed feeling of happiness, and then grew into a belief that not only would my life go on, but also that one day I would dance again. This was not to be for yet another year, but my little seed of hope did not let me down.

As I sat by the window of the train, being whisked away from the dark cave where it seemed I had ceased to live, in my renewed mind

I tried to come to terms with the strange and inexplicable past two years. Understanding is a big part of learning and I wanted to say that I had learnt something from this whole episode. Why was it that I found myself so weak as to be unable to alter my state of mind? Had I somehow brought on my accident because of my negative outlook on everything? From what source had eventually come my seed of hope that, once again, gave me the strength and courage to recognise a pin-prick of light at the end of the tunnel? From the window, the light shone on the trees, houses, people, clouds, and everything I could see. Why couldn't I see, when I needed to, how beautifully the light shines on our world? From the carriage window a whole new world appeared to open up to me. Why then had that world been hidden from me before?

My mind flashed to Portugal, to Africa, to Brazil. It was as though I had mentally switched-off all that I had learnt and observed at that time. Now, as if by magic, suddenly I could be aware again, could sense and feel exhilaration and excitement. Had I understood and learnt from that period in Stockholm? Certainly I felt my sensitivity, which I had had before, was now further heightened. Perhaps for some reason I had needed to sink to those depths, and come out whole, in order to be able to develop strength in my sensitivity. It was too soon then to draw any firm conclusions. These were to manifest themselves later in my life and career. At that moment on the voyage from Stockholm to Bergen - from, as it were, darkness into the light - I remember that I felt such immense relief, such tremendous joy, that I wanted to sing out and involve everyone around me.

My physical condition certainly did not warrant me considering a future in continuing to dance. Indeed I had resigned myself to the fact that no medical help could alter the situation, and that a future in the theatre was now out of my hands - I had no future. But I was free. Free of the thick black cloud that had suffocated me and brought me practically to the end of myself. I was on the way up, and no matter how long it took I wanted to feel physically and mentally whole again. I wanted to be able to say to myself that it was not for nothing that I had tasted hell. It was not long after my return to England that my new-found perseverance took me on an unforgettable journey that brought me into contact with human angels who helped me to understand. A voyage which ultimately led to the end of the tunnel, a cure for my chronic back condition, and a continuation of my career in dance at the age of twenty five after three years of disillusion.

I could not say, on arriving in Newcastle upon Tyne, that I had come home. I had left the family home eight years earlier at the age of sixteen, to take up full time training at the Royal Ballet School in London. Although my separation from a very happy family life was something that affected myself and my adolescence very deeply, I had nevertheless already concluded that a career in dance would negate the eventuality of my returning home. Also my parents had subsequently moved house to another area that was unfamiliar to me. Our little dog, whom I had loved and played with as a child and young adolescent, had long since died. My world had become quite estranged to the earlier life that I had so much enjoyed. Nevertheless, the loving parental warmth that is the family bond, was so welcome, so deeply welcome, that I found myself much more in touch with who I was and my own feelings, and therefore my feelings for others.

I secured work as a waiter in a large hotel in the centre Newcastle. I slowly learned to laugh and have fun again as, amid the long and poorly paid working hours, some very comical and potentially catastrophic situations presented themselves, as was inevitable considering my total lack of experience. However I managed to endear myself to the other employees. In turn, I enjoyed their uncomplicated personalities immensely, consistently comparing the dramatic change in my own present personality with that of a mere few months previously. Three months of work as a wine waiter taught me a great deal and could possibly have given me a new start in life, had there not been a marked improvement in my back condition. Itchy feet, together with a bitingly cold north winter wind, both contributed to my urge to get moving and start dancing again. I gave in my notice at the hotel and took off to warmer climes, to Portugal, to Lisbon, and to the Ballet Gulbenkian once more.

This proved to be an untimely mistake. The country that I had left had undergone a revolution to oust dictatorship politics and introduce democracy. Ballet Gulbenkian, although still functioning, now had a different atmosphere. The dancers were becoming discontented with Milko Sparemblek, who was finding it increasingly difficult to control a company where new and liberal ideas were beginning to manifest themselves. I had returned to Portugal, not with the intention of trying to take up where I had left off three years earlier, but in anticipation of being able to get into dance training once again. I soon discovered that I had tried to return too quickly. Familiar nerve pains of electric shock dimensions put paid to daily company classes. After a month of spending and not earning, I was left with only the means to return to London from where I hitch-hiked back to Newcastle, my tail between my legs, the prodigal son returning home for the second time.

My parents, understandably, were worried for me and tried their best to convince me that perhaps I should be turning my attentions to something a little more secure for my future. Blind to their concern and subsequent pain, I left Newcastle once again with a small rucksack, a little money and a lot of warm clothes. I headed, not south, but north. I left, not by train, bus or by car, but using a prominent thumb as I hitch-hiked up into Scotland amidst January snows, not knowing for how long or where in particular I was going. This move was a massive step in the right direction although I didn't know it at the time. What I did know was that I had to bide my time until I knew that the right moment had arrived to commence training again. At least I had no more doubts that eventually I would again be able to take up my career as a dancer. With this in mind, I blindly set off in search of peace of mind in the wild landscapes of northern Scotland,

In my naivety I had not considered, as perhaps others would have done, the possible consequences of my seemingly hair-brained idea. I quickly found out that winter in Scotland can rapidly produce arctic conditions, becoming at once a very dangerous place to someone without shelter. However, this naivety served me well for I headed fearlessly into the cauldron, albeit an icy one, and came out three months later a far richer man than when I went in. It is perhaps true to say that we are in control of our own destiny. If this is so, then it did not appear to me that I had been making a great success of mine recently. But those three months of extraordinary adventure, travelling by a thumb in the middle of winter to the furthest corners of Scotland's Highlands and Islands, on a financial budget that was totally unrealistic to say the least, led me to think otherwise. For the first time I began to consider the possibility that maybe I was in fact being guided, in my life, in the decisions that I was making.

In contrast to what had happened in, for example, Africa, where I had wanted to both experience and learn from my experiences, I found that in Scotland I wanted primarily to learn and that the experiences were being laid out before me to make this possible. The first month of my journey took me to the east and north coasts of Scotland, along the west coast, and then via the Isle of Skye to the Outer Hebridean Islands of Lewis, Harris, Uist and Barra. Contrary to my expectations, the weather was idyllic. Everywhere I went the local inhabitants and vehicle drivers all said the same thing. Never had they experienced such a calm and beautiful weather at the time of year. I was not unfamiliar with the Scottish Highlands, having had many a camping holiday there with my parents during the school summer holidays. On those occasions, more often than not, we would be camping in mud and deluge. Never had I visited Scotland outside that time of year and so I was quite surprised by the unbelievable lighting conditions, effects and colours that lend such a wonderful charm to Scotland in good winter weather. Mountains, seascapes and deep fjords are readily available in many parts of the world for those that seek them. In my opinion, what makes them stand out so significantly in Scotland is their combination with dramatic natural lighting, such as exists at dawn and dusk, or before and after a storm, or during a snowfall. It can completely mystify the eye of the beholder.

As a child I had been fascinated by Scotland's wilderness, and I can recall often feeling emotionally moved by the wonderful loneliness that I sensed in its grandeur. Many of our holidays had been times of 'chagrin' for my parents, as day after day of relentless rain, and three muddy sons, took its toll on their patience. But for me the rain and mist were an integral part of Scotland's mystical magic, so much so that even now the rainy periods here in Italy, years later, still give me the feeling that I am back in those heather-clad moors and mountains.

However, during those first four weeks of my journey in January and February of 1975, the familiar horizontal grey line cutting off the mountain tops and showing the low cloud level, was not in evidence for one single moment. Even on the few exciting occasions when an exhilarating electrical storm would whip-up from nowhere, showering hail and snow over everything, the weather would change so rapidly that cloud and mist were not given a chance to remain still for a moment. North-west Scotland is a land of very ancient bare rock and peat bog. In winter the hillsides and valleys bearing vegetation turn a rich brown. When it has rained, and at the instant the clouds clear to reveal a blue sky of which even Mediterranean lands would be proud, the glistening rock, the browns and blues, all combine to create out-of-this-world effects which in moments can change again into a completely different setting.

This was the backdrop into which I stepped on leaving Scotland's lowlands behind in the luxury of a Swedish Volvo, which took me on my first thumbed lift from just north of Newcastle upon Tyne, to Inverness over two hundred miles away. I remember clearly feeling a peace within me, that seemed so unfamiliar, as we headed over the Cairngorm Mountain-Pass that had been declared closed due to a recent heavy snowfall. The sky was cloudless and the land was pure white everywhere. Ours was the only vehicle on the road in either direction. One had to presume that the Volvo was on the road for it was not discernable, having melded in with the rest of the scenery. Everywhere, enormous herds of deer had gathered in the lower valleys because of drifting snow higher up where they would normally be located.

At the barrier that closed half of the road just north of Pitlochry, my driver had asked me if I wanted to risk the journey over the blocked pass with him, stating that it was imperative that he arrive in Inverness that evening. I had not hesitated, and so we had set off, spirits high, with the adrenalin flowing. Near the top of the pass, and at this stage worrying as to whether in fact we would get through, we met a snow plough coming from the opposite direction. Its driver gave us an incredulous stare, as we approached him at what had already been a snail's pace for some considerable distance. With the road now well defined and reasonably clear, our pace quickened. Once we were over the pass and heading down the other side, with a glorious sunset developing over the western hilly snowscape, we began to breathe and relax. In the lower valleys the snow had melted from the road and normal progress was resumed.

Later that evening at Inverness, having passed some ten hours in each others company, and particularly while approaching the Cairngorm road pass, we found that we had each valued one another's company. Philosophically speaking, we had warmed to each other. It seemed quite natural then to want to prolong our discourse. This we did over a superb dinner in a rather higher class of restaurant than I would have preferred, considering my attire. My host not only met the bill but also found and paid for a room for myself at the Guest House where he was staying.

This was the first day and night in Scotland on my journey, and I recount it to show what I mean by being personally guided. Perhaps the reader will also credit me with honesty when I say that every driver I managed to hail with my thumb brought magic and wonder to the journey. Whether it was the breadman who left me by the side of the road with meat pies and scones, or the travelling librarian who knew someone at the next village who would give me a bed for the night, or the local school mistress who insisted on making a twenty mile detour of what would have been a twelve mile drive in order to show me the exceptional beauty of the coastline. Or the travelling salesman who asked if I wouldn't mind stopping at the roadside hotel for a drink, and who then insisted on my joining him as his guest in the restaurant. One situation followed another as I always managed to get myself to a destination for the evening, whether I was paying for it or not, as the case may be. And, in warmth and comfort, and always a friendly atmosphere, I would reflect on the day's adventures and arrive at the conclusion that I could not possibly control or organise such a series of events, much less attribute them to good luck. My little seed of hope was growing at last and already, during the weeks to come, would expand so quickly as to make me feel that I must surely burst with overflowing joy.

Mrs. McKlennan, the curly, white-haired proprietor of the bed and breakfast Guest House at Castlebay on Barra, the most southerly of inhabited islands in the Outer Hebrides where I had arrived earlier in the day from the more northerly island of Uist, was intrigued with my explanation. A hitch-hiker on holiday - how could I explain it otherwise - in early February in the Outer Hebrides. Madness. "You'll be having a nice time with the weather then," she stated with a disbelieving glint in her eye, her polite response interrogating and searching at the same time. The wonderful lilt, that is the gentle accent of the island folk, left me dreaming. "Och, come along at seven o' clock and have a wee bite to eat. I've someone here that you should perhaps like to meet."

Mrs. McKlennan would normally be closed to tourists at this time of year as I later discovered, along with practically every other landlady offering modest bed and breakfast accommodation on this seasonably, very popular, tiny island with its extraordinary mediaeval castle standing in the middle of a sheltered bay; a stone's throw from the shore. My lift along the road south, from the tiny ferry boat from which I had alighted onto the island with just one other person, was with the local driver who had come to collect my ferry companion. He had said that there would be little chance of any further cars arriving at the ferry for the rest of the day. "Where are you staying for the night." "Well I hoped I might find a cheap bed and breakfast somewhere at Castlebay," my tone forming a question rather than a statement. "Och, Doreen McKlennan's got a student from Australia staying with her at the moment" my driver replied, and said to his friend "We'd better drop him off at her place."

The student, I later presumed, was the someone she wanted me to meet over the "wee bite to eat" that evening. After a short climb up the hill behind the small port of Castlebay, to view the splendid castle against its scenic backdrop of countless rocky Hebridean islands to the south, I once again experienced this incredulous, poignant feeling of wonder that I desperately did not want to begin to take for granted. Karen, Mrs. McKlennan's Australian student, a beautiful young lady of about twenty-five with a personality so sweet and so gentle as to melt in your mouth, politely and a little formally told me her background. She had come to Sterling in Scotland, her ancient family seat, as a student and, as she had a few days free, had come here alone to walk and to reflect. She had organised her accommodation beforehand with Mrs. McKlennan,

Mrs. McKlennan left the dishes on the table and silently exited from the dining room. When dinner was over, Karen explained to me that she was leaving Barra on the car ferry from Castlebay to Oban on the mainland, the following morning, to begin her return journey to Sterling. I felt a flush of sadness sweep through me. "I've made a friend while I have been here who is camping in a small tent on the grass down by the shore. I'm going to see him now. I know you'd like to meet him after what you've told me about yourself. You'd better put on your jumper and coat, as it's quite chilly down there". As with all my other recent experiences, the prospect of a chilly evening inside a tent by the sea shore, in mid winter, with this lovely lady and her newly-found acquaintance, intrigued me in my desire to understand where all this was leading me. When you meet someone for the first time, and instantly and instinctively feel that you have known that person somewhere before, then you know profoundly that such a meeting was not by mere coincidence. Such was my first introduction to Ted, a tall, lean and muscular American, who welcomed not only Karen but also myself into the warm hospitality of his humble abode - which had been his home for four years.

To my mind Karen and Ted, who were acquaintances to each other for only a few days and soon to part without presumably ever seeing each other again, were angels sent to give me not only renewed faith in the human race, but also to guide me forward into a new world of fantasy and the conviction that anything is possible in this life - and dreams do really come true. I knew Karen for but a few hours in this physical life, before she left on the ferry without giving either Ted or myself a contact address. Ted I knew a while longer as we teamed up later and travelled through the Hebrides and eventually onto the Isle of Skye. That evening in Ted's small two-man tent, with two candles glowing with warmth and light, an Englishman, an Australian and an American sat cross-legged on Scottish soil and communed late into the night.

Each of us had a sad tale to tell. Each of us had hope in our hearts that something had mystifyingly brought us to this place and therefore together at that time. On reflecting now exactly twenty years hence, I feel strongly a very deep feeling of oneness with two total strangers that I never have experienced since. It was for just a moment, and for that time only, but it has lasted a lifetime. I have never lost touch with Karen's spiritual warmth, or with Ted's amazing philosophy on life, after we parted for the second and final time two months later. I knew they had been there at that time to help me become aware of an important lesson, without which I could not advance in my life. Just as, and probably also, I had been there for them.

I believe that when such precious moments present themselves to us, and we are at the same time fully aware that they are out of the ordinary, unless we allow such incidents to follow their natural course they are of no purpose to us. If however, without the intention of prolonging or profiting from such heavenly gifts, we can look beyond ourselves to what we are being told, we can view life very differently to the superficiality that otherwise becomes the norm. In any case, this was my experience during the course of that amazing evening. In total and unpretentious simplicity there was an outpouring of three souls, each seeking to understand rather than be understood, resulting in my being able to view my depression in Sweden in a far more positive light than I had done hitherto. To see the fact that, because I so wanted to dance, and to dance with my total being, my gift was denied me for a time so that I might realize how it was to be used in future years. The fact that I had actually become open to examining my previous life in this very significant way, and in a place that epitomised peace, suggested to me that in my future life I should try to be more aware of the important influences within and around me - and not seek to be so much in control of my own destiny.

As Ted and I watched the ferry depart from Castlebay quay with Karen, the following morning, unashamedly allowing our emotions to rise to the surface and to overflow in my case, we gave thanks spiritually to the presence that was leaving our midst. Feeling lost for a moment, we looked at each other. That evening Ted and I talked again late into the night as though Karen was still with us, but we never then or again mentioned her.

Living for four years in a tiny two-man tent in western Scotland seemed to me to be a formidable penance. I could not but think that Ted was punishing himself for leaving his wife and two children behind in America. This may in fact have been so. But as the days following developed into times of real physical challenge for me, I started to open my eyes and, through Ted, to see just how much joy and satisfaction could be gained from so little. Ted travelled with a fifty kilogram pack in which there was everything that he required to survive and, in many ways, survival it was. I never asked from where his sustenance came and he never offered an explanation. This rugged, yet highly intelligent and educated man in his mid-thirties, had reduced one-man camping to the finest of arts. In the following two weeks, as his guest, I gained a lifetime's experience on survival in the hardest of weather conditions. Two days after leaving Castlebay, my own backpack having been augmented with dismantled cardboard boxes for good ground insulation when sleeping, the idyllic weather that the highlands and islands had enjoyed for well over a month suddenly erupted into hurricane force winds, with gusts in excess of 100 miles an hour.

The reader may well feel that a little poetic license is being used here, but this is not the case. In Ted's four years of camping experience, he had learnt to erect and dismantle his tent, as well as live in it, in every type of weather that the Atlantic Ocean could throw at him. When the gales started suddenly one night without warning, we both quickly realised that we were camped in the wrong place for such winds: namely an exposed, cropped-grass field. My plan of action was to snuggle deeper into my thin and somewhat inadequate sleeping bag and, amidst the deafening howl, try to forget what was going on around us. Ted's plan differed. As soon as he heard the roar of the approaching tempest, be was out of his bag in a flash and, being already dressed, started to stuff all extraneous objects into his rucksack which had doubled as a pillow, demanding politely but urgently that I rise quickly and do the same. In a moment the cyclone was upon us. Boots, socks, cooking utensils, plates, anything that had been left outside the entrance to the tent, were gone in an instant. Anything inside that was not stowed had to be left, as the tent was immediately lowered to a lower level to lessen its wind resistance. I did not have time to put on my overcoat before I was pushed out of the tent, with Ted following in my wake. In only a few minutes we were shivering in a sub-zero temperature, which was reduced much further by the wind-chill factor.

The night was black and wild. Ted, with great presence of mind, had snatched his pocket lamp upon exiting the tent. He now switched it on and passed it to me to hold as he rushed about, crouched, undoing ties and pulling out pegs, all the while keeping at least one foot on some part of the tent. I felt useless. The wind angrily shook the canvas, tearing at it frantically as it was loosened from its holdings. One of the pliable plastic tent poles had forced its way through the canvas, ripping it in the process. Gathering up the tent, while fighting all the while against the gusts, Ted screamed at me above the roar of the storm to shine the torch around in search of shelter. Crouching also against the force of the wind, I remembered noticing a barn not too far down the track along which we had walked earlier in the evening.. But where was the track. The pocket lamp gave a beam extending perhaps three metres. In the blackness I had lost all sense of direction and, like a demented dwarf, I began to scout in all directions until I found the track? In so doing I had lost Ted but he soon appeared dragging his bundle, as I shouted at the top of my voice and waved the torch up and down frantically to indicate my position.

Hunchbacked, we made our way across the wind and along the track until, thankfully, the corner of the barn wall was caught in the thin beam of light. On the leeward side of the barn we could again talk to one another in a civilized fashion. I was reduced to a shivering wreck, I had neither an outer-coat on my body, nor boots on my feet - which fortunately, a least, bore three pairs of socks. My thick sheepskin coat was extracted quickly from within the bundled-up tent, and also a light pair of shoes from my rucksack that was also inside the tent bundle. In the comparative protection that the barn offered from the holocaust, I madly jumped up and down in an attempt to get my blood circulating somewhere in my body. Meanwhile, Ted began to set up the tent as close to the wall as possible. Within five minutes of arriving at our point of safety, the tent was erected, and we were inside it with candles glowing and water heating on a makeshift stove lit by fire-lighting tablets. Ted vigorously massaged my feet that I had not yet begun to feel, calmly smiling at me, which caused me to relax and then burst out laughing at the uncomfortable though ludicrous situation in which we had found ourselves.

"At least it isn't raining, or snowing for that matter" he spurted out amidst childish giggles. That put the cap on it, and for the next half an hour I battled no longer with the wind, but with tearful eyes and a runny nose as I laughed uncontrollably, and shivered until I ached all over. Thankfully the wind did not change direction for the rest of that long night. When dawn eventually broke, Ted broke the silence by offering to make a cup of coffee. Neither of us had slept, and the howling gale not abated. But the tent was still erect and in comparatively tranquil air. Fortunately, apart from the small rip in the canvas at the front entrance to the tent, there had been no damage and the various articles that had been blown and scattered around the field were recovered.

I thanked Ted sincerely for what he had done that night to save us both from our predicament, and during the day as the wind strength gradually decreased and finally ceased altogether, we returned to a more normal existence. I reflected on how fragile man can be before the angry elements. It is said that silence is golden and how true that rang when the air became still once again after the screaming, high pitched wail that had relentlessly attacked our every sense for over twelve hours. At the time I seemed to be none the worse for the ordeal, and Ted and I continued north into Uist, Harris and Lewis. We walked or travelled mainly by postal bus since hitch-hiking had become less reliable as a means of getting anywhere. I felt sure that Ted's enormous and extremely heavy pack was the reason, acting as a deterrent to would-be sympathetic drivers.

Five days later, on the Isle of Lewis, the storms returned. This time we heard the familiar distant roar at dusk, watching with disdain the low cloud whip up into a cyclone, revealing the accompanying rain. We were nowhere near any visible shelter where we could readily pitch the tent, the only obstructions to an otherwise flat landscape being a roadside house and, a little further on, a solitary red telephone cabin. As the rain started to fall, lightly at first, and then with accompanying gathering wind, much more heavily, we reached the telephone cabin. Leaving our bags on the narrow leeward side, only partially protected from the rain, we both squeezed inside anticipating a worse predicament than that of a few days ago. We were not wrong in our prediction.

Ted immediately ruled out erecting his tent in the rain on a wild and exposed position. It would seem that for the duration of the storm we must content ourselves with shelter in this very upright and certainly not voluminous space. In fact the two cubic metres offered by our adopted temporary accommodation were to become very familiar over the next twenty-five hours, as the continuing storm increased to cater-wauling dimensions. When no alternative measures present themselves in what appears to be a dire situation, it is amazing how the human spirit often accepts with gratitude any alleviating and comforting condition in what is otherwise a black hole.

As the early winter darkness set in, we discussed how we were going to pass this coming night, two likely lads in a box with dimensions not much greater than an upright coffin. There was no light in the cabin which, considering its odd location, probably did not get used more than a handful of times a year. There was a small pane of glass missing, and although this was not on the windward side of the cabin, air currents passing through the space prevented a candle from being lit. It was going to be a very long night, and I thought of people trapped in caves or buried alive under avalanches. Sometimes individuals had been known to survive for days, without food or water, in total blackness, unable to move, buried under rubble and in extreme pain. What was it that, under such circumstances, gave people the will and hope to go on living.

We considered our own meagre predicament. For both of us to sit on the floor was out of the question, as Ted's legs were so long that he could not find comfort in any position other than standing. In a short time the rain turned to snow, and flakes from the outside blizzard were whisked into our space through the missing window pane. Despite all this we probably had the most comforting thing of all - each other's good company. Ted had a brainwave, which in fact decreased the floor area by one-third, but which at least allowed us both to find space to sit. By perching his back-pack upright against one side of the cabin, be found that he could sit on the shelf that had once housed telephone directories and extend his feet to the top of the pack. I was allotted the lower bunk. In the pitch-black of the night, with every article of clothing we could find covering our bodies including our water-proofs, we slept fitfully and talked, talked and slept.

Every now and then we would have to move around and Ted, in particular, modified his own seating arrangement a number of times until he satisfied himself that he could not improve on it. We changed places, but this was not satisfactory. My legs were not long enough to comfortably reach the rucksack and Ted's were too long for the floor space, particularly as it had now been reduced. From time to time he lit his petrol-operated stove and made a cup of coffee to break up the long night. This had to be done outside as the fumes from the burning petrol, notwithstanding the natural air conditioning, were quickly overpowering. However, we did manage to obtain a little warmth on occasions from his fire-lighting tablets which, in the small space, quickly took away the chill from the air despite threatening extinguishing air currents passing through air space.

Thus the night slowly passed, and dawn revealed a very heavy snowfall through the misted windows of the sheltered side of the cabin. Strong winds and drifting had created extraordinary shapes and surfaces. But the gales and snow had not abated, and did not abate for the whole of that day. Any thought of progress to a place where shelter might be found, sufficient to warrant pitching Ted's tent, was a daunting prospect and the thought of another night in this telephone cabin with such relentless sound effects made me feel nervy. Ted was out of the cabin for long periods during the day, presumably to give me the space. As the hours passed slowly, I began to feel less well physically; my tonsils had swollen a little and I thought I might have a slight temperature. Towards the end of daylight, Ted returned for the final time. He was snow-covered, weatherworn and a little fed-up. He had been sitting for practically three hours by the machair at the shore a mile away, challenging the elements. In the end he had been beaten. Stiff and freezing, he had finally allowed himself to be blown by the wind back to our compact but sheltered cabin interior.

After four years of tenting in a comparatively unfriendly climate, Ted was not one to give up lightly. He enjoyed challenging circumstances, thriving on mentally and physically overcoming his natural desire to relent to an easier solution to a problem. When I explained that, with the last of the remaining daylight, I was going to make my way to the roadside house we had passed yesterday to try and secure a bed for the night, he shrugged his shoulders. Asking if I ought to include him in this plan, should it be successful, his simple but sullen-faced reply was "I guess so." When I returned three-quarters of an hour later, having been forced at the house to drink a double whisky for medicinal purposes, my urgent and smiling impression caused him to react more positively.

Gathering up our possessions we fought our way back down the road, this time lit by the beam of a powerful torch kindly provided by the house occupants, to their welcome warmth and hospitality. "I've never in my life heard anything like it", Mrs. MacLeod expostulated when I enlarged on what I had earlier briefly explained to Mr. MacLeod. When I first knocked desperately on their door, and shouted my dilemma through the window to Mr. MacLeod who, considering the circumstances, was understandably loathe to open the door, a heated discussion in Gaelic had ensued between the couple. Eventually Mr. MacLeod did open the door hesitantly and I was beckoned to enter quickly, whereupon the door was quickly closed again. Inside the vestibule, I tried to make my story brief but convincing, stating that I would be prepared to pay for any overnight accommodation there and then. From the living room, Mrs. MacLeod opened the door to the vestibule and said to her husband in English that he should "let the poor man into the house at least, as he must surely die of exposure if he doesn't warm himself up a bit." I went in.

In the instant relief of the room's warmth and comparative silence, I positively glowed. "And is he still in the telephone cabin? och the poor lad" Mrs. MacLeod said, shaking her head and sitting me down in an armchair in front of the peat fire. Meanwhile Mr. MacLeod, slowly coming round to the assumption that I was not a threatening person, was preparing my generous double whisky. Their incredulity on hearing that not one but two men had spent the past twenty-six hours in the cabin was now too much for me to bear. I safely placed my whisky glass on a nearby table as I cracked-up, half-laughing, half-crying, with the relief of finding the occupants of the only house in the vicinity sympathetic.

Now, with both Ted and myself securely ensconced for the night in warmth and comfort, a hot meal in our stomachs and a wildly curious middle-aged pair of crofters sat in front of us, we were able to expound on our experiences of the last few days. Mr. MacLeod told us that the storms which had ravaged the whole of the west coast of Scotland were thought to be the most severe for twenty years. The television news showed bleak episodes of dreadful damage to ships and harbours. All ferry departures were cancelled and daily life had come to a standstill. Scotland was now paying a heavy price for its month of idyllic winter weather, literally the calm before the storm. The forecast was for the weather to abate during the night or early morning, and then return to calm though cloudy conditions.

"And why, for heaven's sake, did not the pair of you come straight away, the minute the storm started." Ted and I looked at each other, and then at the floor, without offering a reply. On looking back, twenty years later, I realize with gratitude just how many important lessons were confronting me then about life. How it was being moulded, how I was being taught to be stretched within my capabilities, how I discovered that risk and overcoming risk bring understanding, and were put before us to take us forward. I now wonder if, as human beings living in a civilisation which is poignantly and conclusively geared towards comfort and security, we are failing to achieve our spiritual potential, with the result that we are robbed of a very important element in living - vibrant and positive thinking. I understand now why I had to be broken down in Sweden, to allow my heart and mind to open themselves up to what I would shortly afterwards be exposed. The time in Scotland had began to show me a new way of thinking, to give me a new kind of energy, a new and vibrant courage to say yes to life on every level of experience.

As I lay in a soothing bath of hot, peat-stained water, I pondered over security, it was true to say that I appreciated tremendously the luxury and serenity of this temporary shelter. I appreciated enormously the generosity and hospitality provided by Mr. and Mrs. MacLeod. Would, I asked myself, my consciousness of that appreciation ever have been so acute had I not initially deprived myself of security - the type of security that fear of the unknown causes us to adopt? Would my appreciation of the freedom, that I was now so richly enjoying in Scotland, have been so heightened had I not inhabited my mental prison in Sweden? That night I came to the conclusion that security, when it was most vital, would be provided but that I could do without it in the meantime. That there was too much living and too much learning to do, to waste time worrying about life and where it was coming from. This would be revealed to me as and when I was ready to understand it. From now on I would live with the philosophy of not taking anything for granted, that what I would get out of life would be what I deserved, and my ultimate appreciation would be in accordance with my quota of input.

Later that night, wide awake and on the edge of the double bed where Ted's body was occupying seventy per cent of the space, I listened to the ceaseless storm raging outside and suddenly thought about my back. It had not been on my mind since that evening on Barra, and subsequently I had been unaware of the fact that I had been free of all pain for a number of days. How very strange, I reflected. Perhaps my back problem had been brought-on psychosomatically and, if so, had I healed myself now that I was mentally together once again? There was still the reality of the motor accident from which the problem initially appeared to have arisen. Had I subconsciously, through thought patterns in my depressed state, brought that upon myself also? So many questions. So many interesting, feasible answers. So much to experience.

I awoke with a start, bumping against Ted's naked back in the process and waking him up. Something was very different. There was a deafening hum in my ears. "The storm, its stopped" Ted whispered, his voice resonating above the buzz in my ears. Suddenly I became aware of an overpowering silence that permeated my whole being. I got up and looked out of the window. In the perceptible foreground, the snow lay over everything and stole the show from a hazy quarter-moon. The stillness was shocking, like the moment before thunderous applause after a frantically energetic dance performance. In contrast to the end of the previous storm of a few days before, when the silence had appeared golden, this silence to me was positively deafening. I could not immediately come to terms with it. Perhaps this was because of what had been on my mind prior to falling into slumber.

Over breakfast the following morning, Mr. MacLeod asked if we were awake when the wind died. I replied that I was convinced that I woke up at the exact moment the storm died. Mr. MacLeod, with a far-away look of wonder in his eyes, stated that he had also been aroused from sleep just moments before the end of the storm, and the transition from savage howling to stillness had been swift and sudden. He had not experienced anything so dramatic in his life before. It was like a cleansing, not only of the earth, but of the spirit. He managed at that moment, in a few simple words, to bring to the surface of my conscious mind a much deeper issue that had been burning within me, and which suddenly became very clear.

The air warmed considerably during that day and the snow gradually melted. By dusk, there were just patches of packed white ice where it had drifted. That morning Mrs. MacLeod had, with her husband, insisted that we accept a lift for the twelve miles to the main road. There we would be sure of finding traffic going south to Tarbert on Harris, the ferry terminal for cars and passengers travelling to and from Uig on the Isle of Skye, where we intended to go. She had charged us for the evening meal and breakfast only, waving the back of her band at our protestations and laughingly saying "Och, away with you. Your company and stories were worth far more by comparison". Mr. MacLeod's 'old banger' was possibly the first and only car that day, to make its precarious way along the snow-covered single-track road to the junction. The already wild landscape had a strange, ravaged look. A few gnarled trees surviving the unforgiving winter winds in their peaty terrain, were distinctly leaning towards the east.

Our heartfelt thanks were given to Mr. MacLead as we took our leave at the road junction, acutely aware that in those first few hundred yards, we were physically free to walk in any direction without the severe encumbrance of persistently strong winds. In good spirits, we trundled through wet sludge intent on arriving at Tarbert that day to enquire about the state of the ferries to Skye. One car passed us that morning. Our spirits were still not dampened when, by three o' clock, we had not succeeded in stopping any of the subsequent three cars that passed us in the afternoon. Contentedly resigned to having to pitch Ted's tent on wet ground for the night, we commenced looking for a sheltered spot along the road. At that point, an open-backed Land Rover with two occupants pulled up, and we bundled our gear and bodies into the rear and braced ourselves for the chilly journey down to the port.

Ted was none the worse on arrival and leapt from the back of the Land Rover. However, I was in a frozen and shivering state, and had to be helped from the vehicle. While thawing out in the terminal's passenger waiting room, I once again became aware that my tonsils were swollen and being accompanied by a curious throbbing in my throat. Ted's enquiries at the booking office confirmed that operations would not be back to normal until the next morning. With some regret, I felt it to wiser seek accommodation again for the night instead of roughing it with Ted in the tent on wet ground, although I did help him pitch camp and make a simple meal.

The following morning, concern crept in as I found my condition deteriorating, exacerbated by a rough sea passage where the waters between the Inner and Outer Hebrides had yet to make peace after the storm the day before. By the time the ferry had docked I reached the conclusion that, as I had no quick and reliable means of travel, it would be prudent to make my way southwards back to Newcastle and my parents' home, before my health warranted being bedridden in a strange place. Ted was sympathetic, but he wished to remain on Uig. We both felt, wrongly, as it turned out, that the parting of the ways had come. That destiny, which deemed that we meet and spend this extraordinary time together, was now also calling to us individually to go forward in our own lives with this valuable experience as a back-up.

We shook hands at a cross roads, where I would shortly secure a lift some sixty miles to mainland Scotland. Then, each looking profoundly at the other, we dropped unnecessary formalities and hugged each other, arms and bodies entangled. Preventing emotion from swelling in an already swollen throat, I thought again of that wonderful night with Karen in the candlelight in Ted's tent down by the shore at Castlebay, Barra. Of the deep communion that the three of us experienced, and which had not forsaken me during the subsequent eighteen days alone with Ted.

We parted without words, the enormous pack hiding his person and leaving me with the image of a snail carrying its house on its back. How often in the coming years was I to recall that image, and muse on the powerful magic spell. My Journey to Newcastle from the Isle of Skye took me four days. My first hitched lift to Lochalsh, a few miles beyond the ferry crossing to the mainland, was a mixture of small-talk conversation and sleep, interspersed with a deepening delirium as the fever mounted in my head. By the time I arrived at the independent hostel in Glen Carron, fighting to keep on top of my sickness, I was exhausted. I slept in a dormitory with two other occupants that evening, and also for most of the following day and night, profusely sweating but grateful that the fever was taking its course.

When I felt fit enough to continue my journey, the worst was over. The fever had subsided and my appetite was slowly returning. Only my continuing painful throat and an awesome weakness prevented me from changing my plans. On the third day, I succeeded in getting to within thirty miles of Newcastle when darkness finally precluded any possibility of arriving in Newcastle that night. The air was very mild and an open barn door beckoned me inside for shelter. Only the roar of occasional passing cars disturbed an otherwise tranquil night. I had telephoned my parents from Kyleakin on the Isle of Skye, while waiting for the ferry, telling them of my arrival in due course but without the details of why I was returning. One can therefore understand their perplexity when, once at home, I explained that I had had the time of my life for six wintry weeks in north west Scotland and that my intentions were, within the next few days, to return to the Highlands with a tent.

During the last thirty miles of my return, which had taken over six hours, my tonsilitis had ceased to exist, my strength had returned and a new excitement was bubbling inside me. It seemed to me, that my story had not arrived at a logical conclusion. That I still had lessons to learn up there among the wild hills and seascapes, where one could really begin to sort out the complexities that can build-up in the human mind. For me, my recent experience had been so valuable. I had been privileged with a new direction of thought, a way out of a black hole, to go on learning, to go on discovering who I was and where I was. Through his example and amazing personality, Ted had struck a chord within me that was now resonant, calling on me to try something new, to risk, and above all to learn and live my life as it was destined to be lived.

Had I not been absolutely sure within myself that I must return to Scotland, and what I was feeling was not simply a whim or an escape, then it would have been easy to follow the pleading advice given to me to think about my future. However I would not, and indeed could not, listen to what to others would be common sense. Neither could I explain precisely what I was doing, blindly following a voice deep within me that had spoken so poignantly during the last six weeks. Within five days, and using the knowledge I had gained from two weeks of intense training from a master, I had gathered together what I believed were the necessary materials for winter survival in Scotland, albeit based on a minimal budget. I had scoured Newcastle's camping and secondhand shops for light weight and compact articles that would have a practical purpose in wild areas and in any weather conditions. I had modified my own existing camping gear to suit my purpose, and when I had put it all together on my back to find the weight unbearable for my slight body structure, I had discarded any extraneous articles that were not essential.

Before departing for the second time, and sensing my parents' frustration and bewilderment, I sat them down and attempted to explain what had happened to me in Scotland. Pearls of wisdom from my still youthful and comparatively inexperienced mind were, of course, not forthcoming. I have now gained the deepest respect for the patience of my mother and father, for their willingness to try to understand, and for not attempting to erect a barrier against my seemingly hair-brained ideas that, to them, must have appeared to be leading me nowhere.

My childhood as the youngest of three sons was a very happy one, having been spent in the midst of a loving family atmosphere. I felt that the balance with which our parents brought us up was perfect. Not too restricting, and yet within disciplinary measures that allowed our boisterous energy to go so far and no further. I often look back to those formative years and see distinctly how they prepared me perfectly for the later development of my character.

Many believe that we are, who we are, before we are born. That we come to this beautiful planet to learn, not so much about what is outside of ourselves, but what is within. The more we discover about ourselves, the deeper we can go. When one comes to the conclusion that there are no limits to the revelations that are to be found, then one starts to be in touch with a priceless knowledge that can shine through the darkest barrier. I am of this train of thought and behind my convictions, in fact behind every decision in my life, there is a guidance. If I am honest with myself, that guidance has its deep roots within my dance. I know now that I came to this world as a dancer. That this was my supreme gift. I believe that I was given life on earth, with all its wonder and its restrictions, to be able to explore the gift that comes from within myself, using my body as a tool.

I had first, of course, to learn about movement and how to put thought into movement. I could not simply take it for granted that I could get from A to B, and pick up or discard various items outside of myself along the way. Dance training teaches us this, perhaps, as no other activity can do. Initially, the movements are foreign to our body's natural desire to move, and the coordination necessary is far more advanced than that usually demanded of the body. In normal circumstances we react in a most awkward fashion, sometimes for years, until the brain learns how to control the new messages it is being given. Once these barriers are overcome, and in some people this can be practically instantaneous as I believe they are born to it, then we are free to develop this new coordination through dance.

As in music and the study of a musical instrument, dance is not only the coordination of mind and body but also of the senses of sight and particularly hearing. If one is to develop dance beyond a classroom activity then all of these elements have to reach the point of being automatically activated. A further element is then included in the already extremely complex process - character. One must learn how to put into dance, which is already a medium of movement totally abnormal to the body, something that we call character and which develops over the years from experiences in our lives.

In my opinion most dancers make bad actors, mainly because I feel that their training is so intense and concentrated that it provides a product at an age when little of life's experiences has been gained. In contrast to acting or a career in music, a dancer's life is cruelly short. The wear and tear on the body begins to show physical deterioration at a time when one has only just become mentally aware, experienced, and observant of the diversity of personality. Early on in a career, one has an abundance of physical and dynamic energy. Later in that same career, one develops the artistry and finesse necessary to convey realistically the message that is meant to be given. Rarely do the two vital elements join forces for much longer than a handful of years.

I believe that from the beginning my dance was an inner communication which found its outlet and expression through both bodily movement and sound. Perhaps this is as I had never really related to movement for movement's sake in my career, without the vital element of emotion. Yes, I could appreciate the cleverness of technical perfection in much the same way that I could appreciate the months and years of work involved in high-quality gymnastics. But to me dance was about saying something emotionally, that perhaps could not be expressed more with words.

At the age of nine, when I commenced ballet training, I was not too aware of my parents' reaction to their youngest son's desire to begin dance classes. To all outward appearances I was not a very out-of-the-ordinary young boy. I was born into post-war England in the industrial north east, where boys grew up to be hard, to smoke and drink beer, and 'hang out' with the lads. My boyhood was spent mainly on the streets where, in the fifties, it was still quite safe to be. My passion, as part of a gang, was to build tree huts and create 'bogies' - a type of cart made with pram wheels - and cause general havoc to the residents of our street.

However puberty and an increasing passion for what I was learning through the dance classes put paid to any continuation of a 'normal adolescence'. I cannot claim in the years that followed, that my school days amounted to the best years of my life. School for me, at the age of thirteen, became a nightmare as I found myself naively desperate to keep my dance studies secret from my friends. Unfortunately my French teacher had a daughter who also took classes at the same dance school. This resulted in insensitive, blind comments that he made to me during French classes, which only he and I understood, but which raised the curiosity of the other members of the class.

Eventually, after months of agony, the word was out. There then ensued a period of two years when I was never allowed to forget that, in the eyes of three hundred pupils of an all-boys grammar school, I was a disgrace to the young male contingent of our rough-and-ready society. At this time my parents offered me the solid base on which I needed to stand. My ballet teacher gave me and my parents great encouragement, constantly urging me on, to make up the lost time due to my late start at the age of nine. I may well, at that time, have been the only boy studying ballet in Newcastle upon Tyne. Not once did my mother or father suggest another direction, only advising that I complete first my studies at the Grammar School before leaving home for more intensive training.

The tide turned when, at the age of fifteen, and through a local newspaper article, the school discovered that I had been offered a place at the Royal Ballet School in London to train to be a professional dancer. The scoffing and jeering that was a daily routine with the stronger and idolised bullies, suddenly melted away. Curiosity and wonder took their place. Through my refusal to give in to a seemingly stronger force, I gained respect at my school and my first big lesson was learnt. Without the encouragement of my parents and their belief in me at this early stage, I could well have opted for a more tranquil and straightforward school life, dropping the idea of dance and melding into the background as so many of us sadly do.

It may be that these first confrontations with adversity helped me considerably, and caused me to think more deeply about myself, and my emotional reactions to outside stimuli, thus paving the way for a greater insight into dramatic dance. For it was soon established, among my teachers in London, that I possessed a greater talent in character dance rather than technical dance ability. This was proven in my first contract with the Gulbenkian Ballet, when I found, as did the director, that I was out of place in corps de ballet lines of syncronised simulations, and much more at home with a character role.

On reflecting where I am now with the dance, I am open to considering that every influence and instigation has contributed to broadening my mind sufficiently to allow me to develop my dance from within me, rather than externally and within a competitive atmosphere. I realize too, that being a success is very dependent on how one individually defines and views success. It is easy to consider oneself a failure in anything because of an inability to match the norms set by the masses who - in turn - are controlled and manipulated by the few. Being now totally at home with who I am and what I am doing with my life, I feel that I can say that I am successful and, in my desire to learn and go forward in life, this counts for a lot.

Of course, had I been able to express this point of view to my mother and father some twenty years earlier, on the point of my second departure into the wilderness that is north-west Scotland, it would probably have gone some way to alleviate the uncertainty and concern with which I left them. Nevertheless leave I did. It was a loving father who resignedly dropped me, with my bulky baggage, out of town by the side of the road, and said goodbye with a look of acceptance.

Three Dogs and a Dancer by Stephen Ward

Chapter 8

Out of the Darkness and into the Light

Scotland - Part 2, 1975

So, once again I returned to the Scottish Highlands. It was mid-March and, although very cold, the nights were becoming shorter. Initially I followed the same route that I took when I embarked on my first trip nearly two months earlier, reaching as far as the Cairngorm Mountains just south of Inverness on my first day. That night, camped by a stream on heather-clad moorland was very much a dress rehearsal for what would become, in the weeks and months ahead, second nature to me,

Although camping was not new to me, I had never before hitch-hiked with a tent and back-pack on my own, nor had an unlimited time before me restricted only by a small, borrowed sum of money. Not for one moment did I ever have any concern or fear over what might befall me, or how I would spend my time. My previous travelling, both before and with Ted, had taught me that the more time one allows oneself, the greater the adventure that one is likely to have. Boredom usually follows restlessness. Although I had spent months of deeply depressed restlessness in Sweden, since coming to Scotland I had succeeded in laying that down and subsequently finding peace of mind. Anticipation of survival and adventure were more on my mind than what I would do with the time, and during my first week spent on the north shore of Loch Torridon, a sea loch on the west coast north of the Kyle of Lochalsh, I had a good share of adventures to challenge me.

The natural transition from dependence to independence, which had been made unconsciously since my first sojourn in Scotland, served me well as I found myself totally alone at nights with only my own thoughts for company. Back in January and February I had been pre-occupied with getting from one night's accommodation to another in the short space of time that winter daylight in the northern areas allows. Concern for my physical condition, and the twinges from the aches and pains I still experienced, had inhibited me from straying too far from the road. The perfect weather that Scotland had enjoyed then, coupled with the often extraordinary lighting conditions, had sometimes been so enticing that I found an inner voice arguing with my more reckless thoughts, saying "bide your time, Stephen Ward, bide your time. The moment will come when you'll be able to appreciate the mountains and enjoy the hill walks."

I had followed that inner voice, knowing that should I have an acute attack of lower back pain some three thousand feet up a solitary mountain in winter, then there could be little hope of my surviving and returning. So I had opted for the social outlet that was very generously and graciously offered. At the same time I found that, contrary to many opinions about Scotland's inhabitants, the local people - whether thoroughbred Gael or a White Settler, as the Hebridean folk contemptuously call the Sassenachs and Lowland Scots who have settled in the area - were not mean or avaricious, but warm, hospitable and giving in every sense. I had been dependent on free travel from place to place in order to secure a roof over my head for the night, and found this generosity to have no bounds. It led me from one door to another, filling me with renewed respect and love for the people

I was now more or less independent, other than for travel, with my own shell and rucksack on my back which fortunately continued to be free of pain. I found that I was finally liberated from all the shackles that might prevent me from appreciating the fabulous wealth of wild and natural beauty that this place offered. I also discovered that independence cuts one off from people, since they may not be around to give help and assistance when it might be required. Nevertheless, in a very different light this new and challenging experience brought with it the final healing, both mental and physical, that I needed before I could move on in my life and return to the dance. It was also a time when I learnt profoundly the difference between being alone and being lonely. One is empty when one is lonely and devoid of communication, unable to reach beyond oneself. One can feel lonely in the most social of situations and when, for example, one finds oneself unable to have a discourse with another other person in the throng of a city. I knew these depths of loneliness in Stockholm, when I was not well enough within myself to relate healthily to anyone else, or even to consider that communication and company may be found elsewhere other than with people.

In the Highlands, with just my tent and myself, I knew that I had already come a long way in understanding since those long, dark months. That I was no longer deaf or blind to positive energy in the form of an inner voice, lifting me up out of the dark and into the light. This was borne out in an initially very strange, but shortly to become familiar, deeply spiritual relationship with wild solitary places. This was particularly so in Scotland, but also later re-discovered high up in the Swiss and Austrian Alps, and quite wonderfully in the Apuanian mountain areas - where I would ultimately establish my home with the acquisition of La Casetta.

This voice at first manifested itself through emotional joy when, quite suddenly and uncontrollably, I would give way to an inexplicable outburst of expression, needing to laugh when no funny thought had occurred to me, needing to cry when this seemed the last thing on my mind. Music accompanied me everywhere, when wonderful tunes that were not familiar would need to be sung out loud and clear, until I was breathless from simultaneously singing and climbing.

The wonderful energy that comes with second-wind, following a gruelling and taxing period of intense physical exercise, is something familiar to anyone involved in demanding activity. It is an opportunity lost for those who have never experienced it. I imagine that many dancers never do, for the exercise involved in dance is most often of a very controlled nature, that rarely goes beyond exhaustion and into another realm. However, those familiar with this condition will immediately be able to relate to it. Accompanied by fitness and stamina, and perhaps a knowledge of breathing techniques, I believe that when one achieves one's second-wind and finds extraordinary ease in breathing and effort, it can bring about a state of euphoria or total well-being. Healthy rhythmical breathing, plus a generous intake of oxygen into the lungs and therefore the brain, undoubtedly produces such a state and can be a step towards finding one's hidden self. I believe strongly that this is what happens to myself when I dance. It is what that allows me to reach a different plane to my normal one, and has contributed to the discovery of an intense communication that spills over into my everyday life.

Initially, my street performances quickly exhausted me mainly because of my unfamiliarity with the movement that I was doing, and the environment in which I was doing it. This resulted in an uneven breathing rhythm and the premature termination of my performance before the second-wind had a chance to make its appearance. By contrast, in latter years the repetition of the movement that now constitutes the physical side of my dance, has given me familiarity and an exceptional level of rhythm, breathing and general harmony. I find that a state of euphoria takes over, which leaves me unchained physically to explore the fullest expression and communication in my dance. I am uplifted in myself, totally fulfilled and, desiring no other feeling, it remains with me long after I have stopped dancing.

Now at Torridon, and amidst a mixed bag of weather that forced me sometimes to remain in my sleeping bag for hours on end with a book from the local Post Office, I whiled away ten wonderful days. The moment the drizzle stopped I was out in a flash, boots on my feet, weatherproofing over my body, and going down to the rocky coastline to splash among the smooth stones underfoot. I felt alive and vibrant as never before. I saw the dance in everything: in the windswept sky, in the remarkable manoeuvres of the gulls, in the extra-terrestrial shapes into which gnarled, leafless trees had twisted themselves, or in their self-same roots that crawled over solid surfaces in search of a foothold. I would gaze for hours over the surface of the water, at the fascinating rhythm of the tides, observing the light as it played endlessly on the water and the distant mountains of Applecross. It was never still for a moment, every second creating a new effect. Much as a light show in a discotheque, but offering a stillness and deepening sense of peace that the latter could never provide.

When the rain held off long enough, I would put a few dried ingredients: raisins, muesli and dried milk, into a plastic bottle where it was mixed with some Complan, and set off with an ordnance survey map and a compass into the mountains. Closest were the mountains of Liathach, Beinn Alligin or Beinn Dearg. The latter lay between the other two and was set away from Loch Torridon, to the north. The first of these three was the highest and ice-capped, as I discovered on my first outing to its summit and amazing knife-edge ridge. I had no knowledge of the dangerous reputation that this edge has in winter conditions, even with experienced climbers. Reckless and full of energy I zoomed up into the mist, encountering fabulous ice shapes clinging to pinnacled rocks that had been formed by the relentless wind, snow and hail off the Atlantic Ocean. Approaching the snow line, I filled my bottle of nourishment with fresh, freezing burn water, consumed half and stowed the rest for use later.

It was soon apparent that my state of well being had got the better of my common sense, which happens all too often in the Highlands. I found myself in a position where I could go neither up, nor down, nor along, and an increasing sense of panic and dread took over. My gloveless hands felt lifeless, all feeling frozen out of their fingers. The feet in my boots were stuck in that familiar first position which, in ballet terms, means completely turned outwards and in line with each other. Secreted adrenalin was draining me. Dimly aware that I could not remain in this freezing state for much longer, my feet gave way beneath me and I slid, perpendicularly, for what must have been three metres before my arms clasped frantically at a jutting ice-free rock, tearing and ripping my padded leggings in the process. Incredibly, I was then able to swing my legs to one side and come into contact with another rock, free of ice, onto which I scrambled.

I sat still for a while, fighting to regain control of my nerves and frenziedly looking around to ascertain my new chances of survival. I rubbed my hands vigorously, until some semblance of feeling and burning pain came to the fingers, then thrust them deep into my trousers searching for warmth from my scrotum and thighs. Within a few minutes I had myself under control again, assessing my new position as a more positive proposition than that of a short while ago. When I descended finally to terrain that was neither black or white, I automatically let out such a cry of thanks to 'whoever' it was that had been looking after me, that I lost my balance again and ended in a heap further down the mountain in a pool of freezing, brown, peaty water. I was unhurt, but grateful that I was safe finally from a potentially dreadful fate. Apart from a bruise or two, burning hands and a large pit at the bottom of my stomach, I was none the worse for wear. This encounter with danger and possibly death, was the first of three similar encounters in my life. The subsequent episodes were not deliberately undertaken but were the unwitting result when I mistakenly over-stepped the limits of common sense.

Later in the week, a day of calm and sunshine took the place of mist, wind, damp and greyness, which I welcomed with an open heart. Upon waking to find the bright light penetrating the double canvas of tent and flysheet, I opened up the zipped closure and peered out dreamily, eyes at half-mast, but not for long. One says that beauty is in the eye of the beholder, and how true this seemed to me on this lovely morning when faced with such a wealth of wonder. From my position near the ground, my eyes captured a thousand miniature crystal balls that reflected the colours of the rainbow, shooting arrows of starlight in every direction, but which proved to be dewdrops on foliage in front of a rising sun. Behind this seemed to be an enormous stage, apparently equipped with an elaborate lighting rig, that produced a three-toned effect of aquamarine blue, rose pink and snow white, glittering with a billion diamonds, out of which rose a dark figure clad in a magnificent sequined costume. Was this only the shadow of a cloud over the sunlit loch.

To the west, nymphs and sprites lightly floated in ethereal eloquence, all the while changing colours and sometimes merging, only to separate again and move independently in a mystifying and hypnotic harmony, then disappear altogether. One had to pinch oneself to return to reality and realize that this was only wisps of the remaining mist, drifting lazily over the water's surface before evaporating into the air. Reaching down from the sky, an enormous hand, a limb of great length, slender and sly, stole my attention away from sprites and sylphs, dipping its finger tips into the fresh, sparkling water as though to scoop up the entire loch and cast it into heaven. Could this just be the angled light catching fine, closely spaced spurs, descending in uniformity from the top of the hills down to the sea loch. While beauty is in the eye of the beholder, a little poetic license does bring that beauty to life in the minds of none-beholders.

At that time, my still primitive mind had not yet learnt to fantasize freely and create apparition within the mind's eye. I simply saw and appreciated. It was not until many years later that I discovered, through a remarkable lady and extremely individual artist and painter, how to creatively use one's visual imagination. How to enter a different world, not through simulation, but by simply allowing the mind time to consider a new approach to what the senses are telling it. I first met that person, Anke Peterson, a lady of German origin and a little older than myself, in the latter years of Focus On Dance. She was mounting an exhibition of her work at an arts centre in Dorset where the company was resident, working and performing. Hurriedly returning from the studio to my office one afternoon after rehearsals, I was stopped in my tracks by a painting lying on the wooden gallery floor, waiting to be mounted on the wall. I gazed for some time at the work, not to figure out what it represented or how I could identify with it, but simply mesmerized by the harmony of shades of one single colour. It drew me into itself so completely that I became unaware of everything around me.

Anke, in a soft and gentle voice with the vaguest trace of an accent, asked from behind me if I liked the picture. Aroused from my trance, I turned to confront a tall and attractive lady whose eyes spoke of suffering. That first meeting with Anke, and a deep and immediate relationship with her work on exhibition, formed the basis for a profound friendship that took communication far beyond any experience I had hitherto experienced. In time, I discovered that her creative abilities were in no way attributable to any study of painting techniques, but had been born out of an urgent and desperate need to express the mental agony that she had suffered earlier in her life.

She had been to hell and back, and in a far greater sense of the phrase than that which I had experienced in Sweden. Anke had discovered the outlet for her talent in an institution, at a stage when it appeared that there was little hope of her regaining a healthy mind, unable for months to communicate in anyway with anyone. Slowly, the burning agony that was her suffering found communication on canvas and the unbelievably dreadful, but at the same time, magnificent expression of pain saw daylight and slowly brought healing. Years later, when we met once again, her work had undergone a metamorphosis. The gradual but definite salvation and blossoming of her spirit revealed an extraordinary story explained in wonderful detail in colour and on canvas,

Not many had discovered the glory of her work at that time, as she had only just arrived at a place within herself where she could come to terms with bearing her soul through the exhibition of her work. During the eighteen months that our friendship lasted, until I took to the streets of Europe and Anke moved to St. Ives in Cornwall to open her own studio, our times together would always be spent in profound, spiritual communication. She opened up a new world to myself, not only of the mind, but within nature about which I was already passionate. She, it was, who taught me which woodland mushrooms were edible and which to avoid. She, it was, who brought fantasy to a simple coastal walk or a drive over the Dorset hills. Anke showed and taught me a new way of looking at life and, because of what I myself had already experienced, I was the perfect pupil - always curious, always hungry for knowledge, always enthusiastic.

Her intriguing personality rubbed-off onto two close friends: Helen Hurden and Mike Trim, both musicians and composers, who ran a professional sound studio together in deepest rural Dorset. They also composed film music and ran a six piece jazz band. It was through the jazz band that I came to know Mike, and I met Helen through dance classes that I was teaching at the time. I discovered that Helen, a participant in my adult contemporary dance class, had been a piano accompanist for London Contemporary Dance Theatre, before meeting Mike and moving to Dorset. She had started to find my class too complex for her limited knowledge of movement and had opted to play for them instead. The jazz band, Konundrum, was my major social outlet in a week that was often fraught and stressful. Eventually, Konundrum was to accompany the performances of Focus On Dance, and this was how I was introduced to the idea of improvisation and its creative value,

Anke had her first introduction to a dancer's world through me and subsequently never missed a performance that Focus On Dance would give in the area. She also ultimately joined the entourage of Konundrum supporters and so met Mike and Helen. During the very final months of our company's activities, Anke consented to an experiment in improvisation, suggested by Helen, involving sound, movement and design. This experiment was very different to anything that any of us had experienced in our respective creative outlets. It had wonderful potential right from the start. Each of us felt that we had been brought together for a purpose with this project, because of the richness in creativity that flowed from all of us, and in particular from Anke who produced reams of fantasy-filled inspiration with pen and paper. The 'Will of the Wisp' decided otherwise however when, but a few weeks later, as our project was still comparatively embryonic, I made the decision to close down Focus On Dance and leave England.

For anyone reading this book, who has managed to get this far, but who is having difficulty in knowing where I am going with it, let me offer this suggestion. Try, even if just for one day, to leave your life behind, whether you are busy or whether you are bored. Get out of town, for it is there that you are likely to be. Leave your Bentley or your 'banger' behind and go for a long walk, preferably up a hill, by yourself, with only your own thoughts. Look out over the land and the sky, and see yourself and your life in it. Then ask these three questions of yourself with as much honesty as you can summon. Is your life your own, or have you become a product. Are you really making your own decisions and getting somewhere with them, or are you playing safe and allowing others to make them for you. Are you fearful of trying out a new direction because of the suffering or insecurity you may go through, or because of what those around may conclude about you.

Look again at the sky and the space, and simply know for yourself that everyone of us has emotional feelings and sensitivities, and that it is dangerous to try to blot them out of our consciousness. They are there for a deep and wonderful purpose, as most of us already know. They are our security and, whether we wish it or not, they manifest themselves. They are our best education for they bring us into touch with who we are, and allow us to search more deeply for life's meaning. Without them we are no longer really alive. We are denied the wonder of the true appreciation of the miracle of life and simply being able to be here, free in a world that could well have been hell but is, in fact, heaven. If we will only open our eyes, as I did that glorious morning in Scotland from my tent.

As tears rolled down my cheeks, eyes wide open, unable to think about or consider anything other than the deep message that was burning in my brain, I had made a pact with myself. I vowed that I would search, not necessarily to know, but to endeavour to be in touch with the meaning to my life. To never say "no" to learning, in particular from experience, and to go forward from this point side-by-side with my emotions and whatever they were telling me. In so doing, I had unwittingly put my first foot on a ladder that, as I later discovered, reaches to infinity. From each step of my ascent the view changed, just as it did on that morning - a voice, a treasure beyond all else, welcoming me into my new world. My little seed had undergone a mind-boggling metamorphosis. Not only was it reaching up, it was also reaching out, it was now reaching down deep and getting strong.

So with that perfect introduction to a new day, I had set off from my tent and away from the Scottish loch, inland to places where I could romantically imagine that no human had ever set foot. As the day progressed, accompanied by sunlight, a degree of warmth - the first natural warmth I had felt since coming to Scotland - presented itself and brought the anticipation of Spring. Beyond the glen, and between Beinn Alligin and Liathach, I had surprised a herd of red dear hinds who, as soon as I appeared, scented me and in the next instant were off to a higher, safer, and more distant level to continue their grazing. These areas are off the beaten track and are called deer forests. They are not advisable terrain at certain times of the year for any but the authorised hunters, who slaughter thousands of deer during the annual cull and produce venison for our tables. We Sassenachs, friends of the fox, enemies of the hunt, naively believe that deer are free to live a natural life in the wild and untouched landscapes of north west Scotland. This is true. However, their deaths are not natural since they are a farmed and controlled animal just like their hillside companions, the sheep - who are as much a 'white settler.'

Mountains in Scotland, unlike mountains in many areas of the world, are readily accessible to anyone with a reasonable degree of fitness and a solid pair of waterproof boots. They are, for the main part, a mixture of metamorphic rocks such as schist and granite, and pre-Cambrian sandstone and volcanic basalt - younger stone laid down over their former much more ancient rocks. At one time they would have been a great deal higher. Time and weathering have now brought them all to within the distance of a day's hike. When one stands at the summit of a Scottish mountain, knowing the satisfaction of having set off from its base with the aid of just two legs and a good heart, one cannot help but feel in touch with life's values of a higher and more profound nature. Providing that the famous Scottish mist has not come down, one is privileged with sights that only skilled mountaineers experience – unless one has cheated and taken a cable car to an alpine summit.

It is not often possible in the western highlands to walk from the summit of one mountain to another without descending almost to sea level. In certain areas practically every summit is set apart and stands alone, dis-connected and distant from its neighbours. For the most part, if the ascent has been made for the views and one has chosen the right weather conditions, disappointment is rare. Generally, great distances can be observed from tops over three thousand feet and, virtually from every summit, fresh-water lakes, sea lochs or the Atlantic Ocean make their appearance. If the mountain is near the west coast, one can easily see the lie of the land, and caste an eye over the thousands of magical islands that adorn almost the entire seaboard.

I was presented with such a sight later that day. Having climbed earlier to the top of Beinn Dearg and, feeling exhilarated on my descent, I literally strode up the northern side of Beinn Alligin to be greeted with a sunset from the icy summit that rendered me helpless. With the cairn as my backrest, I sat bewitched in the cold but calm air, and observed this spectacle with the same intensity and wonder that very young children now watch my street performances. That morning greeting from my tent had set me up for a wonderful mountain hike. The present contrasting, fiery confrontation threatened to shackle me to the mountaintop as I found myself unable to turn my eyes away from the enticement of constantly changing colour on cloud, land and water. Not until long after the sun's rays had left the highest cloud did I begin to think about leaving this majestic melodrama and making my descent,

Two thirds of the way down the other side of Beinn Alligin, and rapidly running out of light, I realised I had made a mistake in not consulting my map. Entering a gully that, from above, had seemed my best descent, I followed the trickle of water. The gently sloping sides became steep, and then almost vertical in the failing light. At a point some five hundred feet down this gully, the peaty stream suddenly cascaded over a rocky ledge and gathered in a pool fifty feet below me. I precariously looked over the edge in dismay, finding no exit from the trap into which I had innocently entered except by going back up the gully to a point where I could scramble out from one of its sides.

Once again, a surge of adrenalin brought on panic as I envisaged attempting to make the rest of my descent as it became dark. My legs, which already that day had climbed a total of six thousand feet, reacted stubbornly to this new demand of effort. Finally, I was out of the gully and heading downward again with just enough light to show up the immediate vicinity. I saw clearly the great asset of a strong and healthy body, which is used to being stretched. Unable to assess my direction of travel, but knowing that I must eventually cross the single-track road that skirts the north side of the loch and which would lead me back to my tent, I made sure that I remained clear of the sound of running water. Being ravenously hungry is an excellent incentive to keep going. The thought of the simple fare awaiting me once I had located the position of my camp, helped me to continue on prudently, resigning myself to a five mile walk once I reached the road.

Just as the increasing darkness meant that I could no longer rely on my eyes to see the obstacles in my way, a dull glow of light became apparent in the east, heralding the arrival of the moon. The starry sky foretold a clear pathway for the moonlight which, it seemed, would also reflect across the eastern stretch of upper Loch Torridon. Unable to forecast how much light I would have from the unexpected moon, I caught myself inwardly praying for there to be sufficient for my descent to the road. When the moon's edge eventually appeared over a distant mountain top, I knew it was going to be nearly a full moon. There, on the side of the mountain, I sat down on a rock and laughed. My laughter gave way to tears of thanks-giving, yet again, for divine help. Eventually the tears turned to a song as I continued on my way. It was a very tired man that munched on muesli and raw carrots that night, by the light of a truly splendid moon, which was now high in the sky. My last thought, before drifting into sleep, was that perhaps the time had come to start thinking about getting back to dancing.

For the three subsequent days, thick clouds and rain rolled in from the Atlantic Ocean making any further outings pointless. I made a hurried visit to the local Post Office for provisions and some more library books to read, and hauled-up inside the tent for the duration of the bad weather. Very tentatively, and bearing in mind that it had been three months since I had last done any disciplined exercises, I commenced some simple stretching exercises inside the narrow confines of my tent. If one's career and, in my case, very life hangs on having a healthy body on which the mind can totally depend, when one loses confidence in the maneuverability of that body, tremendous courage and perseverance is essential for regaining that confidence.

In the days following, I was hyper-conscious that the conditions in which I re-commenced training were probably the worst available anywhere. At any moment I might expect an acute attack of lower back pain that, should it occur, I knew would render me wretched and miserable. However, it did not occur, and it was with an uplifted spirit that I began to think about the future. I dried out the tent and packed it away when the rain ceased, and left Loch Torridon travelling mainly by foot and thumb to Shiel Bridge, on Loch Duich. There I found a knoll above the loch with just enough flat, grassy space among the heathers to pitch a small tent. From my vantage point three hundred feet above Loch Duich, all around me the hills and mountains rose above me, like towering giants scrutinising me on my raised platform.

The rain of the previous days had all but removed the snow and ice from the mountain peaks. As the cloud had condescended to remain clear of the peaks, I climbed up into the arms of my giants and looked down from their eye level, curious to know what intrigued them from their lofty heights. The Five Sisters of Kintail, named after their five prominent peaks rising side by side along the length of one mountain, offer some of the best and most exciting hill walking in the west highlands. A full day's adventure is necessary if one wants to complete the hair-raising ridge comprising the Five Sisters and, after the descent, one must count on a walk of seven miles back to the point of one's ascent many hours ago. I was grateful that my earlier perilous episodes on Liathach and Beinn Alligin were not in evidence as, with the cloud high ,and the snow and ice confined to the gullies, I was able to walk the ridge without incident and with full daylight.

So it was also with the following day's climb up the Saddle, on the opposite side of Glen Shiel to the Five Sisters, and of equal height.

Its horse-shoe gave me the feeling of being on top of a volcano, looking out over endless barren and smooth-rounded mountain tops. Over sea-scapes and lochs, until the eye settled on something quite different away to the west - the black, stark Cuillin Mountains on the Isle of Skye. This small but impressive range of dark volcanic basalt rock has a different story to that of its neighbours. It is a rock climber's paradise offering, albeit on a smaller scale, equally challenging climbs to those found in the Alps. The rock is almost completely free of vegetation, and being both weathered and rough gives an excellent foot-hold for climbing.

Apart from this, the Cuillin Mountains are for the most part isolated and encircled by sea or loch, making it a mystical and enticing place to those wishing to discover it. There are eighteen peaks in all, ten of which are over 3,000 feet. They gather up the mists and rain from the Atlantic Ocean, and hurl their cascading waters into the dark Loch Coruisk, formed by retreating ice and only a hundred feet from the rocky shore of the Atlantic Ocean at Loch Slapin. Loch Coruisk, at its deepest point, is a hundred feet below the level of the Ocean that gives an idea of the activity in this area during the ice-age. As I looked across this wonderland to those distant peaks, fantasy rife within me, I knew I would go there. I knew that I had to allow their strength and solidity, as well as their individuality, to seep into my spirit. I also knew that, from this place, I would return at last to the world and to the theatre. As I looked across to those distant peaks, I knew that all this would happen.

My daily exercises, previously confined to the inside of my two-man tent at Loch Torridon, had by reason of the comparative dry weather now extended to the outside. Displacing the two guy ropes at the front of the tent to create a larger and unobstructed space, and spreading my oilskin before the entrance, I could enact a rudimentary work-out using the top of the tent pole as a rather unstable 'barre.' It was primitive, but as I had access to no better arrangement, I was grateful for small mercies and for the positive response of my body to my careful movements. I knew it was too soon to tell whether I could return to where I left off two years earlier, or whether I would again find and respond to the fulfilling and satisfying work of three years ago in Portugal. But I felt confident that I knew myself better now, and that I could react in a wiser way to threatening thoughts and ideas that were likely to bring with them insecurity and depression.

Acceding to the magnetic draw of the Cuillin Mountains, I left the little knoll with its three hundred and sixty degrees vista. Their dark secrets were eventually to reveal more than I anticipated. From Loch Duich, the road rises steeply to the west and the Mam Ratagan pass, and then descends gradually and gently down a long valley to the Sound of Sleat - lying narrowly between the Isle of Skye and the indented mainland, cut here into two sections by three long sea lochs: Loch Alsh, Loch Hourn and Loch Nevis. The access for vehicles or passengers to the Isle of Skye, was then by ferries from either Mallaig to Armadale at the south end of Sleat, or by the shorter crossing from Lochalsh to Kyleakin at the north end. An even shorter ferry crossing used to operate from Bernera to Kylerhea, where there is much greater tidal flow across the strait. Originally, this used to be the only crossing being part of the historical 'Road to the Isles,' down which the cattle drovers brought their cattle south to the markets in the sixteenth to eighteenth centuries.

My intention in crossing the Mam Ratagan to Glenelg pass was to take this shorter ferry crossing, which I presumed was still in service. But at that time it maintained only a summer service, and is nowadays only a fading memory in the minds of the local people. I discovered this information at the outset of my travels. The driver of the car that stopped by the shore of Loch Duich to pick me up, explained the necessity to make a detour to Kyle of Lochalsh if the

Isle of Skye was to be my destination. His own destination was Arnisdale near the end of the single track road by Loch Hourn, with no exit other than to return almost twenty miles back to Shiel Bridge. I was in a quandry. Should I get out of the car now while we were only half-way up to the pass, and return to Loch Duich to take the main road to the Kyle of Lochalsh. The alternative was to travel on in the car to Arnisdale, with the option of returning with him later in the day to Shiel Bridge, and on to the Kyle of Lochalsh - from whence he came. This I decided to do, and my decision led to yet another interesting situation that was to prove of great value to me.

On the journey over the pass and down to Glenelg, the driver explained that quite apart from being the original Road to the Isles, this area had another claim to fame. In the 1950s, a lowland Scot had taken over a remote property next to the sea, south of Glenelg, and there had written a book which became a best seller, and on which a film was later based. The hair bristled on the back of my neck as I anticipated what he was going to tell me. "The house is no more" he continued, "and the author is not alive now , but the effect that his story had on the reading public is still ….." I interrupted him "Gavin Maxwell, the otters, Ring of Bright Water." "That's right" he said, "have you read his books then?" "I've read both the Ring of Bright Water and The Rocks Remain" I replied.

The first book about Camusfeàrna, the name he had given to the house by the shore, and the otters Mijbil and Edal, and later Mossy and Monday who shared it with him, was obligatory reading for my fifth-form school year. It was one of three books to be studied for the GCE English Literature examination. Already, at the age of sixteen, I found in its pages a wonderful wealth of sensitive and vibrant descriptions of Highland and Island life and their natural beauty. The second book I read later, during moments as a student at the Royal Ballet School, when occasionally I would feel overwhelmed by London's size and impersonality. At such times it helped me to believe that another world existed, other than that which comprised cars, concrete and confusion.

"If you like, I can drop you at the place where the track descends from the road down to the spot." my driver said. It's a bit of a walk though, and you will have to pass through the forestry commission plantations." Ring of Bright Water had been for me, as it had been for many, a book in which one could dream a thousand dreams. The places and episodes came alive under Maxwell's pen. They were an intriguing escape from the unnatural world found in most of our planet's thronging cities. I opted to be dropped at the point in the road where I had imagined, in my adolescence, that dream began.

How strange it seemed then that, on arrival at Sandaig – which was Camusfeàrna in the book - I was empty and unmoved when standing on the site where the house had once existed. There was no desire to linger. I felt a strange and deeply perplexing mood creeping into my being, and I hastened back to the road a mile above Sandaig. The driver who had brought me to Shiel Bridge had said that he would look out for me on his return journey about three hours later. However, when another car approached going south towards Arnisdale, I turned towards it and used my thumb again to seek a lift. During that second drive over moorland and through the forestry, then down to the northern shore of Loch Hourn, I spoke of my feelings at Camusfeàrna. My driver told me, unemotionally, that he had known Maxwell while he had lived at Sandaig and had seen how the man had become obsessed with fate and disaster after his house had burnt down. How he descended into a state of confusion after giving up Sandaig and buying a tiny island between the Kyle of Lochalsh and Kyleakin. And that not long afterwards, he died in an Inverness hospital.

I wondered, coming on this knowledge, if somehow I hadn't sensed the negative atmosphere in that place where earlier Maxwell had brought forth such great expressions of peaceful beauty, and creativity and of harmony between man and the animals. How complex is the human mind, I meditated, and how fine is the balance between the sublime and the destructive. In a pensive mood, I retrieved my rucksack from the boot of the car and politely thanked the driver. I surveyed my new surroundings. Arnisdale, a hamlet of cottages spread-out amidst oaks and birches with a bay of gently lapping water in the foreground, took my eye to the magical sights of the craggy mountains of Knoydart across the loch to the south. Behind the houses, the sweeping screes of Ben Sgritheal rose from the waters to their rocky summit of over three thousand feet. How, I wondered, can this land claim so much unadulterated and inspiring beauty within its comparatively small area? Why, in its bloody and inhumane history, did it seem to bring out the worst in people as well as the best? What would it take to reduce all this majesty to the base level of other natural wonders that have been exploited for human gain, and left to lick their wounds?

Corran was at the end of the road a mile further on, where only a pedestrian bridge crosses the River Arnisdale to the handful of stonebuilt cottages. It brought into perception another dimension, that of the Cuillins on the Isle of Skye, seen over the waters of Loch Hourn and the Sound of Sleat. As I had now obviously forfeited my day-return to Shiel Bridge, and the afternoon light was fading, I strolled over to where a Volkswagen camper van was parked on a strip of grass between the road and the loch to enquire whether free camping was permissible. On approaching the van my curiosity was raised by the sound of an opera and an operatic voice. While these were not artistic mediums that hitherto had had a great part to play in my life, I did not discount them unappreciatively. The soprano voice came from inside this tiny camper, and was accompanied by an orchestra that flowed from a radio or a tape recorder. I knocked lightly on the door whereupon, abruptly the music stopped. The door was thrown open and I was greeted in a not-too-friendly fashion by an imposing, older-looking man, and four pairs of young feminine eyes which peered at me from within.

Brought back to reality, I wondered how such a tall man and four children managed to sleep in the limited space afforded by the camper van. The reply that "no permission was required but only a respect for nature", was promptly given, the door was again closed and the music continued. I found my earlier mood strangely returning after this curt and abrupt reaction. Attempting to shrug it off, I quickly erected my tent some distance from the camper van and went for a walk along the quiet sea loch, climbing a nearby hill to gain a better impression of the lie of the land before dusk.

The sky was clearing slowly, the clouds moving off to the east and not being replaced. A red glow in the west heralded the start of a sunset, as observed earlier from the Outer Hebrides where I had spent a month with Ted and briefly Karen. Maybe tonight we would again have a lovely moonlit evening such as I had experienced a few nights ago while descending from Beinn Alligin at Torridon. I returned to my tent feeling rather lonely. Passing the Volkswagen camper van, I felt a little envious of the light emanating from within and, once inside my own shelter, I lit two candles for warmth as well as light. Lost in my own thoughts, I was jolted back into the present when, from outside, a voice almost shouted "Excuse me." Thrusting my head out of the tent, I was blinded momentarily by the beam of a bright torch shone directly into my eyes. Already I was preparing an excuse as to why I had pitched my tent without obtaining permission. "I do apologise for my behaviour earlier. I see you are on your own. Won't you come over into the warmth and have a glass of wine with us"

My mood had not entirely left me and I felt inclined to decline my neighbour's offer, mentally preparing an excuse that I was tired and would be leaving early the next morning. "My wife has just made a vegetable pie and insists that you come and have a bite to eat as well" continued the voice, and I became curious to know how his wife fitted into my mind's eye's picture of the camper interior. "There isn't too much space, but please do come. My name's Stan". I relented and agreed to join them.

I discovered that Stan was not exaggerating when I stood at the van entrance and counted not four, but now seven pairs of young feminine eyes, as well as his wife and Stan himself. My obvious look of incredulity produced laughter from the lady who introduced herself as Gwen. She explained in a warm and homley voice that it was a squeeze, but that they were used to it. "Besides, there's a bit more room now that our eldest two daughters don't come with us anymore." My mind quickly analysed the situation: nine sisters. Gwen continued, "of course our two sons never much liked the idea of camping with so many girls once they got into their 'teens, and in any case the three little ones weren't around then." She was obviously considerably younger than Stan, but probably also past the menopause. The 'three little ones' peered down on me from an improvised bed in the elevating roof, which later in the evening would sleep a further two, and smiled to identify themselves to me.

Stan closed the door with ten living bodies inside and was preparing two wine glasses. He again excused his earlier brash behaviour whereupon Gwen interrupted him and got straight to the point. "You see Stephen, when Stan is listening to his opera, he's in a different world to everybody else. That's why Brunhilde, Isolde, Sigliende and myself were away for a walk while you were setting up your tent. Do you like opera." I explained I hadn't been exposed to much opera, but that I enjoyed much classical music and was a ballet dancer by profession. Looking at each other, their eyes noticeably widened at my remark and a thin smile grew to a broad grin. Gwen took up the conversation, "We've been coming up to the west coast of Scotland for holidays for years, and have met all sorts of people, but never another performer. I don't think either of us have ever met a ballet dancer anywhere, have we Stan." Gwen continued, "My husband is a professional opera singer. Or at least he has been, mainly in Germany where he was a principal artist, but he is retired now." I suddenly had a great desire to laugh, seeing immediately an extraordinary situation, so far removed from normal reality that it defied logic. A ballet dancer, back-packing, camping and hitch-hiking, and an opera singer travelling in a miniature camper with his wife and seven of his eleven children, meeting in such an unlikely and isolated place such as this, in April

My early departure the next morning was delayed - by four days. In that time I came to know Stan and Gwen, and the seven of their eleven children, each of whom was named after a famous character from Richard Wagner's mighty operas. The days were spent discovering the superb terrain in the vicinity of Loch Hourn, climbing Ben Sgritheall, receiving once again the call to the Cuillins, which were nearer and clearer from my new vantage point. I made sure too I put some time aside for exercise and stretching, although I did feel inhibited to continue this practice outside. But my evenings were pure magic. From that tiny area, with some of the most wholesome cooking imaginable, and endless wine, I gained an operatic education in four evenings and a future fascination and passion for the operatic art.

Stan's forte had been singing Mozart, but now his time was devoted to Richard Wagner and Richard Strauss, enjoying also Puccini and Verdi. During those evenings I was given highlights from all Wagner's operas and many others, plus different versions from different singers, together with expert comments on their various attributes. While Gwen stole time for general conversation. Stan only talked about opera, reliving his years in the theatre. When, two years later, I was accepted as a dancer for the prestigious summer Wagner Festival in Bayreuth in southern Germany, where Wagner had created an enormous theatre specifically for his own work, I had already received the perfect introduction to his music. During the six weeks of my contract, which involved myself in only one of the seven operas presented; Tannhauser, I made the most of the privilege by sitting in on many of the rehearsals that were led by Sir Colin Davis. Stan's introduction to Wagner served me well. Our friendship was renewed in their hometown of Oxford four years later, while I was touring with the Ballet Rambert. When I described how my education in Wagner was given a further opportunity in that summer of 1977, Stan was naturally green with envy.

I continued visiting Stan, Gwen and their family periodically. When my own group Focus On Dance was invited to perform at Oxford Arts Centre, the entire troupe of dancers and technicians stayed with them. Gwen would often write me long, newsy letters and always recall the wonderful time at Corran. I lost touch with them eventually when they moved from Oxford to live in Scotland. I never discovered what I did with their new address and I received no further letters. The day I had chosen to leave Corran for the long journey to the Isle of Skye, only seven miles distant as the crow flies, was the same day that Stan and Gwen Heaver decided to go southwards with their entourage. The weather, always a good topic for opening a conversation, had been quite settled in Corran, and continued to be so for the next three days. Thereafter, a surprise change in the middle of the night produced what now seems to be a comical situation, although at the time it most certainly was not.

On the day of our leaving, Stan and Gwen squeezed myself and my pack into their van and took me on a considerable detour to the Kyle of Loch Alsh. From there I was successful in travelling with another vehicle onto the ferry, and as far as Sligachan. This place has really only one of two hotels built in the middle of moorland, where the Cuillin Mountains are reasonably accessible from a road. I arrived early afternoon and walked along a well-worn path into a superb valley through which the River Sligachan passes, separating the Cuillins in the west from a series of equally spectacular mountains to the east. The walk of about ten miles brought me to the sea at a broad loch, near to the hunting lodge of Camasunary. Along the way I passed the eastern shore of the small fresh water loch of Loch na Creitheach, with steep screes reaching up to the summit of Bla'Bheinn at 928 metres. On the west side, a mighty buttress of volcanic basalt (gabro) rises shear from the lake, marking the start of the horseshoe spiral that encircles Loch Coruisk and which culminates in the highest peak in the Cuillins at the other end of the horseshoe - Sgurr Alasdair at 992 metres.

I arrived at the loch just before dusk and erected my tent in a slight depression in the sandy turf at its southern end. For three days, the clouds from the Atlantic Ocean avoided the Highlands and afforded myself, and the Easter weekend walkers and climbers, some perfect conditions - sunshine, cool and calm air, and clear skies. From the time that I can remember, I have always had an inexplicable association with rock. My home at La Casetta and its garden have accumulated stones in large quantities, which I have brought sometimes over great distances to be used either inside or outside the house. I favour rocky coastlines to sandy beaches, and rocky mountaintops to lush woodland or forested slopes. The Cuillin mountains therefore provided exactly what I required. For three days I lived on mussels that were collected at low tide from the rocks around the beach at Camusunary. For three days I climbed high into the dark, forebidding grasp of pinacled fingers, and looked down into the sparkling waters gathered in the palm of this gigantic hand. For three days I played like a child plays among rocks and stones at the tide-line, feeling no guilt at my happy-go-lucky activities, only a one-ness with all that was around me.

But 'enough is enough' I told myself, as I settled down for my fourth night at this idyllic place. I awoke to loud claps of thunder, spectacular forked lightening, and heavy rain which penetrated both the fly sheet and inner tent The rain also rapidly filled up the depression in which, four days earlier, I had made my camp. As a result, the sewn-in groundsheet became a leaking waterbed, slopping and squelching with every movement I made. A hastily lit candle revealed that I was now in a floating tent. Nowadays, a similar situation would bring a philosophical approach from myself to be thankful for small mercies. But on that occasion I cursed everything: my sodden sleeping bag, my sodden self, my sodden rucksack, my sodden food stores; my sodden extra clothes, my now sodden matches, and also my solitary candle which I had just dropped and extinguished.

Although I deemed this episode to be serious at the time, it was more uncomfortable than life-threatening, and certainly likely to remain uncomfortable for some time. My non-waterproof watch showed it was 3.30am in the morning, which meant that I had still to while-away at least four hours in this wild and wintry landscape. Weary beyond words, and with everything now very wet, I felt wretched and miserable at my inability to escape from this wet wilderness. Not a single bright thought could I summon to alleviate my misery. I envisaged catching my death-of-cold and dying from pneumonia before I had got back to dancing. I saw myself stumbling off the path with a back-pack three times its normal weight with water. Nevertheless, into a mind filled with doom and gloom, came a ray of hope. At Camasunary I remembered vaguely an outhouse or lean-to around the main house. Perhaps, I thought, some shelter might be found there. Putting on my body as many wet clothes as I could bear, I abandoned my camp to the elements and rushed into the night. It was not as black as I expected, since a little moonlight was penetrating the layers of cloud, affording me at least a limited sense of my whereabouts.

However, further dismay awaited my arrival at Camasunary, as there appeared to be no hope whatsoever of any entry to the buildings. Beginning to shiver in my wet and freezing attire, I knew that there was only one course of action if I was to avoid a more serious fate. I therefore resorted to breaking and entering for the first, and only, time in my life. I forced an entry into the empty house of Camasunary and, upon so doing, knew I was now a criminal in the eyes of the law. But this thought did not deter me from turning on the gas supply in the kitchen and, with matches found by the cooker, igniting every gas appliance I could find. I took the sodden clothing from my body and hung each item on a makeshift line across the room, gaining just enough light from the gas stove to see what I was doing. The electricity to the house was switched-off, and in my panic to leave the camp, I had not thought to retrieve my one last remaining candle.

I wondered what Ted would have done in a similar crisis. But then no crisis would have presented itself to him since in the first place - his tent would not have leaked. Secondly, he would be more sensible than to pitch camp in a depression in the ground, no matter how permeable the ground might have appeared. I exercised carefully but necessarily, in order to bring some semblance of warmth back to my body. With the aid of the matches, I hunted for a covering to a makeshift bed, eventually finding some blankets in a walk-in cupboard on the first floor of the house. Secure for the time being, I switched-off the gas supply and lay in comparative warmth on the kitchen floor, wide-awake, until dawn.

Once there was enough light to see, I wearily rose and ignited all the gas appliances again, not so much to warm the kitchen as to dry my clothes. The socks and underwear, although still very damp, would dry more quickly on me. T-shirts were soon steaming and were transferred from above the cooker to my body to make way first for long johns, then trousers, and eventually three sweaters that I had worn on my desperate run to Camasunary. Nothing had completely dried, but at least I was more comfortable than when I arrived. My waterproof oilskins would ensure that they remained in this condition for as long as I was wearing them. Then, carefully ensuring that everything in the house was left as I found it, I left the house leaving behind an explanatory note describing my plight, together with a small sum of money to replace the window I had broken in order to enter.

The tent and the remainder of my belongings were as I had left them - sodden. I packed everything as best I could, and with a dripping and bulging rucksack weighing perhaps not three times but most certainly twice its normal weight, I stumbled back along the path. At least I could gain some satisfaction from the knowledge that a rough walk with a heavy pack was no longer a danger to my back. The urgent pace at which I moved kept my body warm. The path had become a bed of cascading water during the night's downpour. My progress along it was marked by a series of large steps and small zigzag leaps, as and when the burden on my back allowed. The cloud and mist had descended to a level just yards above my head, allowing no imagination of the stark beauty it concealed. Only the path, and the hotel and bar which lay at its end, occupied my thoughts.

When I saw the hotel building again from the path, my heart lifted and a new courage seeped into my spirit. I did not want to be beaten by the elements. I shunned the physical idea that my body was communicating to me - that the warmth and comfort of a hotel room was enticing, but it would probably take the last of my remaining money. In my mind's eye, returning to the road was the only alternative, and with it were also the comforting images of a bed, bath and a brandy. I asked myself afterwards whether this was indeed the only communication that the inner mind could find to direct my primitive consciousness into taking that path back to the hotel, in that desperate situation. The closer I came to the hotel the more I started to think about alternatives. There did not seem to be many. Ted came again to my mind. What would he do? Was there a telephone cabin nearby? Would the hotel have any out-houses where I could find shelter. With some pride, I felt that I had at least come sufficiently far in myself as to consider these possibilities.

At the road, with the hotel a hundred yards away, I glanced around the various tents of all sizes, zipped-up and probably empty, on the soaked meadow by the River Sligachan. The river had swollen overnight from when I last saw it, and now carried tons of water every second away from the Cuillins. It seemed strange that I had thought of Ted for there, set apart from the others, was a tent that looked identical to the one which had become so familiar to me earlier in March. My eyes went automatically to the front of the tent, to the place where Ted had sown up the tiny rip caused by the gale on the Island of Barra. I was too far away to see such a detail, but curiosity got the better of me as a mounting surge of incredulity thrust itself up from the pit of my stomach, matching the surging waters just feet away from my own feet.

I put down my ruck-sack, momentarily grateful for the relief to my shoulders, aware that the odds against this tent belonging to Ted were very large. Fifteen yards from the tent I froze. With a lump creeping into my throat and broad grin on my face, I called urgently, "Ted, Ted". No reply. I ran back to my ruck-sack, and putting it onto my back again, continued towards the hotel. The bar was crowded, with a throng of hardy, boot-clad, hill walkers occupying just about every available space. The deafening buzz of jocular small-talk permeated the walls and misted up the windows. Ted was there, alone at a table, lost in thought with a pen in his hand. On the table was a half-consumed pint of beer.

I looked at him through the heads, his woolen blue hat covering his ruddy cheeks. The epitome of a hardened, weathered but beautifully gentle man. I regained the profound affection that I had developed for him earlier. Knowing, as I approached him, that it was he who had helped me come this far, that it was he who had instilled such a sense of courage and thirst for learning deep within me. And also that it was he who had spoken into my mind at Camasunary, and urged me to pack up my wet tent and walk the ten miles to this hotel where he would be waiting.

"I knew we would meet again." His simple greeting in a soft voice, as he looked up at me standing over him, caused me to lower myself to my haunches with my eyes searching his. "How could you know," I replied intensely. Then after a moment I added resignedly, "you knew." Smiling, Ted asked "do you want a drink," but did not proceed with the subject. His question pulled me out of my intensity and I replied with heart-felt sincerity that "it was really good to see you again Ted. I see I still have more to learn". I bought the drinks, a double brandy and a pint of beer, no longer conscious of my wet and bedraggled condition in the noise and bustle of that highland bar. I listened to his story, adding my own, since our parting that morning by the roadside near Uig - not very far from where we were now.

Ted had spent the greater part of the month in the Cuillins, camping first near Glen Brittle and latterly here at Sligachan. At Uig he became acquainted with a small party of Americans on their way to Tarbert on the island of Harris, having gone there from the Cuillin area. Their enthusiasm for this range of mountains, which they had partly climbed from our present location and also seen from the sea, had prompted Ted to make a visit. During his time in Glen Brittle, while hauled-up in his tent in bad weather, he had reflected over his time in the Outer Hebrides.

He had reached the conclusion that these four years had been an escape, perhaps a necessary escape, to fully understand where his priorities lay. Ted had not been without women during this time, but saw that these experiences were always accompanied by problems, that were sometimes of a threatening nature when he was a third party. Of all his recent experiences in Scotland, meeting Karen and myself, and through our communications the necessity of seeking deeper within himself for answers, had meant the most to him. It had forced Ted to confront himself with what he had done by walking out on his wife and family. He did not know yet whether he could make a wrong situation right, but felt the time had come to communicate with them, if only to let them know that he was safe and well.

"My God," I thought, "who has been teaching who." Ted said that my story of Sweden, and the attempt in Scotland to come to terms with my experiences and chronic back condition, had prompted him to look at his own situation in a similar light. He had known we would meet again but could not explain how he knew, and he also knew that there was a conclusion at which he was still to arrive. I excused myself to go to the toilet, needing a moment alone to reflect on what he had told me. I thought of that night on Barra. Ted told me that he had not slept with Karen, although he had had the deepest desire to do so. He had sensed a spirit within her that was far beyond where he was with himself, as I had also. Had she been a catalyst for Ted and myself, somehow knowing that we had to meet in order for us each to resolve the problems within ourselves, before we could move on? I wondered too whether this re-union with Ted had been preordained, as I now firmly believed it was.

Karen had said to me, quite matter-of-factly, over the dinner at Mrs. McKlennan's, "I've met someone camping in a tent down by the shore. I'm going there now. After what you've told me about yourself, I think you should also meet him". At the time this did not seem so extraordinary. Today I feel very differently. It seems abnormal now for a young and attractive woman, who had met and spent time with a man in such a romantic place as Castlebay, to suddenly and without his knowledge invite a third person into their intimacy. The very fact that we were on a different level of communication from the outset, proves to me that this was no will-of-the-wisp at work. Karen's conscious or unconscious assignment having been completed, she promptly departed taking with her any psychological barriers arising from her sex - leaving Ted and myself to sort ourselves out with the help of one another.

When I look back at those conclusions that I made then, and at the way my life has gone in the subsequent twenty years, I cannot but wonder at the supreme coordination of everything. The amazing logic to which we are blind until a flash of light brings everything so clearly in focus, and then so instantly aware that we wonder how it was that we did not see it before. But I know now that we are only given, at any one time, sufficient for what we can handle at that moment and no more. That it is pointless to try to move ahead of our time and that, if we are only patient and aware, realisation will be there for us when the time is right.

So I joined Ted in his tent, accompanied yet again by a mixed bag of weather. I had used the facilities at the hotel to dry my sleeping bag, and we camped that first night by the river in profound conversation once more. The weather was perfect on the next day, allowing me to dry out the remaining few damp items. It never ceases to amaze me how Scotland undergoes such rapid and total changes in its weather, and it seems the Atlantic Ocean has much to answer for. But it is also the instigator of the very unique attraction, beyond just natural beauty, that this land has for certain people who have a deeper, inexplicable yearning for wilderness and simplicity.

Ted posted the letter to his wife and family - with which he had been battling - from Mallaig, after arriving on the ferry from Sleat on the Isle of Skye. Before doing so, and of his own free will, Ted granted me a great privilege. He asked me to read it back to him before he sealed it. And as I did so, I sensed the broken heart within him and released any concern that I may have had for him, knowing that when the time was right he would make his decision.

Ted's prediction for myself was that I would keep my free spirit, that I would dance again and that I would never lose the inspiration that my time with himself had given me. How right he was. The remainder of this episode can be told quickly. I have dwelt in depth on my feelings during the special time in Scotland, when I still had everything going for me. Perhaps it may serve as an inspiration to other young people who, like myself, find themselves in a mental prison without the immediate strength to break out.

Ted and I parted again, ten days after our reunion. All had been resolved. I headed south back to Newcastle and, after a brief halt, continued on to Switzerland with my ruck-sack and thumb in search of work. I secured a contract at Lucerne, in the northern Alpine mountains. However, shortly after commencing my first rehearsal, I suffered an acute attack of my previous back problem. Once my story was told, the Director of the company sent me to a spiritual healer about a hundred miles from Lucerne. Laying her hands on my back while I was seated in a chair, the healer thrust her thumb deep into the pelvic muscles at a point much lower than where I had always experienced the pain. I shot through the roof. The healer explained that she had succeeded in dislodging the nerve, from its point of irritation, back into its normal place. However, I must not dance again for four days, but after this period

I should be able to work again without fear. And so it was. As simple as that. In the subsequent twenty years of mostly exhilarating and inspiring dance, there has never been a recurrence of my back pain.

One week after this incident, while still camping in my tent, I was walking along the eastern side of the beautiful Vierwaldstätersee - the lake on which Lucerne stands - at a place called Meggen. By chance, I noticed a private caravan site only a stone's throw away from the lake, that had an uninterrupted view of the Alps. It seemed to me that living in a caravan was the closest thing to living in a tent. Soon it would be impractical to continue using my tiny tent as a house, and I therefore made enquiries whether I might rent one of the smaller caravans for the winter. In short, I eventually bought the tiny touring caravan that I first rented on the site. In so doing, I at once became a phenomenon to the elite Swiss residents in this classy vicinity – after they realised I was harmless, and an artist and Englishman working at the town theatre. The car to pull the caravan did not appear for a further eighteen months and this, in turn, gave way to a camper van and later to another caravan. My tent and shanks' pony had progressed to six wheels and two rooms, but I still kept my free spirit - despite all the odds.

I have often thought about Ted and Karen, and that amazing time in Scotland. Later, I returned to the Scottish Highlands on two occasions, before the welfare of my dogs in Italy precluded me from going there again. But I never returned to the same places where I had been previously in 1975. Nor have I ever heard of, or seen, Ted again. What I learnt was for that time only. My newly found freedom and creativity in dance was now taking me forward.

Three Dogs and a Dancer by Stephen Ward

Chapter 9

A New Partner on Tour

Switzerland 1989

"I could take him with me up to Switzerland", I offered to Chris and Karen Redsell one evening over dinner, at Croce, their cottage, where I was now temporarily staying. It was late September and still very warm as a Tuscan autumn got underway. "We seem to get on wonderfully. I know he would be good company and, besides, don't forget that I'm meeting Min in Geneva at the end of October. Think what a surprise it would be for her to see Hector again, for the first time since that evening outside the theatre last year."

At the end of August I had arrived at Fiano with my van, towing behind me the caravan that had stood static on a derelict site near Bournemouth in England. Inside it were all my worldly possessions, which did not amount to very much despite it having been my home for practically twelve years. Since first deciding to live in a caravan in Lucerne, I discovered it was pointless to collect paraphernalia, as there was simply no space to store superfluous items. Subsequently, through this necessary discipline of denial over many years I had virtually lost all interest in material possessions, treasuring instead my adventures and my travel experiences. Now I had brought the caravan to what would be its final resting place, on my own land at La Casetta.

The purchase of the house and vineyard would go ahead towards the end of November. Planning permission had been granted and, during the year since I first viewed the property, I had very nearly earned and saved the extra amount needed that was additional to my original £8,000 investment. I had arranged with my neighbours that the caravan could be parked initially behind their house, where I could stay until such time as I had converted the upper room of the barn into a habitable space, and had created a driveway from the road onto which I could put the caravan.

Chris had booked a flight to Canada, for himself Karen and their daughter Emily, to visit his parents, brothers and sisters whom the seven year old Emily had never seen. Ginger the dog, who had been keeping Hector company before my arrival in August, had been given to a shepherd to work with his sheep. Apart from the Redsell's two cats, all the other animals and fowl that comprised their menagerie had either left of their own accord, found their way into some wild animal's stomach, or died of natural causes. Karen had found it necessary to call a halt to 'Croce's' activities as a sanctuary, drawing a line at two cats and a dog - depending on whether a home could be found for Hector. Chris and Karen were therefore quite relieved to know I would take Hector for the duration of their holiday in Canada and, depending on his good behaviour, that I would also consider giving him a permanent home.

The Redsell's departure for Canada was from Heathrow Airport. Instead of flying to Heathrow from Pisa Airport, which is an hour's drive from Fiano, they opted to drive across Europe in their bright yellow camper van, which was a conversion of an old English ambulance. We planned therefore to drive in convoy to

Switzerland where our paths would diverge. Theirs would cross the Alps through the twelve mile Gothard Tunnel and across Europe to England and mine would go over the 7,000 feet Lukmanier Pass and on to the north east of Switzerland. At a motorway stopping place, we parted with a small toast to wish each other safe and prosperous voyages. Then Hector and I watched them depart in their yellow ambulance, three people whose lives were to become intricately involved with mine, as indeed Hector's own life was about to become.

"Well Hector, young lad," I said to him as his dark brown eyes looked expectantly into mine, jaws slightly ajar and showing a bright pink tongue between canine teeth, "it's just you and me now, isn't it?" At this, he approached me as I knelt down and offered his right paw, which I took in my hands and said softly to him "I do hope we are going to get on well over the next few weeks. If you accept me, I will accept you and treat you well. But you must tow the line while we are on the road." But tow the line he most certainly did not, at least not initially in my eyes. At that very spot by the motorway, I took him for a walk and let him off the leash. No doubt feeling the euphoria of freedom, he promptly took-off and did not re-appear at the parking place until five hours later, by which time it was dark. Leaving me to tear my hair and imagine every possible fate that could befall him.

In the weeks to come I was to find that, like myself, my new companion had a very free spirit that could not be chained. Initially I was devastated when, after only a few minutes into a walk in the mountains or forest, he would suddenly dash off from the track, sometimes dragging his lead behind him. For hours I would image he was either ensnared, shot by a hunter in mistake for a wild animal, or squashed to a paper-thinness on the road. But Hector always came back, no matter how many beatings he received. I began to realise that, just like myself, neither beatings nor retaining him on a permanent leash were the answers. Hector had discovered his instinctive freedom, just as I had a few years earlier. As long as he always came back, I found that I wanted to allow him this freedom to live, run and be what he was, in a natural environment. Due to his disability, I lost my initial fear that he might harm a wild animal, and was later to discover that there wasn't an ounce of aggression in his endearing personality. He simply needed desperately to be free to run; to run until he could run no more, until he had burnt up the frustration that - as a young dog - must have built-up within him because of the accident to his leg.

I slowly came to the conclusion that, as I was not prepared to restrain him permanently on a lead, I must accept the likelihood that he might disappear for a few hours at a time. Future parking places would need to be chosen away from the main roads and motorways, preferably in open terrain where I could watch his progress from a distance, and definitely not near any arable land where I might subsequently be confronted by an irate farmer. In the weeks, months and years that followed, it was not uncommon to find myself sitting for hours in the snow, ice, or rain, at a place to where I knew his nose would lead him, beyond which was the death-trap of a busy road and my parked van.

I began to see my own character reflected in Hector, and therefore came to accept this one uncontrollable trait, even though it was cause for constant concern and worry. Only once in the seven years of our partnership did he fail to make an appearance while we were on the road. After a sleepless night and an early morning phone call to the local police in the county of Appenzell, in north east Switzerland, I was told a dog of Hector's description had been found the previous day, and was presently charming the staff at the police station. Knowing Hector as I do now, and having a better understanding of the instincts of dogs in general, I know he would have made his usual breathless re-appearance had he not been restrained by a stranger who believed him lost. I believe now that dogs are never lost unless deliberately taken somewhere by their owners and abandoned. Their instincts and senses are far superior to ours, as are those of all animals. If for no other reason, this alone is justification for their demanding our wholehearted respect.

It was well into our tour that I began to sense a possible game in Hector's rapid departure into the natural surroundings, once he was unleashed. He did not always disappear for hours at a time. Often, while searching for edible mushrooms, nuts or berries, I would hear his breathless panting moments before he arrived. Quickly hiding, I would wait to see if it was my scent that he was following or some wild creature. More often than not it was mine. His obvious pride and pleasure in re-discovering my whereabouts was as touching and joyful a moment for me as it was obviously for him. He would dash around me, hind-quarters almost grounded; then sit before me and offer me his disabled right paw. This ceremony over, he would then refuse to leave my side, remaining contentedly and patiently while I continued collecting the autumn delights of field and forest.

Cycling from my van to the town centre, I experimented by taking Hector with me and my compact stage and equipment when I went to dance. He was a different dog in a city, much as we humans are I suppose, sensing the need for controlled and restrained energy, as opposed to the abandonment that open spaces afford him. Parking the van close to a pedestrian precinct where I would set up my instant dance theatre, I left Hector unleashed to follow my bicycle. I would put him on his lead at the start of my performance, and he would lie very calmly and contentedly attached either to a post or to my empty bag, which was now devoid of its contents.

The latter procedure was more a deterrent than a preventative measure. When another dog passed by, Hector would often arouse himself and drag the bag across my floor while I was in mid-dance to greet his fellow-kind amicably, cock his leg somewhere near the point of contact, wander back to where he been lying before, and then settle himself once more. This attracted the bemused attention of shoppers, possibly more so than my own performance. But once their attention had been captured, I could usually count on their continued bemusement and concentration on both dog and dancer, guaranteeing a larger 'box-office income' than if I were alone.

"That's for a nice tit-bit for your dog", I would often be told, being personally handed a note rather than a coin in my box. I often wondered if simply possessing a dog, who was obviously not neglected or in need, warranted twenty Swiss francs worth of tit-bit - a sum that kept both of us well-fed for maybe four days. With his tender character Hector would entice young children to approach and caress him, never showing any sign of aggression, offering his paw to those with whom he felt most secure. Thus engrossed, the children would stay for some considerable time, obliging the accompanying parents to remain at the spot and watch my performance. Contented children lead more often as to their guardians, and I would usually benefit from the arrangement being the instigator – through Hector – of their well-being.

Continuing our tour of Switzerland's major cities, before descending to Geneva in the west of the country, I began to understand Hector's out-of-town behaviour and realise that our partnership definitely had a future. In fact his whole presence changed my experience of touring and busking, bringing with it a stricter discipline apart the dance. Each day now had a tighter structure to it, as my needs were not the only ones requiring fulfillment. I discovered that my respect and growing fondness for this gentle creature brought with it a necessity to allow him as natural a life as was possible, given the restrictions that accompanied my lifestyle. I felt an obligation to help him satisfy his needs as well as dealing with my own. In this way I found that not only Hector, but more recently my other two dogs: Puppy and Mossy, have adapted to a system that could potentially bring catastrophic consequences. Three large dogs to control, anywhere other than in the wilds where they can all be free, is a full time job in itself. In an urban environment where community restrictions are enforced to keep canine activities to a minimum, and where many do not allow their pets any contact with humans or other dogs, it constantly amazes me that my current trio are so polite, well-behaved and friendly with the other life around them. Perhaps a deprivation of life through restriction leads to the build-up of frustration and poor deportment towards other dogs and people.

Most of the towns we visited in Switzerland had already been on my itinerary for a couple of years. Since I had been travelling mainly to and from Italy, with England still as my base, I always passed over the Alps and through Switzerland. I found busking in Switzerland to be well-tolerated and highly organised by Swiss city police. During my travels I met some colourful characters also playing the streets.

Alex was a well-known and well-liked one-man band when I first met him in Zurich in 1988. He knew and was known by all the buskers. Born in Prague, he had spent most of his life in western Europe. Alex was a well-organised busker with a slick performance, touring around the Swiss and German cities during summer in the northern hemisphere, and Australian cities during summer in the southern hemisphere. He was a workaholic, passionate about his show and constantly improving on it. For three years running I encountered him at least twice in each year. The first year he was alone, like myself. Then, during the second year I met him again in Zurich with a young female dancer from the Phillipines. Ursula was undergoing an apprenticeship as tap dancer and singer for his act and, although lacking his charm and panache, she made up for this deficiency with visual flair and colour. At this time, Alex was working on a totally new act from his one-man-band performances, and Ursula was receiving training.

When I met both of them later in the year, the one-man-band had been dropped in favour of a new attraction, which comprised a keyboard made from partly filled wineglasses, finely tuned and firmly fixed so as not to move. This in itself was not new. But it was the individual amplification of each glass, and the innovative way that this keyboard was played, that created such an ethereal sound and enticed people towards it. Within four months, Alex had perfected his performance sometimes playing very intricate melodies in harmony. Ursula made progress in her own time and when Alex had played for as long as he could, Ursula would promptly take over and keep the Swiss francs rolling in while Alex rested before continuing again. Thus their days were filled, as well as their pockets, and ultimately their bank account. Not having seen them for a couple of years, I discovered from a mutual friend that they had subsequently married, and retired in some style from the streets to buy a house near Prague.

Mike and Steve, a pair of English 'likely lads', were the remainder of a well-intentioned quartet of young musicians going by the name of 'The Blues Busters.' A few weeks into their first European busking tour, and assured from the start that they would line their pockets with gold, two members had deserted and returned to England. Steve, a broad Cockney, and Mike, the son of wealthy parents from Dartmouth in Devon, were not to be deterred by this turn of events. They modified their act: Steve singing and playing the mouth-organ while tapping out the rhythm with specially adapted boots, and Mike playing the tea-chest, double bass or saxophone, as well as singing himself.

I saw Mike and Steve for the first time in Freigurg, Southern Germany, in 1989 and again a few weeks later in St. Gallen, Switzerland, when we- teamed up together and travelled to the south of Switzerland. With a bright, happy-go-lucky outlook on life, they were good company and we kept in touch by letter for quite a long time afterwards. They received my letters sporadically for they were constantly on tour, and had no permanent contact address in Europe outside of England. Their letters to me were full of anecdotes; where they had been, who they had met, and always how much money they were earning. Eventually they burned themselves out. A long and poignant letter from Mike in Melbourne, saying that they had split after an unsavoury argument, explained that the magic had gone from their performance and the sole motivation of making money had taken its place. He wrote that he missed those years of freedom and creativity. He had met a girl who wanted to marry him, but he did not know if he could do it. I never heard again from either Steve or Mike.

Colin was a kilted Scot playing Scottish and Irish folk tunes on the fiddle. A tall, robust and handsome figure, he was visually very imposing in his national dress which he claimed was his greatest asset. He had little doubt that people were more attracted to his appearance than to the audible part of his act, although he took his playing very seriously. Although not a virtuoso by any stretch of the imagination, his fingers on the instrument were very agile, and the sheer speed at which he executed his tunes were sufficient for people to pause and look in his direction. Whereupon they would be caught and end up by being financially a little poorer.

Colin's purpose in busking was two-fold: he enjoyed the freedom that a solitary existence brought him, and he also needed to save some money. On the few occasions when we met in the same town, we would both take a break and discuss our lives over a cup of coffee. Colin always knew where the cheapest coffee in town could be found. When you are saving money and have to fend for yourself, you know about such things. His dream, his whole motivation in life, was to leave Europe that he thought had gone stale, and travel to Vietnam where he hoped to settle. He did not speak much about his past life and I never asked him about it, but he was very prepared to talk about his future and it excited him. Colin did not make the sort of money that Alex, Steve and Mike could make. He had to play long hours in all weathers, often making just enough on which to live. He slept rough taking a room once a week in a youth hostel to shower and wash the one set of extra clothes that he carried. What I liked about him was his modesty and sincerity. He seemed glad simply to be free and to be alive. He did not ask for too much more. His dream of Vietnam perhaps remains still a dream, but his life had a purpose beyond simply gathering money. I sensed that he was a humbled man and often wondered if he stored in his mind a secret, as many do, over which he pondered.

Perhaps the most extraordinary of my encounters with street musicians was in Frankfurt, Germany in 1989. I was on my way from England to Italy, towing the caravan that was to be my temporary home while converting La Casetta's upper interior into a habitable room. It was two months prior to adopting Hector and the Redsell's trip to Canada. The journey from Dorset, across the English Channel and through Belgium and Germany to Frankfurt had gone smoothly. I had left the caravan on the outskirts of the city and driven the camper van to the centre where, in the enormous pedestrian area of that city, I had set up my dance floor ready to begin a performance. "Excuse me" a polite and gentle voice pleaded in English for my attention. "I'm dreadfully sorry" the blond, long haired young man and owner of the voice continued, "but if you are going to perform here then I have to tell you that, in fifteen minutes, there is going to be a terrific sound coming from the stage over there that will completely drown anything you might be playing on your recorder." "Oh," I said, "yes, I saw the stage set up but didn't realize that anything was going to happen straight-away, I'll just do a couple of dances then, when it starts over there I'll move out of range."

"You're a dancer?" the young man interrogated me. "Yes" I replied, "I dance on the street. What's going on up on the stage?" "It's the Kelly Family in concert." "The Kelly Family, who are they?" "We are a singing and performing family" came the young man's response. "Nine brothers and sisters." Thoughts of Stan and Gwen Heaver in Scotland flashed through my mind. Eleven they had had, though none aspired to 'follow in father's footsteps.' "Are you one of the family then," I asked. "Yes. My name's Jimmy, and what's yours, and what sort of dance do you do?" I considered my reply. "Well, I'm Stephen and I can't really put into words what my dance is about, you'd have to see it." I started my performance and noticed him watching for a while, then he disappeared from my sight as I became engrossed in my dance. About half an hour passed before my show was indeed drowned out by amplified music. I was not disturbed by the sound, indeed I found it quite enticing. As I was packing up to move my show, dwarfed by the erected stage and its lights, and surrounded by an enormous public audience, someone tapped me on the shoulder and asked if I was the dancer. On hearing my confirmation, I was given a slip of paper on which was written a message: 'Some of my brothers and sisters have seen your dance. I wonder if, before you leave, you wouldn't mind coming by the side of our stage and leaving your address. Jimmy Kelly.'

How strange, I thought, as I hooked my trailer with the rolled-up dance floor onto the back of my bike. He must have disappeared to tell the rest to come and watch me. I had not noticed. Parking my mobile equipment against a nearby tree, I went over to listen to the Kelly Family in Concert for a while. Nine he had said, but I counted only five on the stage: two young men, two women - one of whom was quite young - and a boy. They were good. In fact, my immediate impression was that they were very good, singing a mixture of gospel songs, rhythm and blues, and ballads. Each of them had an instrument: guitars, percussion, and an accordion, and each sang.

Why, I wondered, had Jimmy Kelly said there were nine brothers and sisters. I wandered to the side of the stage. There was Jimmy, not yet on stage. That made six. And here was another young girl, perhaps fourteen, rushing by me and giving a small basket full of silver to a waiting pair of arms, before thrusting a beautiful cape over her head and mounting the steps to the stage. Seven. They certainly were a physically attractive family. Such presence, such flair up there under the lights. "Errr... Jimmy. You saw me earlier on, and someone gave me this message". The reply came, "I'm not Jimmy. Jimmy's on stage. I'm Joey. Can I help you." Then, reading my message "Oh, you're the dancer. If you give *me* your address and telephone number that will be fine". "But I haven't got a telephone number, and I don't live here – I live in Italy" I responded." "Well, OK. Just leave the address," I was told.

I left the address, asking him for their's, and then moved back and behind a now much larger audience. Who on earth are the Kelly Family, I asked myself, and why should they be interested in me. I watched and listened for a while longer. As I took up my bike and floor to re-commence my show at the other end of the pedestrian zones, out of earshot of the loudspeakers, the hairs on the back of my neck stood up and a tear came to my eye. Something about a rose. I hesitated for a moment, then I turned. All seven were now on stage singing a song that captured my emotions. "When the night has been too lonely, and the road has been too long. When you think that love is only for the lucky and the strong. Just remember in the winter far beneath the winter snows lies a seed that, with the sun's love, in the spring, becomes a rose."

Who are the Kelly Family, I whispered to myself as I turned to go. I was not to find out who they were for a further five months, or see the two remaining children that completed the nine strong performing group. Or to discover that their father also sang and performed with them, and had sired a total of twelve children. That is until one day a telegram from Amsterdam arrived at La Casetta, at a time when I had forgotten all about the Kelly Family and their interest in me. Why should our paths cross again, an obviously talented and successful singing family group, and a single unknown street dancer?

After Frankfurt, I had continued my journey to Italy with the caravan, a little disillusioned over the non-reaction of that city's shopping populace to my dance performance. While I had been there, my caravan had been broken into and left in a state of chaos. My reaction was to make my way southwards and wonder why on earth I had decided to stop there. The rest of my long drive was fraught with worry. The van overheated while pulling my caravan over the Swiss Alpine and Italian Apenine passes. It also refused to start at all, once the engine had stopped, making it necessary each time to detach the caravan and bump start the van from an engaged gear. This presented no problems if I stopped on a hill facing downwards, with a clear run before me. However, I would need to summon the help occasionally of at least two other people, in order to push the van when no hill presented itself. On finally arriving at Lucca I was worn out and exhausted. A telephone call to Chris quickly produced his old workhorse Land Rover, that pulled the caravan up the long winding road to his house, Croce. The camper van was towed up later in the week, having refused to start altogether when Chris brought me back to Lucca to collect it.

I told Chris and Karen about my strange encounter with the Kelly

Family in Frankfurt, and the odd feeling with which I had been left afterwards. Karen suggested that I send an information pack to them, explaining what I had done during my time in the theatre, and how I now came to be a street dancer. This I did, wondering at the same time why it should seem so important for me do so.

Returning to my travels through Switzerland with Hector, this led us both eventually to Geneva where we would meet Min, my angel and Hector's good Samaritan. Between forest walks, which slowly became less frantic once I discovered that Hector always came back, my time was spent largely in the city confines, either dancing or recuperating from dancing. Of necessity, my primary motivation was to be able to put aside sufficient funds to meet the final costs of the purchase of La Casetta, for which the final contract was to be signed in late November. I also felt it desirable, although not essential, to have some additional funds in order to buy a few materials and start modifying La Casetta once I had taken possession. At that time I was still in ignorance of the subsidence in Fiano village and the embargo on new building work by the local council.

The inspiration that had motivated me to take dance to new levels of discovery, and to give what I found there freely to a street public, had never left me in the eleven months that had elapsed since placing the deposit on La Casetta. Indeed, this severely testing year had convinced me that dance has as much a place on a bright sunlit street corner as in a theatre, and I had danced as I had never danced before. With this encouraging stimulus, I felt richer beyond my wildest dreams. I cannot not claim that I was left with a feeling of fulfillment or a box full of silver wherever I danced. There were times when I felt mocked and made to look ridiculous. Times that left me wondering why I had the audacity to lay my soul bare on city streets that, far from being lined with gold, seemed to smell more of corruption or single-minded materialism.

Slowly I came to see these times as a part of my learning experience, and with each new realization my dance became richer and fuller. Less sparkling but more sincere, less superficial but more communicative. I began to see dance and what it signified for me in a new light, and with this slowly dawning revelation I saw my own life too in a different light. I looked back over the chapters of my life, and saw more clearly how one episode led to another. At every stage conclusions were drawn before I was ready to move to the next adventure.

It appeared to me that the thoughts and ideas that came to me in Scotland, when I was then trying to work through something which was unclear at the time, were both a preparation and a necessity for what was now happening in my life. That my experiences, first with Ballet Rambert, and then with my own dance company, had served to build-up my character and let me know my inner self. As a result, I could now convey the message of my dance in an honest and genuine manner, without ambiguity and manipulative publicity. I was free to practice and perfect my art that was becoming a deeper expression of my soul. I was also beginning to understand the real meaning of freedom, the real meaning to me of dance, and to feel rich beyond all measure as a consequence.

And so my journey over the last months, that had taken me from Italy to Yugoslavia, Austria, Switzerland, Germany and England, alone yet never alone, always on the street, finally brought me to Geneva. My body was still intact and was now far more strong and supple than it had ever been. I had a new companion and friend in Hector, whom I knew with certainty would be sharing my new life at La Casetta as well as on the road. And finally, I had ample funds for the acquisition of La Casetta. At Geneva I was to witness the reunion of my good friend, Min, whom I was to bring back to Italy, and Hector - the dog that had stolen her heart over a year ago.

Although Min knew of Hector's fortunes and return to good health, she was unaware he had accompanied me to Switzerland. She was therefore unprepared for the sight that awaited her on descending from the coach that had brought her from London to Geneva. Her eyes greeted me with a smile that became fixed, when those eyes lowered to focus on the black animal at my side. "Oh Stephen", she said softly. The two words said everything as she approached and slowly knelt to caress Hector, re-living those moments outside the Giglio Theatre fourteen months ago, when Hector innocently put his paw into her hand.

Without further words, she rose and hugged me with a greeting that spoke clearly and deeply of everything that my dance was beginning to signify. From that moment on it was to become my single inspiration, and therefore my simple message.

Chapter 10

A television show in Cottbus

Winter 1990

The warmth in the bright sunshine was shockingly pleasant considering that this was the last day in January. The sky had been a brilliant blue since Christmas, and the air was remarkably clear, affording views from the tiny marble patio at the top of my vineyard as far south as the Isle of Elba, some eighty or ninety miles distant.

I was blissfully happy. Hector was lying at his usual viewpoint, where he had flattened the thick dead grass down to earth level, and was surveying the land beneath him which spread in a magnificent sweep over the village of Fiano, deep down into the valley and out beyond. East to the woodland and olive groves. South to the more distant hills in the midst of which was nestled the medieval town of Lucca, and then beyond to Pisa, Livorno and the mountains of Elba - visible on the rarest of days. West to the sweeping chestnut forests and the first peak of the exotically beautiful range of mountains, the Apuanian Alps. Monte Prana rose almost directly out of the Mediterranean to 4,000 feet; one of the lesser peaks.

All this was visible from the little patio that was my first creative work since taking ownership of La Casetta two months earlier. All this lay at my feet and in the deepest recesses of my being, together with the wonder of the countless blessings that had been showered on me since taking that controversial step out of the theatre and onto the stage of the world, where I now saw my dance and my life in a new and sparklingly fresh light. How could I look out over this panorama and tell myself, with any honesty, that the fortunes befalling me were simply good luck? How could I take my deep contentedness and dismiss it as if taken for granted? Too many wonders had touched me, too many revelations had amazed me, to be blind and deaf any longer to the voice inside me saying "Come on, follow me." I had followed it initially out of curiosity and my first revelation was that I walked without fear. The second was that, thus rid of fear, my eyes were opened to a deeper set of values. In turn this brought me profoundly closer to a clear direction and purpose in my life, from which I have not since wandered nor cared to wander, reveling anew in the day-to-day wonder of the world and its miracle of life.

I looked down on Hector and wondered what he saw. He was such a quiet beast, seemingly simply contented to be in my presence, soaking up the same peace as I from the broad spectrum of shape, colour and contrast that lay before us. Considering that his early introduction to life had been as a city street-dog, he had certainly molded perfectly into his new environment up in the hills above the town, first in convalescence with the Redsells and their dog, Ginger, and now with me. He was naturally at one with nature, as I was, but I was willing to learn from his new example. Earlier, in December, I had found a tiny bird damaged with lead shot but still alive, in the forest where we went daily to run and collect sweet chestnuts. I had brought it back to my caravan behind the Redsell's cottage and put it in a box with straw and simple food. Hector had kept a constant vigil on the poor thing as if protecting it, until it died the next day.

This was the first incident that sparked a thought in me that perhaps, whereas our main medium of communication is the word, all other life has probably developed its own methods of sending messages. I have also thought often that, in our desperation to conquer the severity of our environment and to make our lives more tolerant and comfortable, we have slowly lost our previous ability to instinctively communicate on other levels. There can be no doubt that communication in an advanced form exists in many, if not all, species of thinking life. One does not need to be scientifically knowledgeable to note the wondrous coordination of certain species of birds in migration, or the remarkable miracle that confronts us when observing an enormous ants' nest. Or even the comparatively new discovery that whales speak to each other, over vast distances, using sonar.

It seemed strange that, at this stage in my life, I should begin to discover something with which I had been intimately involved for well over thirty years. Most of that time had been a medium of fantasy and make-believe, and here was something that signified an opposite level - a medium of communication that spoke directly from the soul - the dance. I had also found my movements changing, becoming less aesthetic and artistic, and more real and in touch with who I really was as a human being, rather than an inaccessible spirit or character far removed from my own world.

Once in Zurich, on the fabulously wealthy Bahnhofstrasse where investors store their millions in the underground vaults of Swiss banks, or where elite shoppers ostentatiously demonstrate their largesse in the suave boutiques and stores, I put my arms around the shoulders of a well-to-do stranger. At that moment my dance was leading me and I was following. The lady had, unlike most others, stopped by my floor and become mesmerized by the harmony of music and movement. Her incredulity had given way to tears as she, in her own mind, began to put things into perspective concerning her world. The dance had succeeded in drawing her away from the daily pressure and pointlessness of consumerism, and had opened a door to her emotions.

As she stood with tears rolling down her cheeks, one of perhaps three or four observers by my dance floor, my instincts told me to take her and hold her. Amazingly she allowed me to do this as she unashamedly wept and as others gathered around. Afterwards, when I was packing up, my eyes caught her hovering a few yards away. She approached, apologised in embarrassment for her unprecedented behaviour earlier, and said that she wanted to explain to me what she felt had happened to her. She had not been unhappy, lonely or in any negative frame of mind. On seeing the dance, something had been released within her and had shown her another way, other than the materialist trap into which she had become ensnared. She said that had been shocked out of her entombed mind into a deeper self with whom she was no longer familiar.

Yet another strange incident took place in Rijeka, north west Yugoslavia, very close to Trieste and the Italian border. It caused me to ponder on the reaction that the dance had on people who, within their social system, were not spiritually free to allow themselves to openly react to something that had moved them and touched their emotions. I had found that after three years of street performing in England, France, Germany, Switzerland and Italy, my performances were appreciated by most street pedestrians and generally well tolerated by the police. Encouraged by this reaction, I had ventured from Trieste into Yugoslavia but was very unprepared for what happened. Naively and quite innocently, I had set up my dance floor directly in front of the police station. To my western European eyes, there was nothing immediately discernible that identified the closed and empty office with a police function. The street, a pedestrian zone in the centre of Rijeka, was crowded. It was Sunday afternoon and there was no trading apart from the odd candy stall or coffee bar. The hum of a weird, hushed conversation reflected off the high walls. The street was wide and there was plenty of space for both my floor and a public that, as I noted during setting-up, was going to be quite large.

Quite suddenly, I felt a tremendous surge of doubt on whether I had chosen the right place or time to enact a street dance show. My instinctive feelings were absolutely correct as a most bizarre situation then began to develop. The orderly promenade and hushed conversations around me abruptly stopped. I looked up from my preparations, and promptly felt a wave of uncertainty pass through me as I observed an enormous crowd of perhaps five hundred people, formed into a perfect half circle around me and about fifty feet from my floor. Not one person was out of line, not one voice was heard above the eerie silence.

I placed my little wooden collection box at the front of my performing area, pressed the start button on my recorder and danced my first dance. It went well and so helped me to shrug off the strange feelings that were going through me. When there was no reaction at the end of my dance from the now grossly augmented crowd, I knew I was out of my depth. Not one person stepped out of line, not one person left, not one person came forward towards my box. I felt my only alternative was to continue. At the end of the second dance, a solitary elderly man 'walked the fifty-foot plank' to my box and put in a note with a smile. I thought, quite wrongly, that this public would be a hard nut to crack. I had not heard a single human sound in the street since I had begun my performance ten minutes ago.

In the middle of my third dance, I sensed two pairs of heavy boots rapidly approaching out of the crowd, and only had time to glimpse two uniformed men before my music was abruptly stopped and abuse hurled at me. The voice of one of the men quickly reached screaming pitch as he gestured for me to pack up my equipment, the other asked for my identification papers by continuously repeating "document, document." There had still been no reaction from the crowd, and still not one word spoken. Then, as I was rolling up the dance floor, individuals came forward slowly with defiant but silent eyes on myself and the two policemen. They came from every part of the half circle and quietly placed notes in my box. The policemen were obviously becoming uneasy, glancing both at each other then at the increasing numbers of people coming forward. My box was soon out of sight beneath a mound of notes.

My reaction to the peculiarly aggressive behaviour of the now-intimidated policemen was non-existent, my instincts telling me to remain calm and silent despite the adrenalin surging within me. Then my packing-up was abruptly stopped, and I was ushered into an opened door to the office directly behind me. There I was held by one of the policemen while the other, now joined by a further three policemen, was attempting to disperse the crowd. For the first time I heard voices, loud shouting voices, coming from the crowd. I glanced outside, concerned for my equipment. It was all still where I had been obliged to leave it, including the mound of notes that had become even larger.

When I eventually managed to convey to the policeman holding me that my 'document' was in my vehicle, parked a hundred and fifty metres away, two armed policemen accompanied me to my van and then brought me back to the same office with the identification papers. My collection box and the notes had been gathered during my absence and now lay on the table beside me. I remember thinking at the time, that despite not being in a democratic country, the two policemen and their colleagues had over-reacted, and were continuing to over-react, in what seemed to me to be a very innocent situation. I remembered how strange it was that the crowd seemed initially almost fearful of reacting to my performance. Once the old man had come forward, and particularly when the police intervened, this seemed to open a breakwater, releasing something in them and enabling them to summon courage to be defiant.

Once my papers were found to be in order, including every document on my van, I was ushered out of the office in the same impolite and hostile fashion as that when I entered. My passport and other papers, as well as the mound of notes, were thrust into a plastic bag and thrown at me along with the remark that if I remained in Rijeka then I did so at my own risk - which I could only interpret as a threat.

At this point, I gave vent to anger that was unfortunately directed at a young man, who had approached me and asked me in good English for "my story". I hurled abuse, that I had deemed unwise to vent at the police, complaining that his country's police had no right to treat an innocent artist in such a degrading manner. However, my righteous indignation cooled when I was told that that, because of political unrest in the country, the government had controversially banned all public gatherings. If his interpretation of my dance was correct, he could well understand the concern of the police in attempting to maintain control over people on the street, when faced with my apparent provocation in front of a police station.

He went on to explain that he had watched the entire episode from his apartment overlooking the street where I had danced. He said that my feelings of an oppressed crowd fearful of reacting were quite correct. Somehow, my short performance had succeeded in moving an otherwise passively obedient public to the point of reacting, albeit on a very submissive and controlled level. I invited this young man back to my van and he told me that he was a student, that he contributed to an underground student newspaper, and that he would like to write an article on the day's happening in Rijeka. He was not deterred when told that I had performed entirely innocently, oblivious of where I had set up my stage, and of all civil restrictions resulting from the political situation in the country. I often wonder now, in the light of what was soon to befall Yugoslavia, what became of this young man and perhaps the thousands like him.

Hector had roused himself from his position near my feet and commenced barking loudly, his attention focused on the narrow road that passed my house directly beneath us. A voice shouted from half way up the vineyard: "Stephen, it's the postman. There's a telegram for you. I'm going to get started on the wall again".

The voice belonged to Dennis Hann, an Englishman, a good friend of mine and a stonemason by trade. When I had written to him and his girl friend earlier about the purchase of my house, I had promptly received a reply telling me he had split with Gillian, was between jobs and that his dog had just died. If I could give him a bed and food, he would like to come out to Italy for a 'change of air' and to help me get started with the building conversion to my house. I leapt at this remarkable chance since I had no experience at building work, and I knew that Chris Redsell's time to help and advise me would also be limited. Chris had kindly offered to keep an eye on me, stage by stage, but the work would have to be carried out by myself. With Dennis here for two months until the end of February, I could now be sure of completing a large proportion of the interior walls for the first floor room. With the experience gained, I could also hope to finish the rest of the work by mid-April when I was expecting a visit by my brother, his wife and my nephew and niece,

Dennis arrived in magnificent weather at the beginning of January, expecting to commence work on the exterior walls. When I explained the dilemma of the local council's halt on building, of which I only became aware of in December, we decided to cement-in foundations under the two feet thick walls at ground level. I had been assured by authorities that, once planning permission was granted, I could then commence work on the interiors of the existing building. The seemingly massive task of under-pinning the stone walls, considering we had no cement mixer, was abandoned when dug under the earth floor and discovered that the barn was built entirely on rock foundations. Deciding that the ground floor could remain temporarily as a store, we commenced work on the first floor interior walls, removing first the soft limestone plaster that had been thrown haphazardly onto the stone rubble wall to fill up spaces. Cement took its place, and finally white plaster.

Having had no prior experience in this kind of work, I found it a little tedious at first. Gradually one wall was completed and all the dust and rubble removed, and I began to imagine how the room would look. I took courage. Considering Dennis was working without payment, his unfailing enthusiasm for the project, and dedication and hard work set myself a good example. I took on his professionalism with excitement, knowing it was my own home we were constructing. In the years to come, I would look back on this happy time and remember it with a smile,

Dennis was staying in my caravan behind the Redsell's house. Hector and I slept in the camper van alongside the caravan during the week. At weekends we went to Lucca where I danced, twice on Saturday and twice on Sunday, earning enough for our food, and for the tools and building materials for our construction work. As well as being an obvious pleasure, the weekend performances had become a necessity. On returning to Italy with Min in late October, I believed I had ample extra funds - together with my £8,000 legacy - for the purchase of the property and the associated legal costs, leaving me about £1,000 with which to get started. But after signing the contract in November and totting-up all the costs, I found that instead of being a thousand pounds over, I was actually two hundred pounds down. There were so many unforeseen extras and, lacking the ability to translate the legal procedures, I was not sure of my financial commitments.

Remarkably the original proprietors of the property, Lena and Bruno, lowered their price on the spot by the exact amount that I lacked in cash, sensing my unease and generously reacting accordingly. I left the cool, dark legal office in central Lucca, as the new proprietor of my first property without a single penny in financial reserves. Strangely, I felt remarkably happy about my financial position. It was a new beginning. I knew my purchase would bring big changes in my life and somehow it seemed right to step forward naked, as it were. I had no fears that all would be well. Nor did I need to have for, in the coming months, it seemed that one opportunity led to another and everything was in the hands of a spiritual grand plan. I owed nothing, and had no intentions of running-up any debts. I had no ambitious or urgent plans for my house, and was entirely content with the tiny space that I had to myself – which seemed enormous after living so long in the tiny confines of my caravan.

After receiving Denis' letter with his offer to come to Italy in January, I decided to go to Lucca four times a week in order to earn the money to fund the construction. I started to develop a reputation as 'the dancer of Piazza San Michele.' As soon as I arrived on my bicycle pulling my rolled-up floor behind me, children would flock to my reserved spot to get the best view, and always I came away with a box full of notes and coins. One Saturday afternoon in the crowded Piazza, I unintentionally donned my ballet shoes for a clown's hat. Upon my arrival riding my bicycle, there was an extremely loud explosion that caused thousands of pigeons to take to the air suddenly in a 'whoosh' of wind and sound. This was the signal from the worn rear wheel of my bicycle, that it had given up the unequal struggle of supporting sixty kilograms of dance floor and sixty kilograms of human flesh and blood. The wheel simply disintegrated after the explosion, lowering the cycle onto the rear forks and myself onto my feet, immobile. Instantly the crowd had gathered around me, not to watch my performance, but to commiserate and join with me in laughing at the ludicrous situation.

With almost a month in hand before Deniss' arrival, I busied myself with two projects. The first concerned the little marble patio, which commanded the best view of the area and looked east, south and west over the hillsides, valleys and mountains. In the coming months it would be used often as a place of repose and recuperation, after the hard physical construction work to which I was not accustomed. Directly above this patio, at the topmost corner of my land, Min and I were unwise in digging out and preparing the earth later for my first vegetable garden. Unwise, because in the summer of 1990 I quickly discovered that in order to keep my plants alive, they needed copious amounts of water in the morning and evening.

This water came from the cistern on the side of the house a hundred feet below the level of the garden. After four or five ascents, and with each ascent involving two buckets full of water, a rest at this little patio was as essential as the water for the plants. Now, six years on, an irrigation system has been developed that collects and distributes the rain water, maintaining the garden in all but the driest summers. However, for four years, I painstakingly carried ten buckets of water daily from the bottom to the top of the land, a vertical height of some seventy feet, during the hottest months from May to August. Eventually, I told myself that this was crazy and that a new system must be devised if I were not to go to my grave trying to maintain the garden.

The second project, completed shortly before Deniss' arrival, and which years later gave me the idea for the irrigation system, was the revelation I had in November 1988 when first ascending through the vineyard to the highest point of the property's terrain. Here, in the company of Bruno and Chris Redsell, I had the vision of a dancer - myself. I knew there and then that I would become the owner of the property, and that one day I would dance on this very spot, a free spirit, flying in the glorious space all around.

The project was for a large terracotta tiled terrace between two olive trees. As a dancer, I may not have had two left feet, but neither did I have a mathematical brain. When it came to calculating the number of tiles I would need for the terrace, which needed to be large enough to accommodate my four-by-five metre dance floor, I had thought that eighty tiles would be sufficient. They would also need to be laid on sand rather than cemented, as I did not intend to secure planning permission for my terrace. I excavated a large enough area out of the inclined hillside, dragged about a ton of sand from the road to the top of the land and hauled, not eighty, but one hundred and sixty very heavy tiles to the site. Finally, I stood on my completed terrace and once again imagined a dancer, but this time more vividly. The unpredicted cost of the extra tiles had again reduced my meagre savings to nothing, but again I felt that all would be well.

However, I reckoned without the weeds and roots. After four frustrating years of removing them from the sand foundation three times a year, I belatedly hit on an idea of terminating this weed growth that would also conserve all the rain that fell on it during the course of the year. Not, I hasten to add, through the use of any form of dangerous weed killer, but with a huge tarpaulin that I found dumped in the forest nearby. The tarpaulin was placed under the tiles to collect the rain falling onto the terrace, where it ran off and was collected in a large subterranean container, to be then channeled through a Japanese rock garden containing five small pools, arriving eventually at a pond alongside my now augmented vegetable garden.

The question might be asked why, in six years, I had not plumbed in the water that is so readily available at the top of the land in order to water my gardens. First, I see little point in using expensive and precious drinking water to produce vegetables that would eventually cost more than those available in the shops. Second the satisfaction gained from knowing that one is using what is given free-of-charge from nature is immense. Third, and in retrospect, had I simply used a permanent though expensive water supply, there would have been no incentive to create a delightful Japanese garden to channel the water, which today brings me such great pleasure. And I might still to this day be pulling weeds from the sand under my terrace.

Hector, scampered off after Dennis, looking back at me to see if I would follow. They had taken to each other immediately, Dennis giving him the same fuss and attention that he gave to Sam, his dog who had recently died at the age of sixteen years. Our lunch break over, Dennis was keen to get back to the dust and rubble. He was appreciating the comparative winter warmth of Italy, and the work on the house was helping to erase from his mind the memories of his beloved dog and girl friend. The telegram lay on the low stone wall, at the entrance to the upper room where we were working. Why did one always initially anticipate bad news when opening a telegram. My thoughts turned to my aging parents. Could the news signify an urgent return to Newcastle-upon-Tyne in England. My heart responded to this thought with a quickening of its pace. Surely someone would have telephoned the Redsells if any news needed to reach me urgently.

It was from the Kelly Family, the singing troupe whom I met in Frankfurt the previous year. 'Would I be prepared,' they enquired, 'to travel to a small town south of Berlin called Cottbus, in order to participate with them in a show being recorded for German television in two weeks time. Could I please telephone the family as soon as possible with my answer.'

I pondered for a moment over what I had just read. Dennis was busy chipping away at the mortar inside the barn. I knew I must rejoin him soon, but a moment of quiet was needed to put this sudden offer into perspective. I had spoken only a few words to two members of the Kelly Family: the one who had watched briefly my dance performance in the pedestrian zone of the city, the other brother whom I had mistaken at the side of their enormous stage. After watching their performance that day, I had felt then that our paths would cross again, although I did not anticipate it would be in such a dramatic fashion. While I had later sent them a Curriculum Vitae and photographs of my time spent with Ballet Rambert and Focus On Dance, neither of us knew much about each other. But perhaps this invitation would provide the opportunity to discover just who were The Kelly Family.

My telephone call to Amsterdam that evening revealed more about the Kelly Family. I spoke to Dan Kelly, the father and manager of the group. Dan explained that he had been intrigued to hear the reports of a dancer performing on the street and, when my information pack had arrived with my background, he decided that he wanted to meet me. The television recording at Cottbus was to be focused exclusively on the Kelly Family and their guests, a two hour performance before a capacity audience of around four thousand. He was planning on three guests, who were each to be professional performers in their own right. Two of these guests were already providing inputs to the Kelly Family's performances: a Flamenco guitarist of Spanish origin, and an American/Asian percussionist, both of whom were internationally known. He would like myself to be the third guest and felt sure that, in time to come, I would also provide an input to the Kelly Family's performance as a dance teacher. If I was prepared to come, all expenses would be paid and a cash fee given, the amount to be decided by myself.

I asked him whether, given the importance of the occasion, he might not feel he was taking an enormous risk in asking a street dancer to participate in a television show that was promoting his group. Particularly as he had never seen me dance, or knew what my performance through the dance signified. His unexpected reply showed me that here was a man of integrity and worthy of my respect, and which became evident later as I came to know Dan Kelly and his family better over the following three years. Dan said that his life, and the life of his children, had been weaved around risk. He had learned to discern which risks were less or more risky than others. Already through my own statements to him, he had sensed an honesty which intrigued him. Moreover, he had confidence in the opinions of his family who had seen me dance. Continuing, he said that although the Kelly Family had won success through their music and creativity, their beginnings had been very modest, first in the home and then on the street, with nothing other than voices and a couple of instruments. Although they were now enjoying their success, they never forgot their humble beginnings. He was sure I had a story to tell and that, risk or no risk, he would be intrigued to meet me - that in itself was worthy of a little investment.

I could not help laughing. In a short telephone conversation, this man for whom I could conjure no physical picture, had aroused my curiosity. He seemed to stand-out in a conforming world, and had unknowingly succeeded in giving me one of the greatest compliments of my life – his own confidence in myself. I decided that I must meet him. So I told him I would do it, but that he should be prepared also that my dance may not fully complement the Kelly Family's own performance. I was asked to telephone again in a couple of days, when my travel arrangements, a rendezvous in Berlin, and the passage across the then border into East Germany would be confirmed together with the exact requirements of my services.

I eventually arrived in Berlin in a state of nerves, and rather regretting my decision to make the journey from Lucca to Berlin by train, rather than taking a flight from Pisa airport. After receiving the information on when I was required to be at the television theatre in Cottbus, as well as Dan's requirements that I should prepare some simple steps for the Family to learn and present at the performance, I was asked to arrange my travel accordingly. Dan said that when they knew my exact time of arrival in Ber1in, he would arrange for me to be met at Checkpoint Charley - the now defunct point of passage between old East and West Berlin – and I would then be transported to Cottbus. A visa for my entry into the Democratic Republic of Germany would also be made availabe for me.

It all seemed to be rather an adventure, and an occasion to which I always rise. When I went to the train station in Lucca from a teaching commitment on the Thursday evening, for the performance on the Saturday evening, it should have been a straightforward, twenty hour journey to Ber1in, via Florence and Munich. Expecting to be away for three and a half days, I had left the dog with Dennis and was quite unprepared for what was to follow.

I arrived at Lucca a few minutes before the train departed for Florence and, once seated comfortably in the warmth and light, I checked again my travel itinerary. The reserved return ticket to Berlin took me first on an eight minute journey to Florence, where I would then wait three-quarters of an hour for the overnight train to Munich, on which I had reserved a couchette. On arriving early Friday morning in Munich, a further connection would take me to

Berlin that afternoon. I would be met by a certain lady who would bring me to Cottbus in time for a Friday evening rehearsal. There I would formulate a simple dance demonstration for the family, which would be completed at leisure during the Saturday before the show.

A short distance from Lucca our train stopped. As the minutes ticked by with the train still at a standstill, the other passengers in the crowded compartment started looking at their watches, as I did myself. Voices began to talk about the delay and ultimately became raised, and I felt myself breaking-out in a cold, nervous sweat. Arriving in Florence, I was the first off the train with just thirty seconds before the scheduled departure of my connection to 'Munich. Was it too much to ask, I thought, that one train might be one minute late in departing to compensate for the other that had arrived forty-five minutes late? It was too much to ask. My connection had departed on time, and I was now left to rearrange my voyage to Berlin before alerting the Kelly Family of my new arrival time. I prayed that they were still in Amsterdam.

This would have been fairly straight-forward, albeit maddening for the sake of one minute, if I could find someone in Florence Central Railway station at 9 .00pm who could help me. I needed the new times for my departure from Munich, and arrival in Berlin. However, the station Enquiry Office was closed. The staff in the two Ticket Offices stated that they did not have any information on arrival times in Berlin of trains that departed outside Italy. They suggested I contact the station police and, upon being directed to their office, it was of course also closed.

In my dilemma I telephoned Amsterdam. I was passed quickly to Dan Kelly, who said that the Kelly Family were leaving Amsterdam that night and could not be contacted by telephone from Western Europe once they had entered East Germany. In all likelihood, he continued, my arrival in Berlin would be too late to warrant a further three hour journey by car to Cottbus at night. He suggested I book into a hotel for the Friday night and that he arrange for me to be met at 9.00am on Saturday morning. I hung-up the receiver feeling frustrated and depressed that this potentially important opportunity in my life was getting off to a very bad start. The next train for Munich left in three hours. I realized that if I were to pay a further fee for a bed on this train, which the ticket office informed me was obligatory, then I may not have enough cash to pay for a hotel bed in Berlin. I did not have a bank account and so could not pay by cheque, nor did I believe in credit card use and abuse.

I returned for a third time to the Ticket Office to secure a re-imbursement for my now useless couchette reservation, together with a new reservation on the next train. I was met with a sour stare and a shake of the head. With this I both lost control of myself, and surprised myself at my ability to express my anger in Italian. A telephone call from the Ticket Office official promptly brought a policeman, who told me politely that it was too late to get a reimbursement and I would have to wait until the Enquiry Office opened in the morning. I summoned my self-composure and explained calmly and quietly that, had my train from Lucca not been forty-five minutes late, the problem would not have arisen. I was travelling to East Germany to participate in a television production. I demanded a couchette on the next train to Munich to replace my lost reservation, and stated that it was imperative that I knew immediately the new time of my arrival in Berlin. Inwardly, I was fuming and furious at the incompetence of Italian railways and their staff, whether or not I had any justification.

The policeman looked blankly at the official on the other side of the glass separation and, after a few mumbled words had passed between them, beckoned me to follow him. At a private office in an obscure part of the station, a further discussion between the policeman and another employee eventually produced written proof on a chart that my train from Lucca had indeed arrived forty-five minutes late, and half-a-minute before the departure of the overnight train to Munich. More charts were produced which showed the status of couchette bookings on my new train at midnight, and finally a voucher was given to me that I was to present at the Ticket Office.

"And my new time of arrival in Berlin?" I almost shouted. Further blank stares of repressed irritation met me, as it was quietly discussed whether it would be necessary to ring Rome or Milan to find this information. I could not believe what I was hearing, but twenty minutes and three telephone calls later I had the information I required. The new time of arrival in Berlin would be six hours later than at first planned. Thinking it unnecessary to telephone Dan Kelly again at ten o' clock in the evening, I resigned myself to a long journey and a shortened rehearsal with the Kelly Family in the theatre in Cottbus.

I smiled my thanks to the policeman, wondering at the same time why it was necessary for one to become irate in order to obtain this service and information, which should be readily available for twenty-four hours a day. Now of course, it would be, thanks to the unifying influence of the European Community and modern technology.

On Saturday morning I presented myself at Checkpoint Charley at 8.30am, having had a reasonable night's sleep in a moderately priced hotel near the station. By 9.00am there was a constant flow of people, mainly tourists, through the narrow gates in the massive concrete wall that successfully separated this huge German city in two. My eyes searched continually for a young lady who could be bearing a sign with my name or that of the Kelly Family. At 9.30am I began to wonder whether I should be met by this young lady on the east or the west side of the gate. Until now there had certainly been no one waiting for me on the west side. How could I get through the checkpoint barrier without a visa? Surely the meeting place must be the west side, whereupon we would go through the barrier together.

By 10.15am there was still no obvious sign of anyone and, as the queues at the barrier were getting longer, I opted to join them and explain my dilemma to the border police at the control point. When my turn came at 10.45 am, and aware that precious time was slipping away, I explained to the border police that I should have met someone who had an official visa for me. My passport was handed over. As I was nervously explaining that I was due to participate in a television recording later that day in Cottbus, a slip of paper that had already been prepared was compared with my passport, and then both were thrust into my hands. I was through. I realized then that the visa had been waiting for me all the time with the border police. I prayed that I would not be too late to meet my contact.

On the other side of the wall, in a state now approaching panic, I looked around for someone who might be there to meet me. There were various people waiting, all men, and eleven bore plaques with names. None showed my name. On the opposite side of the street was a single young lady, gazing in a slumped fashion into a shop window, a large piece of cardboard in the hand by her side. I rushed over to her. Sensing my approach, her face reflected a comical look of disbelief, she thrust her card in front of her chest, and upon it were the words 'The Kelly Family and Stephen Ward.'

Simultaneously we both laughed and blurted out our individual stories. Mine, that I had waited since 8.30am on the wrong side of the barrier, hers that she had been about to telephone the theatre to alert the Family Kelly that I had not arrived. I warmed quickly to this lovely young lady whose name was Ursula. Her manner and personality were so reassuring after my forty hour ordeal that had been fraught with worry. She explained that, due to the delay in my arrival, the person in whose car we were travelling had left to attend to an important task before driving us to Cottbus. We would now not be able to leave before 2.00 pm. It was a journey of about two and a half hours. My mental calculations told me this further delay made it impossible to prepare anything with the Kelly Family before the start of the television recording, which was scheduled for 8.00 pm., and may even preclude my own participation as a dancer.

A wave of dread crept over me. I realized that I had bungled everything, kept everyone concerned waiting, and not only caused myself a lot of aggravation and unnecessary worry, but had also been responsible for the last-minute changes of plans of others. If only, I thought, I had taken a flight instead of deciding to travel to Berlin by train. Ursula telephoned the theatre and passed the telephone to myself when she finally managed to speak to Jimmy Kelly. A young man of about twenty-two years of age, Jimmy had been the person who first spoke to me in Frankfurt to warn me about the loud music, and was instrumental in my invitation to Cottbus. I was taken aback when, after making the most profuse apologies for the complete upset in plans, Jimmy's voice calmly told me not to worry, and hoped I had not been too inconvenienced by the delay. He was looking forward to meeting me again, and to introducing me to his father, brothers and sisters. He said it may still be possible to arrange a dance for the Kelly Family, and that he felt sure that I would participate in the first part of the show with my dance. This would only require a quick lighting rehearsal and a sound check with my music.

At first I could not take in all that I had just heard. It seemed more important to Jimmy and perhaps the Kelly Family that we meet, than the fact that I would be arriving twenty-four hours late, and just three hours before a television recording before an audience of four thousand. Relaxing over a much-needed cup of coffee in a nearby bar, Ursula suggested she take me on a personal tour of East Berlin in the three hours that remained before we left to drive to Cottbus. Afterwards we could have lunch at her flat, where we would be met by her friend at 2.00pm who would take us on the journey.

With a gradual acceptance of an unalterable situation, I began to put aside my thoughts on how I was going to face the Kelly Family and perform that evening. It is quite remarkable how concentrated thought can render one completely oblivious to the senses, seemingly switching them off until they are again necessary to bring us back to reality. And so it was that I suddenly noticed the stark contrast to what was now around me, with the environment that I had recently left behind in West Berlin. As we walked through the comparatively deserted streets, bare of shops, advertisements and petrol fumes, into dilapidated though still magnificent squares, dominated by superb architecture, I began to relax. Ursula explained to me the history of the city and its buildings, the complex political past that had led to the split of Germany after the second world war, and subsequently of Berlin - the majestic, cultural and political centre of Germany.

I responded that my first impression of West Berlin was one of a consumer-orientated centre of commercialisation, intrusive publicity, blatant profit and sensual pleasure. As a young woman born and brought up in East Berlin, and having the opportunity to see both the western and eastern cultures, Ursula felt that my assumptions were fairly close to the truth. Walking through the quiet, historic streets, I ventured an opinion that the West German government were making a point about monetary success and the rewards that went with it. Knowing little of the social and economic backgrounds, I nevertheless concluded that I would never allow myself to be stifled in such a tinselled and suffocating environment.

Ursula looked at me wryly and smiled. She said that only a few people from the 'West' felt this way. The vast majority could not cope with the silence, could not come to terms with the material contrast, and could not wait to return to the other side of the wall and feel safe in their make-believe world. "Don't get me wrong" she said, looking into my eyes seriously. "There are good and bad in all forms of power. It is a fact of life. Communism has been just as responsible for human misery as your western commercialisation. But perhaps the one thing in its favour is that communism endeavours not to bestow on its populace the overwhelming greed to have more than one's neighbour".

I said I felt all political ideology was manipulative, was ultimately a question of brainwashing, and inhibited individual spiritual growth. In the West it was necessary for each of us to slot into cogs that kept the massive consumerist machine ticking over, allowing us no time to ask ourselves who we are and where we are going with our lives. Our anxiety was to conform, apprehensive of what might happen should the consumer machine be allowed to stop. In the communist East, the effort to make all people socially equal had made it necessary to keep them equal, giving them modest comfort and security, but releasing feelings of boredom and dissatisfaction with their lives. Perhaps, I ventured, Communism had created as big a machine as the West, albeit on a different dimension.

Changing the subject, Ursula asked me about my dance and why, as she had heard from Dan Kelly, I did this on the street rather than in the theatre. I stopped as we reached the entrance to the building in which was her small apartment. "Do you know", I said to her, "you are one of the few people in my four years of street dancing who have been curious to know why I choose to perform in this way. It seemed simple at first, but if I think deeply about it now, the answer is very complex. When I was a teenager, I was ousted from my social group at school because of my desire to study dance. I think that ever since then, I have been searching to find a way forward without the 'prop' of a social group. Later in my life, I arrived at the conclusion that most of my experiences have brought me forward. The ones I remember the clearest are those that were made alone, where the decision was mine and I did not think twice about making it. Whereas earlier, I used to wonder why I did not fit into a so-called way of life. I now accept that the way of life that I have chosen is normal to myself, and ultimately will help me come to understand the mystery of life and death - rather than just simply living and being afraid to ask too many questions."

Continuing, I said "I find that most of my time now is spent alone, not in loneliness, but far from it as I understand more and more how to be in touch with the deeper voice of peace within me. I discovered that, as a society, we seem to be less able or less willing to communicate with each other. We have the means of communication at our fingertips, in instant, mind-blowing technology that brings information to us from every corner of the world. However, this information and the knowledge behind it, is not ours. The conclusions are not drawn by us. We ourselves are able to communicate this information to others through memory and speech, and it would seem that the line is drawn at this point. How many of us, when we talk to others, communicate on any other level. Are we becoming oblivious to the fact that, as rational human beings, we are slowly losing our abilities to talk with each other about ourselves?. We slowly lose our curiosity to know and understand the individuality that lies within every person, from which we can learn and come to terms with our own individuality. Or would this be too dangerous and too close to upsetting the wheel?"

Over a glass of wine in her tiny but cosy apartment, Ursula said she felt much as I did, but asked "what has this had to do with your dance and where you choose to perform it?" I went on. "A few years ago I had my own dance group that I built-up from nothing. I had four, very young but talented dancers. Fresh out of dance school, these dancers had started with another company which later closed through lack of funding. They approached me and asked me if we could start a new group together. At that time I had just left the Ballet Rambert, had a little money, and was well-adjusted to living simply and cheaply in a caravan. We found some free studio space to rehearse to put a programme of contemporary ballet together. With help from a director of an arts centre, we prepared a lecture demonstration linked to workshops and contemporary ballet performances, and offered these to schools and school teachers as a means of coordinating dance classes with their own pupils. The approach was very successful, and within a year a whole series of educational activities and dance performances had been put together."

"The original idea was that, as a new dance group operating away from a large metropolis, we were more likely to attract funding if we concentrated our work within education. This proved to be true, and we found no shortage of schools desiring our services. I found my dancers were also motivated by the creative aspect of schoolwork. When feedback was received from the school teachers about the benefits for the pupils, and their increased awareness in the creativity and coordination of movement, I knew we were beginning to use dance as a form of communication. Later in the four year life of our company, before our future was terminated by an indifferent education authority who curtailed the funding of our activities, we were taking our workshops into many establishments: physical education colleges, acting schools, centres for the handicapped, schools for young delinquents, schools for the disadvantaged, as well as the secondary education schools."

"I became fascinated by this process of communicating to young people, the vast majority of whom had never had the slightest interest in dance or what it signified in our world, let alone to want to participate in such an activity. We had first to win them over in order to get their attention, and then to arouse their curiosity and eventual interest. It was not always an easy task. We met them initially on a personal level, showing we were not superior or on a different plane. Each step was analysed to make the continuity accessible and yet challenging. We had to convince our participants continually that they were making their own movements and to give encouragement when often fascinating things would result. I discovered I was able to look at movement and how we enact it, and communicate this to people who had never thought about it before. I was also able to receive from my students some exceptional choreographic ideas that came about simply as a result of opening the mind to creative thought on coordinated movement."

"The communication was completed by our group finishing the workshop with a demonstration of choreographed dances, relating to our teaching, and showing how dance could be used to both send messages and to give ideas to those receiving. If relevant, this could be followed by an open discussion where students could talk about their discoveries. The more I became involved with this educational project, the more I found myself wanting to make my approach as real and as human as possible, in order to reach young people at every level. Young people who were intelligent or otherwise; who were athletic or physically disabled; had social hang-ups or problems at home; were destined to become ballet dancers, or those who were destined to be un-employable or drug addicts. In short everyone. I believed wholeheartedly in the possibility of using creative and coordinated movement, with music or rhythm, as a means of motivating people who were often unmotivated by the process of education itself."

"When the vital funding to continue this work was not forthcoming, and my dancers disappeared to seek other paid employment, I found it impossible to attract work without the back-up of my company's name. Having already some experience of dance improvisation on the street, and finding that I enjoyed it, I left for Europe in my camper van to clear the air and change my ideas. Mistakenly, I imagined that to be successful on the street, I would have to do as most other street performers do: be animated, create an ambience of fantasy, be virile and impress my public. All these things I did, initially, to my cost. Whereupon I discovered that I could scarcely maintain the pace necessary to fill my collection box with sufficient money on which to live."

"Slowly I started to listen to what I was being told from within me. I began to see that I had taken a retrograde step from Focus On Dance educational projects to street dance entertainer. Was my dance communicating anything now I asked myself? What about my feeling at approaching dance on a more real and human level? What about the reactions I had witnessed from the students when something had touched them strongly, opening a door to their inner selves and feelings. I had believed once that the dance could do this, why had I abandoned the idea?"

"At the same time, over a period of about a year, an extraordinary series of incidents had happened to me, leading to deep revelations that took place in me. As a result of these experiences, some joyful and some painful, I analysed all the different challenges I had set myself in my life to see where they were leading me. I couldn't really talk to anyone about them. They were my own personal experiences that meant a lot to me, and the character they built within me, but they were of no interest to anyone else. Then I had a thought: maybe I cannot talk about my adventures and what I felt about them, but the character was still real, it was myself, and that was something I could dance about, something that I could communicate. As a consequence, my performance started to change. It was no longer a performance and no longer a show. It became, slowly and over a period of months, what I had been trying to give to my students in my work with Focus On Dance: a true expression of the dance within the dance. The true communication that exquisitely and wonderfully opens doors to other people's souls."

"I had wished to bring my ideas on creative movement to all levels of society, without exception. Now it appeared that the natural development of what had then seemed important, could also be given to the person on the street who, in fact, embraces all levels of society. The remarkable thing is that, together with this change in what I was presenting on the street, came a big change in energy concentration. I was no longer throwing away my energy, but directing it with more force and strength into expressing what I was now saying. The result was a more powerful dance, more energy reserves, and longer performances. My audience had also changed. Not wishing to cope with such a stark confrontation, many passed by deciding that I must be an extrovert exhibitionist and out of my mind. Those who allowed the dance to open a door to themselves, watched with a a different concentration than before, and gave generously afterwards."

It was now 1.50pm, and Ursula's German friend and our chauffeur to Cottbus, had just arrived. He explained that following my delayed arrival that morning, and his six hour return journey to Cottbus, he felt it best to bring his own arrangements to an early close that day. Hastily eating some of the remains of our lunch, he beckoned for me to collect my belongings and make my way to the street, where the car was waiting. My mind, after a considerable lapse, got back into gear again and I began thinking of the television recording and the Kelly Family. As if reading my thoughts, Ursula, then half way down the stairs, turned to me and smiled "I think you'll like Dan Kelly and his crazy family, after what you've told me."

I suddenly thought of Karen, the Australian girl on Barra whom I met fifteen years ago. She had said almost exactly the same thing before introducing me to Ted, the American who had been living in a tent in the Highlands for four years. Ted had helped me to understand myself, as well as showing me an alternative way of living which, in a slightly different way, I had adopted in years to come. I caught myself smiling wryly, becoming ever more curious to know how Dan Kelly and his 'crazy family' were going to affect me and my life; assuming my very late arrival did not rock the boat too much. On the return journey to Munich, then Florence, and finally back to my tiny house and the weeks of building ahead, I had time to reflect over this visit to Germany and at the inexplicable feelings with which I was left. I could only ponder at the wealth of experience, the richness of contrasts and, above all, the deep sense of communication on all levels.

Ursula and her friend decided to stay and watch the television recording, taking overnight accommodation in the same hotel as the Kelly Family and their guests. I had accepted their offer to drive me back to Berlin early on Sunday morning, thus avoiding a delay of several hours while the Kelly Family's entourage packed up and returned that way themselves. During the drive back, they asked me about my conclusions regarding the Kelly Family, and indeed the whole experience. I didn't know where to begin.

On our journey to Cottbus, my companions and I had arrived outside the theatre at 4.15 am, after a very fast and animated drive from East Berlin. During the drive, I was given their opinions on East Germany's social and political system that was totally foreign to my knowledge or experience. I remember receiving the same stimulation nearly twenty years earlier when, in Salisbury, then Rhodesia, I risked wandering into a bar in the coloured quarter of the city, and became immersed in conversation with some poor black citizens - rejects in their own country.

During our journey, Ursula and her friend listened patiently to my thoughts on the disadvantages of Eastern European politics and its puppet governments, put forward in ignorance of any real experience. They then showed me an alternative way of looking at socialism, with its advantages and disadvantages, giving me a stimulating confrontation with the issues at hand. It brought home the bigotry and selfishness of ignorance. That drawing conclusions on what one only hears, without being prepared to experience something at first hand, is not the path towards tolerance, compassion and understanding in a world where one desires to live in freedom and alongside one's neighbour. This would be an important lesson for me in my future life of dance and communication. I heard that quiet voice within me saying "beware, Stephen, not to attempt to express anything through your dance other than that which you have either experienced yourself, or are prepared to experience, and therefore to conclude with yourself."

The whole Kelly Family of nine brothers and sisters, met my nervous stare as I entered the rehearsal room at one side of the theatre. They were deep in discussion about costumes for the evening's performance. As I announced myself, Jimmy Kelly came forward to welcome me, then introduced me to each member of the family in turn. I was offered fruit and fresh orange juice and generally made a fuss of. There was not the smallest reproach from anyone at my late arrival, and when my apologies were offered to the eldest family member present, Kathy Kelly, they were gently deflected with the suggestion that I immediately meet their father, Dan Kelly, to discuss how I would be involved in the television recording.

Having spent fifteen years of my life in the theatre, theatrical personages were not new to me. My first impressions of Dan Kelly were of just such a personage. Kathy brought me from the rehearsal room into the vast auditorium and stage, from where the evening's performance would be filmed. In the first row of seats was a group of about ten people, among whom one man stood out in appearance from the others. He was a small man with long, flowing grey hair, and a 'Father Christmas' beard and moustache matching the colour of his hair. His single garment of attire hung from his shoulders and touched the ground around his feet: a sparkling, full length, white robe that disguised perfectly a body of ample proportions. He was a man in his early sixties.

The first impression of a theatrical personality quickly evaporated. Despite the audacity of his attire, I was greeted and welcomed by Dan Kelly as though I was the star of the show - instead of being a very late street dancer incognito. This was a jolly man who seemed to have an appetite for fun, yet within him I detected a deeper side, perhaps of suffering, that cautioned me not to make light with him.

He suggested that, as the film crew and the lighting and sound technicians were all present, and if I were up to it, could I do a rehearsal straight away of the dance that I intended presenting that evening. Without a further word I changed into the costume that I had brought, and completed a quick warm-up for my body. Then within a space on the enormous stage, most of which was taken up by sound equipment and instruments, I performed my four minute improvised dance as though I was doing it on the street. I was asked to repeat it, and this time the side and top lighting accompanied me as well as a following spotlight. This made me uncomfortable initially, as it had been five years since my last performance on a professional stage with a full range of theatrical lighting.

In the interim, my eyes and equilibrium had adjusted to using daylight, and my complex movements had adapted accordingly. However, experience and professionalism soon took over, and I began to relax into the new environment, convincing myself that this was just another street location. Four cameras tracked me, including two mobile cameras on stage. At the end of the second rehearsal, Dan beckoned me over to him, the expression on his face beaming approval of my intended contribution to his family's performance. I was introduced to a young man whom I had not noticed before. "Stephen, this is Thomas Stachelhaus, a very good friend of mine and my family. He is a professional photographer and does all of our publicity photographes. He wonders if you wouldn't mind doing one more rehearsal so that he can get a few action shots".

In my next and final rehearsal I felt a little of my past theatre life return, as I relaxed totally into the ambience of the place, recalling also the numerous times I had been before cameras, either live or in film studios. Afterwards, Thomas approached me, thanked me and said he would get a copy of what he had taken to me via the Kellies. Dan called me over again to where he was seated. Kathy had joined him. She explained briefly the order of the programme for the evening. The audience would be allowed into the auditorium at 8.00 pm, and filming would commence between 8.30 and 9.00 pm. The first half of the recording would show the Kelly Family with their teachers: myself, the Spanish Flamenco guitarist, and the American/Asian percussionist. The latter, Nippy Noya, approached our group and was introduced to myself. He asked whether I had ever danced to percussion. I replied that although I had not done so on stage, I had danced on occasions with professional jazz musicians and enjoyed the improvisation.

Dan suggested that we try an improvisation together to see if it would be suitable to insert into the first part of the programme. I was in my element. Nippy, I discovered, had often accompanied dancers with his percussion and, once we had organised the start and the finish, the remainder was relatively straightforward. The lighting men arranged their visual creativity, and the camera men made a few notes. Thomas was busy with his camera. Afterwards, everyone agreed that this impromptu collaboration should be included in the recording that evening. I found myself enjoying the instantaneous rapport that existed between the producer, camera crew, sound and lighting technicians, photographer, musician and dancer. The electric atmosphere within which something could be quickly and professionally created was very definitely a part of me. I reflected that, within an hour of my arrival, I had completed two rehearsals of my own dance, and then had created a brand new dance with music and lighting in preparation for a recording that would take place in less than three hours time - with people I had never met before. This was a rare opportunity, and everyone had their own particular stimulus. Communication and, above all, trust and the total lack of personal manipulation, brought out from each of us our best and most exciting contributions.

Afterwards, Dan told me that he felt both dances would be an asset and good contrast to the rest of the show, but wondered if there was still time to prepare a brief dance with his sons and daughters.. Kathy went on to explain that as a child and adolescent, she had studied seriously classical ballet and other members of the family also had some experience of dance. I changed quickly into my rehearsal clothes and followed her back to the studio where, between children's games, costume sorting, discussions, feeding and music making, there was general bedlam.

However, all these activities ceased abruptly when Kathy, with a loud shout, got her brothers and sisters attention and asked everyone to gather around her to explain our intentions. I said that as time was now precious, I would need their complete concentration for the next hour, anticipating this was going to be difficult given their broad range of ages - plus the excitement of the coming performance. But I was very wrong. As I began to put a simple dance together, my fascination for this family increased to amazement when I saw their ability to coordinate movement. So began an admiration of their motivation, and ultimately the respect that developed over the six years to date of our relationship. Ultimately though, it was my own inability and pressured attempt to do something professional in the time remaining and my nervousness arising from a lack of preparation, that finally led Dan to call a halt to our frantic rehearsal.

"Stephen", he gently called from the back of the studio that he had quietly entered. "I can see very well that, given time, you can do something with the Family. But do you not think it would be better to save the opportunity for when we have a little more time? Perhaps, for this evening's performance, the contribution of your dance will serve our purposes far better than trying to make an audience believe the Family are not only singers and musicians, but dancers as well. I am not, however, ruling out that this miracle may happen one day when there is more time. What do you think?" My response was the signal for everyone's relief and we all laughed, and the mounting tension within the room was immediately broken. I went to Dan, and apologised to him for my inability to produce what he had been seeking. Then, in complete sincerity, I added that I was amazed at the potential I saw within one single family, and that I hoped he would consider me in a future role as their dance teacher.

The moment that followed I will never forget. It serves to remind me that there is a destiny in our lives that is open to everyone, regardless of sex, creed or colour. Many of us never achieve our goal in our lifetimes. Many never have the courage, or the necessary encouragement, to get on the road to our goals. Some die before reaching the end or having drawn any conclusions. Others get caught up in public and media attention, and are not strong enough to maintain their original purpose.

Those that achieve the end of a road, changed only through enlightenment and experience, and not from outside, gain strength. They open doors to others' realizations along the way and carry on forward. Open to learning, open to giving and receiving, open to growing and open to seeking perfection within themselves. Every road is different and we cannot, I feel, follow it by leaning on others. Each has his own way. In this respect we are alone and must remain alone to overcome our fears, uncertainties and insecurities. As we go along this road our burden becomes lighter. We realise that we have gained the strength to step beyond our negative thoughts, and we cannot or do not want to look back. When this astounding revelation occurs, we see, quite simply, that we are not and never have been alone.

As I looked into Dan's friendly eyes, I felt a surge of emotion seep through me as I saw a tear creep down his cheek. In a moment his entire expression had changed to one of intense feeling. He took my hand in his own as his nine sons and daughters began to draw around us, themselves sensing a unique moment. "Let me tell you a little about the Kelly Family" he began. Angelo and Miteh, the two youngest members of the Family whom I had not seen in Frankfurt, sat on either side of me smiling. "A long time ago in America where I met my wife, the only mother of my twelve children, I was involved successfully in buying and selling antiques. My Irish origins were always close to my heart and, as our family started to grow, we moved to the north west of Spain. Music and dance became family pastimes. I had a passion for music, and my wife had been a dancer before she met me. The children grew up in a world where I wanted to protect them from the materialistic values that I saw in other American families, taking them over and changing their spirits. My wife and I educated our children ourselves in the best way we could, trying to give them values in their young lives that would serve them well in the future."

"In northern Spain we had no television but had a lot of friends. When my wife and I began to see our family respond eagerly to singing, music making and dancing, we invited our friends and sang and danced for them. Even I danced then, and they were wonderfully happy times. As each child arrived we became poorer as a family, and my business began to fail, but in spirit we were richer by far. My eldest daughter, Kathy, and my second eldest son, Paul, began dancing lessons with a very good teacher who had danced himself. Carlos Itoiq lived close to us in Spain, and began to teach those who were old enough to learn classical guitar. He is our guest tonight. Listen to him. He is a master of his music, as you are in your dance. Soon we found ourselves invited to different places just to sing and play. We bought an English double-decker bus and travelled to Northern Europe. Somehow the dance got left behind as our music became the bread-winner. We performed on the streets, my wife always with a baby in her arms. We were poor, but we were also a closely knit family unit that had the magic motivation of music and melody."

" Then my wife died tragically shortly after giving birth to our youngest son. Of course I was devastated. Her dying wish was that I not forget the dance in our necessity to survive; and that the music and dance should go side by side. In the eight years since that date we have struggled on our road to success. We had to be a little hard, and had to fight. But we are still a family unit and we can say that we have come through with integrity. Isn't that so, you guys."

"Sure is father", Jimmy Kelly spoke for all. "And do you know what is so amazing is that when I saw you dancing on the street and called over my brothers and sisters, we all recalled our mother's wish." Dan took up the point. "You see, Stephen, along the way we have met dancers, teachers who were prepared to introduce the dance to my family, but it did not work out. When Jimmy described you and your dance, I was intrigued. But it was when your package arrived, with all the details of your background before you took your dance to the streets, that I knew you were a man after my own heart and that destiny would bring us together. When I saw your dance for the first time this afternoon, I understood your course and your struggle, for it has also been ours for many years. And when you tell me of the potential you see within this family, then perhaps you are an answer to prayer, and we may yet see ourselves as the Kelly Singing and Dancing Family. What do you say?"

What could I say? I was too overcome to say anything. Instead, over Dan's hand which still held mine, I placed my other hand and could only manage "Thank you, thank you all." Pulling us out of the emotional corner we were in, Dan suddenly shouted "Well that's it, now get your 'arses' back to work. Johnny, Joey, Jimmy, Paddy, go and tidy-up the stage and get the instruments off to the side. Barby, Patricia, have you sorted out which costumes everyone is wearing? Then get them to the dressing rooms. Miteh, Angelo, get some food to the stage crew. Kathy, show Stephen his dressing room, and then lets go and find the producer again for some last minute checks. We're on the road in two hours, so come on, look lively." Dan glanced over his shoulder at me, smiled and winked an eye. "He means what he says" Kathy said when we entered my private dressing room. "You have moved him. He's not the man to be open like that with everyone." I went for a walk. My body was on fire. The hairs on my head felt as if they must be vertical. What an extraordinary introduction to the Kelly Family.

Considering the little preparation, my contribution in the first half of the show went perfectly. I enjoyed both my dances, finding perfect control in the first, then throwing myself into the impromptu improvisation in the second with Nippy Noya. As the Family came on stage and showed their own prowess, first with percussion, then with guitar, I understood why Dan had wanted to include dance in their performance. His sons and daughters were multi-talented in music and song. Would they not one day also include dance in their shows, he no doubt wondered. The second half of the show, which included Dan himself, was nothing less than a riot. With Nippy on percussion, the family really let their hair down, and gave a hot-blooded, slick and invigorating performance that received a standing ovation from the audience. I felt very privileged to be included in their success.

Now, on the train that would shortly reach Florence, I compared my state of mind with that of eighty-five hours ago. The return journey had passed very quickly. I had written most of my thoughts down on paper, feeling that they were too precious to simply remain as thoughts that might be forgotten. When I finally arrived back at Croce, where my caravan and camper van were parked, I was on the receiving end of a tremendous and touching welcome from Hector - who was the only presence at the Redsell's cottage. He leapt about and rushed from one side of their land to the other in a way that I had never seen him do before. I began to see how difficult it would be for us when, in the future, I would need to leave him. He had become such a big part of my life.

The Redsells were away. Inside the caravan, Dennis' belongings had gone, and the tiny space was spotless. An envelope on the bed with my name on it offered an explanation. My anticipation was correct. It said that the past three days alone had proved to him how much he was still in love with Gillian. He begged my forgiveness and hoped that everything had gone well in Germany.

He finished by saying that he had left instructions in the barn on how to complete the construction work. Hector calmly entered the caravan, sat down in front of me, looked with his big brown eyes into mine, and lifted his right paw up to my knee.

Chapter 11

A Journey from a Vineyard in Tuscany to Amsterdam and the Kelly Family

Spring 1990

The next time I met the Kelly Family was towards the end of May in that same year, and I was able to spend up to a month with them. Min had come out to Italy for three weeks, to stay in my finished upper room in the cottage after the departure of my brother-Christopher, his wife and their two teenage children, and she accompanied me to Amsterdam in my camper van. Hector came with us. It was his second long journey, and he seemed very content to be making it in the company of his two favourite people.

Min had come to La Casetta four times since Hector had acquired his new master: once in the late summer of 1989 when we had met her in Geneva and then travelled back together, in late autumn when I had just purchased the property, a further time in March when work was nearing completion and I had the opportunity to tell her all about the Kelly Family, and finally a few days after the recent departure of my brother. She would be coming again in July. With every visit she grew fonder of this curious black dog, as did I.

He seemed to speak into our hearts of peace, friendship and freedom.

It was a novel experience for me to have guests in my own home, and fortunately my first guests were people who knew what to expect from me. My brother, Christopher, and his wife, June, lived in a large stone-built converted barn on the outskirts of the coastal village of St. Bees, in western Cumbria. Being an architect, he had a hand in the conversion of his property although he bought it as a finished project. He was naturally very curious to see, with his own eyes, the potential of my own tiny house and vineyard in the years to come.

Until their arrival, the weather had been kind with warm, dry and sunny days. I worked day and night in the two weeks prior to their arrival, in order to have some semblance of civilization at the cottage, although I anticipated this to be on a fairly primitive level. The experience I had gained with Dennis, plus further advice from Chris Redsell who popped in often to make sure I was following instructions, had served me very well. As I cleared the final debris of dust, fallen cement and plaster from the tiled floor, I smiled contentedly admiring the first major building achievement of my life.

Being fascinated by stone, I decided at the outset that I would enjoy it in my cottage. The south-east and south-west walls were cemented over and plastered, leaving their respective windows framed in the original stone, which I had cleaned and polished. The north-west wall contained the entrance, and had been done in a similar fashion. The remaining wall lacked any windows or doorways, had been carefully restored with Dennis' expert help to reveal the original stonework. I was proud of the overall end result.

Notwithstanding the generous fee for my participation in the television show in Germany from Dan Kelly, money was still short and certainly insufficient to furnish my small space with new items. The previous summer I had brought back a carpet and armchair in my van from England, that had been given me by my parents. My other trips in Europe had produced a dining table, five chairs, some curtain rail, a few picture frames, a bamboo kitchen table, a wooden single bed frame and a foldable single bed. All in good condition but needing a little attention. Objects that were no longer wanted by their previous owners, and which I had found discarded in various places. Hector and I had often to bear the presence of these items for a considerable time in the limited space inside my vehicle, until being able to unload them at La Casetta. Charity stores in Switzerland had also produced two mattresses, a secondhand sideboard and a kitchen sink. In Lucca I found a settee with a ripped cover by the side of the road.

Min stayed for a week in March, while I busied myself with plastering. She went to Lucca with Karen Redsell and they bought some material cheaply from Lucca's street market, and made new covers for the bed and settee and curtains for the windows - simply panes of glass wedged between the stone and outer brickwork frame.

The final plastering was completed four days before my brother's arrival with his family, and I arranged my house. I had spent the last of my money on a temporary roof over the space outside the first floor room, between the outer cottage wall and the retaining wall. Here I completed a small enclosure for a chemical toilet, on the other side of which was space for a 'fair-weather' kitchen with a battery powered pump to raise water from the rain-fed cistern beneath the space. However, when the weather changed the day before my brother's arrival, the idea of cooking in my exposed kitchen had to be abandoned. The two burner stove and bottle of gas that Chris Redsell had given me, was moved into the house itself until a more protected kitchen could be constructed. But my temporary, 'fair-weather' kitchen has now served me well for nearly six years, and will probably remain permanently temporary until the local council decide that my 'temporary home' can become permanent.

Having followed my ill-informed advice, Christopher, June, Peter and Emma Jane landed at Pisa airport prepared for warm, dry weather and were totally unprepared for the winter gales that now ensued. Having spent weeks and all my money in getting everything ready for the comparative comfort for my guests, I discovered too late that my house lacked the most essential comfort of all – warmth. The walls had not dried out, nor did they dry out during the two weeks of my family's stay, contributing immensely to the damp and humid conditions inside the cottage. Wind, which hardly ever reached the protected position of my home, whistled constantly between the spaces in the windowpanes and the brickwork, through the old wooden door, and even through the roof tiles. On a number of occasions it even lifted the plastic corrugated roofing over the temporary kitchen and bathroom. A small gas heater that I brought into the house from my van was ineffective, and made no impact to the cool temperature inside. Subsequently, I have learned that April in Tuscany is invariably wet, before the long dry summer that can start as early as May. But I have yet to experience another April as cold or as windy as that in 1990, when snow lay only fifty metres above us.

By far the most comfortable of my guests were my nephew and niece, Peter and Emma Jane. They were were in my caravan on the Redsell's land nearby. As it had been my home for many years, of necessity the caravan had been thoroughly insulated and a powerful gas heater installed, which could warm up the small caravan space in less than ten minutes. Although not cold, the temperature inside the cottage was not what one could call comfortable. Fortunately, my brother and sister-in-law were hardy, outdoor types, and entered into the pioneering spirit with which my derelict barn had been rapidly converted. A portable gas lamp, plus two paraffin lamps and numerous candles, gave atmospheric and adequate lighting for the evenings as well as a little extra heat.

Then two days after my guests departed, Min returned and with her came warm, calm weather that rapidly became hot. Spring had finally arrived and, within a week, the vines exploded into leaf transforming my property into a Garden of Eden. The grass had remained uncut since the previous harvesting of grapes by Lena and Bruno, and was becoming a headache. Although it also contained a bank of beautiful knee-high wild flowers, I could see it would have to be kept under control. Chris Redsell came up with a solution, asking me if I would share the cost of a secondhand two-stroke strimmer, my half to be paid when I could come up with the money.

Min whiled away her time, titivating my tiny home with her feminine touch, and helping me to prepare the plot for a vegetable garden at the top of the land. She raked up mountains of hay in my wake, as I ploughed through a jungle of every imaginable type of wild herbaceous plant. Cutting grass on a steep, terraced, hillside vineyard is an art that I have only recently perfected. The first attempt in May 1990, with a strimmer that seemed to constantly jump out of my hand and then stall, was a task that tested my temperament. In the long grass, I had no idea of what I was cutting, at ground level, nor was I in full control of the machine. I found it difficult to avoid severing the new growth of vine stems with the razor-sharp, gyrating blade at the end of the four foot shaft that I was unsteadily holding. In a very short time, the unfortunate result was that I succeeded in damaging my potential crop of grapes not only for that year, but also for many years to come. Some of the severed vines never recovered, and just dried up and withered.

It may be thought I would have learnt a valuable lesson that Spring. But the following year I again cut the grass too late, obliterating more vines and damaging others. I began to understand that taking care of a vineyard involved more than just simply picking the grapes.

I was not without help or advice that first year. Antonio Barzanti, a young and talented flautist, was introduced to me by Chris Redsell. At that time, a musical collaboration between the Redsell's and a young professional pianist was just starting, and I became involved in the project by adding dance to their music. I discovered that Antonio managed single-handedly a hectare of mature vineyard on property belonging to his parents, where he lived with his brother and sister six miles east of Fiano. Having studied flute for three years at the Paris Conservatory, Antonio spoke fluent French. We were therefore able to communicate as, until that time, my Italian had not developed sufficiently and I was struggling to cope with a thousand other things new to my experience.

With his undoubted talents, Antonio should have continued under the masters with whom he had studied in Paris, and who had great hopes for his future. Being a country lad at heart, born and brought up a few miles north of Lucca in the mountain village of Borgo in Mozzano, he had missed this simple life in the more sophisticated atmosphere of a music conservatory in a grand city. He had returned home after securing his diploma from the conservatory. Therefore, he enthusiastically entered the collaboration with Chris and Elizabetta Fiorini, a pianist, whom I discovered amazingly was also a dance teacher. In fact Elizabetta's first passion in life was dance, and she would have followed a career in ballet but for a knee injury that halted her studies in Rome, and which at that time were almost complete.

Gueseppina Consoli, her mother and a piano accompanist herself, had encouraged her desperate daughter in this new direction. Although never having been able to enter into a life in the theatre, as a consequence she had found herself in the rare position of being professionally trained in both music and dance. As a consequence she and her mother had moved from Rome, and Elizabetta had opened a ballet school in Borgo in Mozzano, while Consoli taught and played the piano privately. Indeed, it was Consoli who had organised the series of concerts to which Chris, at that time working with an orchestra in Rome, had been invited to play during the summer in which he and Karen found their home at Croce. Suggesting perhaps that it was no coincidence that Antonio would meet Elizabetta, Chris and myself, all of whom had settled in the area at various stages.

Chris and Karen had been desperate to move out of Rome. The Tuscan countryside around the beautiful home of Consoli at Celle di Puccini - the family seat of Italian composer, Giaccomo Puccini – made an immediate impact on them. It was during this time that they found a property to buy in Fiano - a dilapidated sheep pen, overgrown with brambles and costing, together with adjoining land, a mere £2,000.

I had originally met Chris in England, when he was co-leader of the viola section of the Bournemouth Symphony Orchestra. After their daughter, Emily, was born they decided to close their now completed house in Fiano and move back to England. But later, when Emily had reached five years old, they had returned to Fiano intent on following a simpler life, with Chris accepting musical work wherever it was offered.

Thus it was that four professional talents, all of whom had opted for something that the city lifestyle could not provide, met early in 1990 at a house on the top of a hill, set amidst a vineyard, above the village of Borgo in Mozzano. A stranger combination would be difficult to imagine: pianist, flautist, violist and dancer. But in such an creative environment, with the absence of available performing artists, how could beggars be choosers. Antonio's father, Mauro, who spoke only his own language, busied himself in the kitchen where he was perfectly at home with Italian cuisine. His mother, Penate, took Chris, Karen and myself on a guided tour of their magnificent hilltop mansion. It commanded spectacular views over the valley of the River Serchio, that separated the Apenine mountains from their smaller but more spectacular neighbours, the Apuanian Alps. Elizabetta was content to remain in the company of Antonio and his brother and sister, deep in an animated discussion that I could not understand.

Our tour of this 400-year old, four storey, beautifully restored building was a little out of context considering that we were in the heart of Italy, and our guide was the lady of the house and of full-blooded Italian lineage. For the descriptions and explanations that she gave us were in that lilting, musical sound that is so familiar and welcoming to my ear - the Scottish accent. Penate, although born in Italy, had moved in her early childhood to Britain with her parents and they had settled just outside Glasgow. It was not until adulthood, when she met and married Mauro, that she was enticed back to Italy and this lovely part of northern Tuscany. Later in the day, the project discussions now at an end, Antonio took me around his vineyard and explained the various stages of maintenance and care.

Winter was the time of most work, when the vine was dormant and the sap deep in the roots. He demonstrated the art of pruning and talked about working, weeding and feeding the land encircling each stem. In spring, as soon as new growth became visible, sulphur and copper treatment was applied to protect the plant against the many diseases and sicknesses that can afflict it. These treatments are applied by spraying and, except before and during the flowering in

May, continue every two or three weeks through the summer until September. In summer the long stems, and in particular those bearing fruit, are pruned to concentrate the sap energy where it is required. From July, and once the burning heat from the overhead sun is gone, the foliage is removed from around the swollen fruit to prevent humidity leading to a fungal disease, and to allow the fruit to profit from ripening sunlight. The 'vendemia,' or harvest, would vary from year to year but was never earlier than the end of September or later than mid-October, depending on how hot and dry the summer had been.

This was a lot of information to digest all at once, and much of it went over my head. However, Antonio offered to come over to Fiano to see how my vines had been pruned. Earlier, while Dennis was still with me in January, we had taken advice from local people in the village and pruned the whole vineyard. We did not really understand what we were doing. Antonio said encouragingly that I would get a harvest, but next year I should gain more knowledge about the pruning if I was to keep my vineyard under control. In May, and before I left La Casetta with Min and Hector for five weeks, Antonio came with a sulphur-powder sprayer, showed me how to use it, and then left it with me. The cold weather in April had delayed the development of the new spring growth, and I was able to spray the vineyard twice before leaving for Amsterdam.

During May, Min and I made a chance discovery that set my mind thinking about a hot water system for my house, that would cost nothing other than my energy and effort. After six years of experimenting with this system, I can now claim that it is viable, if not always dependable. A safe and free method of alternative energy, the only materials necessary are plenty of fresh grass and a little water. The discovery that decomposing grass, and all organic matter in large enough quantities, can produce heat of up to 70°C was a new one for myself. While I now know that this knowledge will be familiar to any gardener, to myself at that time it was unbelievable and needed to be exploited.

A few days after gathering all our cut grass into a massive haystack at the top of the land, I was amazed one early morning to see wafts of vapour rising from it. Thrusting my hand into the haystack, I removed it quickly and wondered what was the source of the heat within. As I went down to Min, who was preparing our breakfast, my mind was already considering how I might profit from my discovery. "Oh, didn't you know that freshly cut hay produces heat," Min said, "in olden times, farmhands working in the fields used to bring a prepared dish of food with them, put it in a haystack and let it cook slowly." Astounded, I replied "you mean it's hot enough in there to cook." Amused, Min responded to my question "well I don't know much about it, apart from what I've told you, but I don't think you could heat a house with it, if that's what you're thinking."

I was excited. "Maybe not a house, but perhaps a hot water tank. I'm going to put a couple of containers full of water in there to see how long they take to heat up." By evening, steaming hot water was poured from the containers. This sparked a plan within me for my kitchen and bathroom whereby the rainwater, that was collected and stored higher on the hillside above the house, would be heated by passing it through a haystack outside the bathroom.

As departure for Amsterdam was now imminent, I could take no action on the plan until I returned in July. In that month, and amid rehearsals for my role as a dancer in the music festival that Chris was organising, I installed a primitive plumbing system that provided 'haystack hot water' for my kitchen and bathroom. During the same month, Elizabetta also held her first summer dance course for young people at Signora Consoli's lovely home in the hills near Celle di Puccini.

However, La Casetta was now closed, and Min, Hector and I set off on the road to Amsterdam where we hoped to reach in three days. The journey went smoothly as far as the Belgian-Dutch border apart from two minor and amusing incidents. The first was in Switzerland, where we had left the main road to exercise Hector and to break our journey. We parked on a grassy verge by the edge of a forest, just off a narrow farm track so that any vehicle using it could pass us. On returning from a walk in the forest, during which Hector had elected to remain with us, though unleashed, we found the camper van surrounded by cattle that preceded a cortege of brightly costumed, local people. About twenty animals, brightly ornamented around their heads and horns, were creating a cacophony from an array of cowbells of all sizes and tones set around their necks.

Bemused, we watched from the forest edge, as I held Hector by his collar. When the procession passed and its sounds had faded in the distance, we released Hector and approached the camper van, and were dismayed to find the grass round it churned-up from heavy hooves sinking deep into the soft, damp earth. Getting the camper van out from this bog proved impossible, as the rear wheels only embedded themselves deeply into the ground. Fortunately, a tractor passed by half an hour later. We hailed the driver, who stopped and kindly pulled us back onto the hard surface of the farm track.

Before leaving Switzerland, Min bought some presents of Swiss chocolates for her friends and family in England. Most of these never reached their destination. They was used in France as barter for petrol which had run out when we were close to the French-Belgian border. Unbeknown to ourselves, the day that we had chosen to cross France was a national holiday and, as the day before this was a Sunday, we found nowhere to exchange lire into French francs - not even at the border crossing from Switzerland. Unfortunately, as the petrol gauge in the camper van did not operate, I could only estimate the amount of fuel in the petrol tank. Having exhausted all reserves of petrol in attempting to find any place willing to exchange our money, I looked for a local farmer who was willing to exchange chocolate for petrol. But it was not a simple task to find anyone. The first farmer said no. The second had only diesel. The third, however, a long cycle ride from where I had left the van, was more accommodating and seemed quite pleased to receive the equivalent value of twenty litres of fuel in sumptuous Swiss chocolate.

Again mobile, we journeyed on into southern Holland and were only two hours from Amsterdam when a more serious incident occurred. Evening was drawing in and, tired from our journey, Min and I were looking out for a lay-by where we could spend the night, before completing our journey the following morning. Suddenly there was a tearing, searing screech from the rear of the vehicle and our modest speed was dramatically reduced - the camper van's steering gone from my control. Fortunately motorway traffic was sporadic and, as a complete halt was not only imminent but inevitable, I managed to manoeuvre the vehicle onto the emergency hard-shoulder on the right hand side.

Min held Hector while I left the camper, went around to the rear, and was aghast when I saw the odd angle at which the van was leaning. This was certainly no puncture. The left rear axle was now supported on gnarled and distorted metal, its wheel gone from the recesses of the arch. Some presence of mind told me to retrieve the wheel that might be lying on one of the driving lanes, a potential death-trap for an oncoming, fast moving vehicle whose driver would be unaware of any obstacle in the fading light. Sure enough, the lost wheel lay in the left-hand fast lane, a hundred metres behind us. On retrieving it, however, with the brake drum intact, I saw despairingly that the rear axle had completely sheared off.

An hour and a half later, by the beam from bright halogen lights, the camper van was slowly and precariously being winched onto a recovery vehicle. Min and I watched the procedure glumly. Hector remained in the camper van, yelping to be released. Against our pleas, the mechanic - who spoke only Dutch - gesticulated that the dog must remain in the vehicle while we travelled with him in the cabin of the recovery vehicle. The camper van was then secured by chains with the offending rear left side hoisted-up onto wooden blocks. Thus we travelled to a small, quiet Dutch village that was well away from the motorway where, by two o'clock in the morning, the camper van was parked on the forecourt of a small garage with its three remaining wheels two feet off the ground. Hector's panicking pleas reached a crescendo but had to fall on deaf ears during our journey to this site. He was again quiet and content when reunited with us in the camper van, where we remained for a further six days.

This was the time it took the charming Dutch secretary at the garage to locate another secondhand Bedford rear axle, and all the other innumerable bits and pieces that were required, at a location a hundred miles away. Min and I were given a car and detailed directions, and sent to collect them. After cleaning and preparing the axle, fitting and testing it, the garage mechanic eventually removed the camper van from its elevated position on wooden blocks and presented me with quite a modest bill.

Throughout the six days, we continued to use the camper van, sleeping and eating in the full view of the garage and the village high street, just feet away. I had telephoned Dan, explaining our predicament, and apologising for the delay in our arrival. He offered to send one of his sons to bring us to Amsterdam while the camper van was being repaired. But I declined as I was uncertain when my vehicle would again be on the road, and I preferred to remain with it until we could all drive to our destination.

Min, who posses the ability to communicate and relate to others at a deeper emotional level, had formed a friendship with the garage secretary during our stay at the garage. When the secretary's time allowed, they were often to be seen deep in animated conversation over a cup of tea in the office adjoining the garage workshop. In contrast, Hector and I remained in the camper van for many long, boring hours, the mechanic working silently and methodically, almost unaware of our presence.

This quality in Min made me realise that we all have a place within us which various stimuli can reach and can open us up not only to others, but also to our own conscious minds. I have often observed how quickly people, who receive sensitive and interested sharing communion from another person, will develop a deep bond with that person who may even be a complete stranger. Such a catalyst can succeed in opening doors to ourselves that we may not know are there. I have also seen Min hurt and perplexed, apparently without cause, when emotional barriers go up suddenly when sometimes others feel too exposed. Perhaps this is because we feel at once a weakness entering our minds when confronted with perplexing emotions, which we feel unable to control through failure to realize and accept their existence. In a world of security, where all seems to be so much under control, it is intolerable that we might lose control of ourselves thereby showing weakness and failing to maintain the superficiality of the norm?

Perhaps we have also distorted our interpretation of 'weakness.' But surely, it is only in confrontation with ourselves over what we feel are weaknesses, that we gain the wisdom and the strength to overcome and surmount them. It seems to me that weaknesses manifest themselves in very personal, individual ways, and with them we cannot conform to a general pattern that is applicable to everyone. If this is so, then by refusing to recognize deeper issues within us, the answers to which lie only within our own minds, we falsely protect ourselves from ourselves.

When we located finally the canal in which the "Sean o' Kelly" was docked, the Kelly Family's coastal boat home, we were welcomed with great warmth by the entire family. Min stepped on board feeling relaxed in what could have been an unnerving situation. However, she soon found herself challenged and tested on her own ground. I too was taken aback when, during the two days before Min's departure for England, Dan Kelly disconcertingly challenged her every statement and conviction. He dug deep into her soul with his mischievous eyes, drawing out truth, and expecting every argument to be accompanied by honest or well thought-out answers.

The conversations were mentally exhausting as we found ourselves confronting a sharp wit, an analytical brain and a man who seemed to have his own answer to everything. He enjoyed the fact that neither Min nor I would accept passively his direct and challenging statements. He rose exuberantly to the challenge of a good argument and a battle of wits that, to a degree, I found stimulating and thought provoking. However, Min was bewildered, perplexed and threatened by his seemingly brash behaviour, which was obviously designed to test us. I think we both passed the test. Despite what was shortly to happen to him, Dan has maintained a respect and certain admiration for both Min and myself over the years since that time.

Together with the members of his family, Dan succeeded eventually in endearing himself in a very particular way to Min's sensitive, yet strong and loving heart He touched and stimulated a deeper emotion which aroused questions that were perhaps latent within herself, and were certainly in my own self. I asked myself how this family had remained such an entity, with old and strong values in a world - particularly their world - that seemed to scorn such values. Why was it that the energy and aura emanating from both their manner and their music, stimulated within me a self-interrogation, and at the same time helped clarify hidden issues simply through their projection. From where, I wondered, came the capacity for a single family to live and work in such unity and harmony.

Dan was severe with his family, when he felt that individuals were not using their commonsense or intelligence to sort out the problems that inevitably would arise. These problems were either among themselves, through their complex personality entanglements, or arose because of the family structure within which they were obliged to live in order to remain a harmonious unit. Above all else he encouraged logical and constructive thought, discussion and assertiveness, being at once prepared to acknowledge and accept another point of view if he felt conclusions had been drawn wisely.

Min and I had a lot to stimulate our thoughts during the time we were alone, either taking Hector on walks in this somewhat dilapidated area of Amsterdam, or sitting quietly together in the camper van. We looked deeper into ourselves and talked more openly with each other, as a result of the influence on us by this intriguing family. There were moments when we felt an uplifting energy, the power of their song and music touching us as they played and sang together in the intimacy of their home after an evening meal.

Min had left Amsterdam, and I began teaching the first dance classes in the boat's hull, which had been emptied of a mass of paraphernalia for this purpose. My fascination for the brothers and sisters turned to amazement as I saw, during only a few days, an understanding of the instinctive rhythm and coordination in each individual of the family, regardless of age. Within a week, they had all succeeded in defining dance in relation to rhythm, forming a solid base for the classical ballet techniques that were to come later. I taught four two hour classes a day. For three of these, the Kelly Family were split into logical groups. The two younger members of the Family, Angelo and Miteh, took the first morning class of introductory movements. They mastered these within a week, and simple technical steps were then introduced into their class and progressed according to their level of understanding.

The boys' class, which included Paddy aged 13, Joey aged 17, Jimmy aged 21 and Johnny aged 25 years, was an enlightening experience. During my career in dance theatre, I had had only one opportunity of teaching boys in a separate class from girls. The male participation in dance education is vastly smaller to female participation. Therefore, in all but the biggest or most important dance schools, male students normally take their classes alongside female dancers where they are always in a great minority – often being the only male participant, as I found out myself during my early training. These four diverse and amusing characters were therefore privileged to have separate classes from their sisters. The content of their classes progressed quickly from the dull and mundane to the sharp and energetic, which is the essence and challenge of a male dancer's training in classical ballet. I found that their abilities were fairly even despite their various ages, with particularly Paddy finding within himself a natural flair for the controlled and stylized movements.

The third class was a girl's class made up of Barby aged 15, Patricia aged 21 and Kathy aged 27. Earlier in her life, Kathy had trained seriously under a 'master.' Her greater knowledge and experience therefore gave encouragement for her younger sisters to emulate her abilities and work towards a higher level. A fourth class was held later in the day, which had a looser structure and was in the form of a workshop. This provided the Family with an opportunity to come either together or in groups, where they could work on various choreographies using different structures and guidelines. Here they needed little guidance, applying themselves straight away with a great deal of imagination and creativity. At once I was inspired by their spirit of cooperation, and their enthusiasm and energy. Their understanding of what I had taught them was as if they had that knowledge already, needing only the catalyst to unlock it and set them free to activate each other.

All of my nine students possessed the essential elements of poise and projection that, through their own performance, were qualities which seemed to lie naturally within them. They were able to combine style with the technical aspects of my training far more readily than most other students I have taught, and our rapid progress towards the more complex and interesting delights of dance were guaranteed. Stimulated by their enthusiasm and ability, and excitement at the realisation of their talents, The Family progressed at a rapid rate, until an event happened during the fourth week of my visit which was to affect us all.

Meanwhile, Hector had a friend among the countless dogs in the vicinity of Panamakade, where the 'Sean o' Kelly' was moored. He was courting, and was as determined as any young male who is courting a maiden, to be with his bitch for as long and as often as possible. As I anticipated, Hector was very popular with everyone on board except Colin, the Family's four foot high deerhound - an enormous dog, a little neglected and very docile. In fact Colin was so docile that he gave Hector a very wide berth when in the vicinity of the boat. The entrance to the 'Sean o' Kelly' was by a narrow, twenty metre pontoon which stretched from the land to the boat. Whereas the Family allowed Colin to be on deck, but not in their living quarters, Hector had the run of the boat being smaller in size and a great deal cleaner.

I left him free of any restraint since the entire area was quiet and virtually free of traffic, and he took up quarters during the day on the warm, sun-heated deck near the entrance. He would welcome everyone on board, strangers or dwellers, but not Cohn who would remain static on the pontoon fearing Hector's low, gutteral, warning growls. On occasions, the growls would reach a worrying level if Cohn decided he was being treated unjustly and attempted to break though. But, unless Hector was removed from his 'guard position, Colin never managed to get past him and reach his accustomed place. Neither was there any skirmish between them, and they would amicably tolerate one another on walks together. It was only a question of who reached the pontoon first, as to whether there would be any warning reprisal. Should it be Colin, then Hector would pass cautiously by him at the entrance to the deck. In other places on the boat except the entrance, they called a truce, which was maintained throughout this and our future visits.

For the first two weeks of my stay, Hector gave me no cause for worry. If he was not immediately visible during the day, when I checked his whereabouts between classes, one call would always produce a wagging tail of a happy and contented dog. He seemed reluctant to wander far from myself or the camper van, to which he always returned at night, perhaps at a loss to find those delectable wild smells that only fields, forests and mountains can bring. Despite Spring being very warm that year, he would not entertain the idea of sleeping outside, preferring to suffer the heat in order to remain close to myself.

Around the dock area there was plenty of evidence of other dogs and during the course of the day, numerous animals passed along the footpath between the camper van and the boat with their owners. Twice a day a group of six mongrels would pass this way, herded by Maria, a forty year old Dutch lady living on a barge in a deserted neighbouring dock. I came to know Maria well through our mutual fascination with canine behaviour. However, unless I called to her in advance, Maria could no longer observe her dogs activities or recognize myself as she approached the Sean o' Kelly. Maria had glaucoma, a degenerating condition of the eyes that leads to total blindness, and her condition was already well advanced. But with the aid of contact lenses and glasses she was able to walk without a stick provided she was on familiar territory.

Thus passing the same places every day, avoiding the same obstacles, and following the same pathways, she was able to blot out the inevitable realisation that she would soon be blind. Maria was glad of some sympathetic conversation in English, a language that she had mastered perfectly, like many of the Dutch. When I told her that I had lived for fifteen years in a caravan, she invited me to spend an evening with her so that I could see the conversion of her barge - of which she was very proud. Hector discovered an empathy with Maria's mongrels and, on the rare occasions when he did not respond to my call, I knew that he could be found with them.

It was during the third week of our stay in Amsterdam that Hector disappeared. On returning at dusk from a walk with Hector at the end of a tiring day, I lay down in the camper van with the door open and promptly fell asleep. Awaking in the early hours of the morning, chilly and hungry, and seeing Hector was not inside, I called quietly to him. There was no response. Rousing myself, I set off to search for him, passing first by Maria's barge, then retracing the steps of our evening walk. My concern grew when there was no sign of him. Eventually, feeling it was now too late to be wandering around a residential area calling for my dog, I returned to my van and slept fitfully until the morning. The door to the van had remained open during the night to allow for Hector's entry when he returned. But the following morning still produced no dog and, during the breaks between my classes, I went out to call him and check whether he had returned.

After the third group class, Kathy suggested I cancel the final session and offered to alert everyone of the change in schedule. It was late afternoon and I felt tense and frustrated. By dusk four hours later, I had visited every street, canal and footpath in the area, calling for hector and asking passers-by if they had any information on the whereabouts of my black dog. In despair, I decided to return to the Sean o' Kelly and telephone the police, when a car stopped beside me. A man of my age asked me urgently something that I did not understand. My apology in English produced a smile and he repeated the question in my language. "Are you, by any chance, looking for a black dog, about this high?" he gesticulated.

My dark mood immediately changed to hope, as a surge of adrenalin forcibly thrust me to the side of his car. I said that I had been searching everywhere for a black dog who had been missing since yesterday evening. He laughed and gestured for me to enter the car, causing me to relax for I knew that I would now find Hector safe and well. But I was unprepared for the sight that faced me when entering the living room of his house, with his wife welcoming me with a glass of wine. In the dull light from a single table lamp, I became aware of two black furry bodies lying snugly together in a dog basket. On closer scrutiny, I was taken aback to see that Hector was one of these bodies, entangled in the legs of his new friend, sound asleep. At my whispered call, his eyes opened and he nonchalantly acknowledged my presence. He did not move, and neither did his partner.

I looked up at my hosts with disbelief. Their eyebrows lifted, both heads turning slightly, concentrating on my reaction. "I can't believe this is my dog," I said quietly. "I have never seen him with another dog in such obvious intimacy. Is she on heat?" "That's the extraordinary thing, you see," answered the man, his wife smiling at me, "she's not on heat, or having phantom pregnancies, or anything. Yet since this dog of yours arrived yesterday, we have simply been unable to separate them. It is a mutual feeling between them. Our dog, Meep, pines as soon as we separate them. They sleep, play, and even eat together in perfect harmony that, personally I have only observed before in humans." "If you could see them play, urged the wife, "it's like poetry. We are sorry that we do not have a video camera to film them, as their tenderness towards one another is quite out of the ordinary, particularly when you consider that Meep is not on heat."

I was amazed. Never before in the twenty months that I had known Hector, had I seen him show any interest in his own species apart from an occasional sniff, or when mating smells took over his senses. Subsequently, never have I also observed any similar behaviour between Hector and any another dog. Later, when comparing the interplay between my other two dogs: Puppy and Mossy, mother and off-spring, and their obvious affection for one another, I would often recall the intimacy of Hector and Meep – a wonderful smooth-coated, black retriever. Hector had never before, or since, slept with another dog and neither have I seen him play with another dog. He certainly has never allowed another dog near his food. While this includes Mossy, another male, it also extends more strangely to Puppy with whom he has also mated.

The husband, Jo, continued, "Meep has not yet been with another dog. She's thoroughbred with a pedigree. We wanted to take her to stud so that we could keep one of her puppies ourselves. Then we intended to sell the puppies and have her spayed. His wife, Ineke, took up the point. "We wanted to know, after seeing how they were with each other, whether you would let us keep your dog here for a few more days until Meep comes into season. We want her so much to have Hector's puppies, as obviously they have something between them that is so rare that it should be allowed to come to a conclusion

Ineke topped-up my glass and motioned for me to sit down in an armchair. Hector then roused himself, disentangled his body from his mate, sniffed inside her ear, then gradually wandered over to me and sat with his chin on my knee. Meep slowly raised her head and followed him, approaching and greeting the stranger in their midst. We all laughed at these actions and slowly my story came out. I was not from Amsterdam, only visiting a family on a boat nearby for a few weeks. In fifteen days I would be returning to Italy and my home. Looking up, I saw the pained glance from Ineke to her husband. "But perhaps I too could keep one of her pups. I expect to return to Amsterdam maybe twice a year. If somehow my visits could be timed to coincide ......"

But I was cut-off by Ineke. "Look" she said, "it's going to start." I sipped at my wine curious to know what was 'going to start.' Then I began to appreciate why Jo and Ineke were now in such a deep conversation. Hector had moved from my side to join Meep, whose eyes did not wander from his stare as he approached her cautiously. In a subtle movement, he slid with his neck and then his breast onto Meep, who rolled onto her back to accommodate him. In the next instant they were together yet strangely Hector was not aroused, there was no erection and no attempt at mounting. How could there be: Meep was not in season. There was something that was tender and beautiful in their behaviour, no dominance, no submissiveness.

In our human ability to communicate with one another, and our analytical observations of each other, we draw conclusions on how to react to stimuli that set-off patterns of behaviour. Those who study animal behaviour may be able to explain why our pets respond in certain ways to particular stimuli. But I had no knowledge on which to base any conclusions. I was stunned by this extraordinary example of canine 'contact improvisation.' There followed a long silence between us as Hector and Meep settled into their bed again. Jo broke the mood "would you consider letting them remain together here so that we can see where this is leading. It would be awful to separate them at this moment."

I knew straight away that I could not separate Hector from Meep, should he desire to remain. What I had seen had struck deep. Our dogs had shown us that respect and consideration for our domestic animals' welfare can and should be as important as that of ourselves. So I left their house late that night, torn between wanting the company of my own friend, and trying to accept his new need - a part of the freedom that I had wanted to offer him. As I was about to walk through the door, I turned instinctively and called Hector. He looked at me and told me with his eyes that he wanted to remain with Meep. I understood, accepted it and left, wondering if I had lost something that meant a great deal more than I had ever visualised.

For three days Hector remained with Jo, Ineke and their dog, while I concentrated on my classes. One day Dan inspected my camper van and noted its deteriorating body where various bumps and scratches had now become rusting holes - hanging appendages in some areas. He enquired whether I would object to having a few repairs being carried out. He added that Johnny, Jimmy and Joey would do the work for free and all materials would be provided. I demurred. He assured me that it would be a pleasure for them, and they would do an excellent job as they had already had experience in body work repairs. In the days that followed my reports to Dan on their progress showed my gratitude. Within a week they had restored the exterior of the camper van to its former glory, having carried out a first class job. They stripped the offending parts down to bare metal, methodically filled-in all holes, and smoothed the repairs until the desired aesthetic form was achieved. The final spray of paint was the test and, after it had dried, I found that I could not fault their work in any way.

On the fourth day of Hector's honeymoon, I returned to the camper van for a short break following my first class of the morning. The boys were just gathering up their tools before changing and going to the boat for their own class. Paddy, who had been helping them this morning, said to me quite casually, "Oh Stephen, Hector came back about an hour ago. We let him in the van". I threw the door open, my eyes wide, and called him. In a flash he was off the bed and all over me, in an excited frenzy that caught me unawares. Having been a prodigal son myself, earlier in my life, I understood immediately the joy and acceptance of a deprived father, as I rejoiced over my dog's return. Although time was limited before my next class, we fussed and played with each other and then I left him, leaving the door of the camper van open. Feeling that had I not done so, it would be trying to keep a friend who - of his own free will - left his companion to come and see me.

When I returned later, Hector was still asleep on my bed. After my final class in the early evening he was gone. However, a brisk walk to Jo's house found him again snuggled-up to Meep. This state of affairs continued for six days until the weekend, when Jo and Ineke had planned to depart for five days for the north of Holland, taking Meep with them. My departure was also imminent, since I was to accompany the Kelly Family to Germany for eight days, where they would be in a studio recording a new album of songs. I would need to take Hector with me and I worried in advance as to how he would be, away from Meep,

Thirty-six hours before leaving Amsterdam, I was on board the 'Sean o' Kelly, chatting with Kathy about the progress of the dance classes. Hector was lying nearby. With Meep no longer around, I needed to keep a close watch on his movements so that he did not disappear again with the intention of trying to find her. "Kathy, Kathy, are you there." Jimmy's call from the entrance echoed around the iron structure of the boat, in an urgent and blood-curdling tone of voice. Kathy, raised herself abruptly, and rushed out to meet her brother who confronted her, panic-stricken and out of breath. "Kathy, its father. Come quickly. Something's happened to him. He's in the car park."

Kathy did not wait for the end of his statement. She rushed out through the entrance of the boat, instinctively calling to Johnny and Joey to "get out here, quick". As I followed in her footsteps, I passed Jimmy, ashen-faced and fearful, struggling to gain control his emotions. My interrogating glance caught his face, and saw that he had experienced something awful. As we ran together down the pontoon, with Hector following, shouts and commands sent other running bodies back to the boat. I quickened my pace, unable to prepare myself for what I might witness, once I had reached the scene.

When I arrived, followed urgently by family members bearing blankets, clothes, pillows, water, I saw Dan's death-filled eyes, unable to focus, and heard his breath locked seemingly in his chest. He was on his back floundering, arms and legs waving in awkward, spasmodic movements, as though he were drowning in slow motion in deep water. Angelo and Miteh, who had just arrived on the scene, began to cry piteously and were taken away by Patricia who tried to console them. Putting Hector in the camper van, I stood eight metres from where Dan seemingly was fighting for his life. I was strangely aware that, amid this serious crisis, there was no confusion. Only methodical and practical activity - a superb and automatic communication between each of the remaining six members of the family. Urgency: yes, strong orders and advice: yes, but no panic, no indecisiveness, and no lack of obedience to commands.

Feeling like a fish out of water, I observed quietly the drama unfolding before my eyes, studying reactions, and noting the caring and emotionally controlled actions that gave their father his best chance of survival. Within minutes, sirens could be heard approaching fast, and in a moment the drama was no longer visible. The ambulance had whisked Dan away, taking with it two of the older family members, leaving the others behind in stunned silence and hypo-anesthesia in the open space of the car park. Jimmy broke the mood with an incredible reaction, over which I have long since reflected, wondering how such a young man could have the answer to the need for emotional relief. "Come on, you guys," he said. "Get your instruments. We are going to play and sing while we wait for news. Come on, come on."

I went to my camper van, took hold of Hector, and I prayed for help for Dan and the members of his family - a multi-talented and unique unit of nine individuals who, on the verge of a very important project, were now faced with the biggest crisis in their lives. Then, when I stepped into their living room cabin and heard them singing and playing, something moved inside me. All heads were bowed, the enthusiasm and energy had gone from their music, and yet a spirit permeated the room as their prayers found expression through song. Minutes went by. The two youngest were comforted by their elders when they gave expression to their worst fears. Only song offered security during those anguished moments until word came.

The ring of the telephone cut through a guitar chord. In a split second the receiver was lifted, and six people waited to hear whether 'Papa Kelly' would be coming home. Jimmy's practical voice, emotion hidden temporarily, acknowledged the information from the hospital, his eyes moving from one person to another. His first words were to Angelo and Miteh "Father is in hospital. Kathy and Johnny are with him. He's going to stay there for a while. We can't go and see him. Kathy wants you two to be good and to be strong for father. He needs us now to be strong for him."

Miteh began to cry and to call for her father. Angelo, just seven years old, held his older sister and said, "Miteh, father wants us to be strong, remember what he always said about being strong, remember ....." "You two", Patricia's firm voice broke the tension, "get out of here and go and tidy your bunks". When they were out of the room, Paddy remaining at the door to ensure they were not eavesdropping, Jimmy relayed the news from the hospital to all those present. "Kathy says it's too soon to know if father will pull through. He's had a severe brain hemorrhage. Johnny and she are staying. None of us are to come to the hospital, and she will ring every hour to let us know what is going on".

"My God", whispered Patricia, "don't you become paralysed with that." Joey piped up, "We don't know anything yet, Patricia. it might not even be whatever they say it is". "Get Miteh and Angelo back in here. Paddy, call them Come on, let's play music. We can't stay here like this. Think of the little ones." Patricia took charge, putting the kettle on the stove to boil. I got up to go, unable to say anything. As I passed her she put out her hand to touch my shoulder, her face filled with emotion. "Stephen, I'm sorry. Please excuse us. I don't think any of us could cope with any more classes today, but maybe tomorrow it would be good for us, especially for Miteh and Angelo. Please......."

I nodded, looked around at everyone then left. I wanted just to walk, and to think. I walked with Hector for two hours, eventually ending up at Maria's barge where I announced myself and entered. Her warm, welcoming voice gave relief to my anguish and compassion. When I left two hours later, I felt clearer in my own mind. Maria's sensitive understanding helped to put my thoughts into perspective. I telephoned Min, who was in England, to give her the news and question her on the causes and implications of a cerebral hemorrhage. Being a trained and experienced nurse, she told me everything about a cerebral hemorrhage.

I repeated this later that evening to the Family, when I returned to the Sean o' Kelly in order to get the latest news on Dan's condition. The two younger members were now in bed asleep, so the others were able to talk to me freely. Johnny had returned to the boat, with Patricia taking his place to join Kathy at the hospital. Empty and drained of energy, he looked at me and smiled without expression. All other heads were lowered, bodies either slumped forward or backward. Instruments lying at their sides were as silent and as lifeless as their players.

The telephone made everyone jump, and Johnny picked up the receiver. A faint glimmer of a smile, his eyes widening, caused everyone else to close in around him. "He's stable." But after a long message from Kathy on the telephone his thin smile had disappeared. "What about the recording the day after tomorrow. Should we cancel? We have to make a decision." A long pause. "OK, I'll be there early in the morning." Johnny put down the receiver slowly, gathering his thoughts, then gave us his message.

"Father's condition is very serious. He's alive and stable but he's had a severe stroke which might leave him paralysed for life. At the moment he cannot communicate anything at all, and the hospital tells us that this may be the case for quite some time. They say it is vital he keeps his will to live, and that we can help him get better by being with him constantly at the hospital once he has recovered sufficiently to be able to see us. We must encourage him to live and to move. Kathy says it could take a long time, maybe even years, but it will only happen if his mind will let him. He will have to make himself move, it won't happen automatically. He will only do this if he sees and understands that we really need him and want him still to be our Papa."

"Kathy has rung Helmut in Germany, and he will be here tomorrow. She's going to ask if we can delay the recording for a day or two and then go ahead with it. It's what father would want, and it will keep us from moping around here. So Kathy, Patricia, Jimmy, Joey and I are going to take shifts in two's to be at his bedside, all day and night. Paddy: you and Barby, Miteh and Angelo will come with whoever's here to the hospital from time to time, so that father sees us all and recognises us. We have to talk to him. We have to encourage him, and we have to let him know that we are strong and can cope with everything until he gets better. Kathy says to rehearse as much as possible. She asks you, Stephen, if you can keep the classes going with whoever is here. They've given her a room at the hospital. She can stay there for the time being, but father will have to be moved to another hospital. Kathy's trying to sort out a place where he'll get the very best care. We've just got to go on. We've got to, I know that Mother would have wanted it - and father too, if he could tell us".

Johnny turned to Jimmy. "We'll have to try and organise a schedule with Helmut, where some of us can be in Amsterdam while the others are in Germany for the recording. It's crucial. We can't just leave father, especially if the doctors say it's vital at this stage that he recognise us and somehow understand that we need him, more now than ever before." I asked Johnny whether he thought that, in the circumstances, it would be better for me to leave and come back later in the year. The Family might then benefit from the dance classes without having the weight of Dan's stroke, the recording, and the total re-organization of their lives, on their shoulders. "You'll have to talk with Kathy, Stephen, I'm sorry. But personally

I think she'll say 'don't go'. I think we really need you as well, at this time. She'll be coming back for a short time tomorrow, and I'll ask her to have a word with you. I'm sorry, Stephen, that you're in the middle of all this. Incidentally, how's Hector, is he getting over his girlfriend?"

Later, when I was out in the fresh air with Hector at my side, I wondered how many people would have asked me a question like that in a similar crisis. How many would even consciously put their minds to thinking about anyone else's tiny problems in face of their calamity. "Would even I," I asked myself? While I was a teacher for the Kelly Family, it seemed that it was I who was being taught by them in a quiet and subtle way – even though they were unaware of it. Again, this reinforced the principles that I had already adopted in my approach to life since those years in Scotland: to search, not necessarily to know, but to be in touch with; to never say no to learning and growing from experience; to be aware of emotional feelings and what they are telling me; and, to never take anything for granted in life. And to use these principles to lead me forward, with no other security than my belief that we do not walk alone.

So here was a family that was about to face the greatest test of their lives. A family whose security lay in the bonding between each individual, and the independence that Dan had instilled in them. Their education to date had been one of survival, in understanding human issues, and learning from experience. They had suffered poverty, deprivation and the loss of their mother. Dan, in his grief and despair, had weakened momentarily and sought escape in alcohol. But the Family did not go wrong, disperse, fall foul of drugs and sexual abuse, or fall prey to money. They demonstrated their integrity by hanging on to the moral codes that brought them strength and success in the commercial music world.

I left Amsterdam for Italy sixteen days after Dan's hemorrhage, and saw the Family recover from their crisis. Within three days the family had rallied, organised and prepared for what was to be a two year period of management control of their company. Each family member adopted new responsibilities. New schedules were formulated to cope with their work, and split their time between Amsterdam and the recording studio in Germany. The Family's popular singing style would be maintained at the highest standard for their new album, where many of their songs were their own composition. The Family showed their professionalism by concentrating on the work at hand while, at the same time, returning in groups to see their father in Amsterdam. It proved to them that, if they remained together and gained strength from their determination, then they could continue to survive.

During the first days, only individuals were called to the studio by Helmut, while the others remained in Amsterdam I gave dance classes at the studio, either in the studio, the foyer, or outside on the garden terrace. It was improvised and sometimes a little disorganised, but it worked. I returned with the family to Amsterdam at the end of the recording session, and witnessed their reunion with Dan at the private hospital to which he had been moved. In fact it was a celebration. The Family told their father how well their work had gone, and of the two new songs that were set to music and included in their new album. I told him of our progress in the dance classes and my opinion of his exceptional family. He showed, through expression in his eyes, that he understood and approved of his family's actions. However, the trials of the Kelly Family were really only just beginning, and it would be a further five years before they could show that they were on top of everything.

I left for Italy with plans to return to Amsterdam again in January of the following year. Hector was taken to Jo and Ineke's house to be with Meep for a last time. Their mutual reaction made it heart-rending for me to take Hector away, and I was left with no alternative but to promise that he would come back as soon as I was in Amsterdam again. Leaving the city, I stopped unannounced at the hospital to visit Dan, and Kathy greeted me. She told me not to worry about Dan, he was a strong-minded man and she hoped he would recover fully from his paralysis. Standing by his bedside, I sensed the frustration in his mind, and how he would need to learn how to re-direct the messages from his brain to his body. A formidable task, and one that would demand interminable patience. Kathy said, "We will not let him rest until the day when he once again joins us on stage."

During the long journey home, I was pre-occupied with what had happened over the last few weeks. "Who are the Kelly Family," I had asked myself in Frankfurt ten months earlier, when I saw them for the very first time. Now that I knew the Kelly Family better, I realized that I was no nearer the answer to my question.

Three Dogs and a Dancer by Stephen Ward

Chapter 12

'Giamboree'

My neighbours, Chris and Karen Redsell

Summer 1990

"You won't believe what's happened at La Casetta. The vineyard has just gone mad - out of control. Its a jungle of foliage". Min hugged her favourite dog who thrust his black and tan muzzle between her thigh and arm, his individual and personal way of greeting, the right paw lifted and waiting to be taken in response to his gestures. She looked up at me as if to thank me for bringing Hector to the airport to meet her. I went on, "the weather's been terrific. You look great. Did you have a good trip." "Wonderful, as smooth as anything. It's good to be back, and I can't wait to see La Casetta in the summer. When am I going to be able to have a haystack hot water shower?"

"Thank you also Stephen, for picking me up here at Pisa," Min said. "Well, we couldn't exactly leave you to find your own way, now could we." "Well, no, I guess not. How's Hector been." "Fine. He's really settling down well, and loves his new home. Romps through the vineyard like it was a forest, well, actually it is. I'm only a quarter of the way cutting through the grass. It all needs doing again since May. They've had a bit of rain while you and I were up in Amsterdam, and it's all back up to nearly hip height now. You can't have a hot shower just yet but I'm working on it. I've got the plans sorted out on how I'm going to pass the water through the haystack, and then into the bathroom and kitchen - which I still have to construct. You'll see, you'll see. Let's get going".

Min had decided to come back out to Italy for six weeks and put out feelers to find an abandoned property for sale. Her Italian roots, as well as her frequent visits to Italy, had showed how much she felt at home in her father's country. Although born and brought up in Oxford, and prevented by her Italian father and French mother from speaking any language other than English, her Latin blood was proving too strong an influence to allow her to continue living in England. I had already been back at La Casetta for two weeks when Min arrived in mid-July, amidst the tremendous heat. My journey from Amsterdam had gone smoothly. I had driven slowly along the motorways, being apprehensive of my camper van with its altered rear end. However, it had given no trouble and apart from one adventure along the way, Hector and I had enjoyed our return journey - anticipating our arrival at La Casetta.

The adventure took place in Switzerland, on the edge of the Alps at a place near Lucerne. There, fifteen years earlier, I had recommenced dancing after overcoming my debilitating back problem, which had stopped my career for over two years. I had parked the van for the night at a favourite site off the main road, by the lake on which Lucerne stands. Dusk was approaching and, in the little daylight that was still available, I collected some wood to make a small camp fire. Being some way from the danger of traffic, Hector had been left free to survey his new territory. I did not think he would wander far since, behind us, slabs of granite swept up that were too steep for a dog to climb, and the lake close by also limited his travel in that direction. Soon afterwards I wondered if I had under-estimated Hector's climbing ability. As I settled in front of my fire for a pleasant evening, I heard Hector's high-pitched bark - which he only uses when needing help - way above my head and coming somewhere from among the slabs of stone. A second cry from Hector reached my ears and, without using my common sense, I left everything and immediately began my ascent up the steep, bare rock.

If I had had my 'wits about me,' I would have changed out of my casual day shoes into stronger boots, and picked up a torch and a dog's lead. But Hector's urgent calls drove me on without thinking. Halfway up my precarious ascent to where I imagined Hector was trapped on a rocky ledge, I began to get my thoughts into perspective, and realised that my own hasty attempt at rescue could well end up as myself needing to be rescued. In the failing light I could make out vaguely the terrain above me. Forest growing steeply began to intersperse intermittently with bare rock, above which Hector's now continuous cries were coming a hundred metres away. He had obviously made his way up through nearby woodland and, once he had seen the camper van or myself, had attempted to descend not knowing that the trees gave way to bare rock.

My own ascent was not straightforward. In daylight, I might have considered descending the same way alone, but would definitely not attempt such a descent with a dog in the dark. Hector's cries had risen in pitch. I was afraid now to call him in case he should decide to try and come down to me, lose his footing and fall, which would mean death or certain injury. I continued to climb, adrenalin and the desire to save my dog urging me on until, almost in darkness, my outstretched hand received a wet lick. Immediately I tried to calm Hector, for the place where I found him clinging to solid rock did not afford any space for a boisterous welcome. My huge relief at finding him safe and uninjured was tempered by thoughts on how I was going to get myself and my dog out of this dangerous predicament. By this time there was scarcely any light left to plan a descent. However I could see that, not far above, the forest took over from the almost vertical rock, and that this would afford a safer and more secure route down, in the dark.

Since Hector had already descended to the point where I found him, he was quite capable of retracing his steps once he understood my intentions. As we approached easier terrain, I considered the necessity of spending a night on this mountainside, wedged for security between the tree trunks and shrubs. But it was growing cold, and in this inhospitable place I concluded it would be best to attempt a descent. I cursed myself for not bringing Hector's lead and wondered how I might restrain him in the pitch-black night, where I could now hardly see my way forward. However, as we headed up into ever thicker forest in order to avoid the bare rock, Hector was perfectly at home, seeing where I saw nothing, stepping fearlessly where I blindly stumbled. While my every footstep had to be calculated and confirmed by my hand's sense of touch, he was free to make his own descent. Our recent positions were reversed. Now it was myself calling to Hector to stay close by, and it was he who was guiding me through this dark mountain forest. Finally, after what seemed a long time, I became aware that I was no longer in pitch-blackness, and was able to distinguish some reflected lights from the surface of the lake below.

I took a tentative step forward, but then almost lost my balance as I realised that there was nothing between myself and the lake below. Reacting instinctively, I froze and clung onto whatever I could grasp, in order to prevent myself falling. If I had done so, I would probably not have stopped until my body reached the lake. I climbed once again to get clear of the precipice. Hector, had left me initially but now responded to my fresh and urgent calls. I heard the sound of his movements through undergrowth, eventually reached him and took hold of his collar as we moved upwards together. He must have wondered why my progress was so painstakingly slow, but the gradient was steep, and the terrain full of obstacles and brambles. Adrenalin surged through me, and my senses were now fully alert to any sudden change in terrain.

I felt sure that Hector now realised that I was totally dependent on him to guide me safely down and out of this nightmare. He was constantly by my side. When he went up, I went up. When he descended, so did I - albeit at a snails pace. He was my eyes and, like a blind man, I knew I had to trust he would get us down safely. Gradually the steep gradient began to lessen and I knew that I was out of danger; he had not abandoned me in my true hour of need. The adventure was not over until, finally, I sensed a rise in temperature from the ground, and realised it was the ash from my fire. Hector had brought us back to the exact point of our departure, a conclusion that bonded our trust in each other, and showed me what a true friend I had in this dog. By the light in my camper van I saw that the time was 3.30 am

When I arrived back at La Casetta, I could see that in future years I would have to consider carefully whether I should be absent for so long in the Spring. The vines had not been pruned correctly, and their growth had produced a jungle of runners that camouflaged completely the neat rows that I had left in May. The cut grass had, in five short weeks, grown in height to almost a metre in places.

As soon as he knew I had returned, Chris brought our jointly-owned strimmer down to La Casetta. "You have a bit of a job here" he said. "Plenty of fuel, though, for your hot water system". I wondered if he was being facetious about my scheme that I had explained enthusiastically to him before I had gone away to

Amsterdam. I set to work straight away, eager to impress Min who had written to request that she be allowed to come in July. During the next two weeks at La Casetta I had the good fortune to locate a bath, a washbasin and a ceramic double kitchen sink at local dumps, scrapped but in good condition. I scoured the roadsides for good stone, found ample, and brought it back in my camper van, in half ton loads. This stone would be used to build a dry-stone wall in the two metre space between the house and retaining wall, where the vineyard began. I chose dry stone because my kitchen and bathroom needed to be temporary structures that could be dismantled, once the local council's embargo on building work in Fiano was lifted.

In a two-by-two metre space on the outer side of this wall would be the haystack, installed into which would be an old boiler, also reclaimed. Fifteen feet above this, in the middle of the vineyard, a defunct commercial freezer served as the reservoir from which water would be fed by a single tube to the boiler. Inside the wall, the bathroom would extend one and a half metres to a bamboo screen, beyond which would be my kitchen. However, I had only progressed to getting a fibre glass roof over the kitchen and bathroom, and laying the floor in rough-cut marble found at a disused marble quarry, before Min arrived mid-July. Stones for the wall, and cut grass gathered in large heaps to prevent it drying out, lined the terrace above the house. In just a little more time, all systems would be set to go.

"It's going to be great, Stephen", Min said encouragingly, as I explained my plan to her when we arrived back from the airport. "I see what you mean about the vineyard. Did the garden up at the top come to anything?" "Come and see," I replied, "you'll be amazed." But in fact the garden was not that amazing, when I compare how my vegetables grew then with how they grow now, in such a favourable climate in the rich Tuscan soil. In May of that first year, Min I had painstakingly prepared the ground, removing weed and grass roots thickly embedded up to a foot deep in the earth. However, having no manure or natural compost, we planted our seeds directly into this comparatively sterile ground and left them to fend for themselves. It was fortunate that the seedlings did not shrivel up and die, for June in Tuscany can often be a rainless month, overhead sun drying and parching the ground in days.

But our seeds germinated in the damp, warm conditions and, to my inexperienced eyes, had grown sufficiently to warrant continuing to water them. Little did I know then, just how much water the plants would need to keep them alive in soil that seemed to be in a permanent state of dehydration. Our crops in the weeks to come were miserable in comparison to my present-day harvests, when the physical labour of hauling water twice a day from the bottom to the top of my land is taken into account. However, our efforts had produced something, and that was reason enough to be glad. And the summer was ultimately to shower so many other blessings onto our heads that, by its end, we would feel rich beyond measure.

Elizabetta Fiorini, the professional pianist and dance tutor, had asked me to participate as teacher and choreographer in her second annual summer course for young adults. The two-week course would involve intensive classes and workshops in dance, music and drama, with students able to be involved in any one or all three activities. There were also groups in design, scenery and costume making, the ultimate intention being to present a short theatre piece with dance and music for family and friends. The course had attracted twenty-five young people from various regions in Italy, and the final production was to be 'Adam and Eve,' by the American author, Mark Twain.

I thought that this was a formidable task to accomplish in just two weeks, with young adolescents of diverse talents, whose main priority was likely to be having a good holiday with social outlets. However, I under-estimated Angelo Biondi's ability to bring these young people together under a common cause. Angelo, a long standing friend of Elizabetta in his mid-forties, was experienced in teaching drama and production and possessed the rare ability of bringing-out the creative best in people. He oversaw the directing, casting and producing, and got the twenty-five students to work together as a unit by firing their enthusiasm, observing where an individual's talents could be exploited, and then adapting the production accordingly.

Chris and young flautist, Antonio Barzanti, were responsible for the music tuition of those students who were already accomplished in playing an instrument. Elizabetta and myself gave workshops and classes in dance, and other teachers also attended to give introductions to costume and set design. The first week was designated as a 'getting to know you' period, when workshops were interspersed with outings to places of historic or holiday interest in the area. As they began to relax and make friendships during this week, the students' individual personalities and creative flair were assessed by Angelo and Elizabetta, providing a basis for their approach to the production. The students themselves were encouraged to openly discuss their ideas, the intention being to include as much of their creativity as possible in the production. Their abilities varied greatly, and some sensitivity was needed in casting to ensure that everyone's talents were given an appropriate opportunity.

With so much to consider, the end result could well have been confused, badly prepared or difficult for an audience to follow. However, the performance given on the large terrace in front of Consoli's villa, to over a hundred people, was a tremendous success. Tears were shed by the young students at the end of the evening, and addresses exchanged and continuation of friendships promised.

As I stood back from the throng of the post-performance champagne reception, I reflected on my good fortune in having come to live in this beautiful part of Italy. Of having met some wonderful people through Chris and Karen, who had similar ideas to my own, and who had permitted me to be part of an event which would remain in young minds for some time to come. I thought of the value of expression in helping to create a stable, healthy and motivated mind, particularly the initial molding of that mind. I reflected on my own youth and the chance that I had been given to follow my desires. I thought of my work with Focus On Dance, and the extraordinary wealth of expression that brought joy and satisfaction to many of the thousands of young people. Sadly, I also considered the ever lessening emphasis now put on artistic expression in the material world.

A child will find expression naturally, instinctively and uninhibitedly through voice, movement and play. Curiosity initially sets a creative track, and discovery and the use of logic moves the child along the path. It needs to sense there is a purpose in its discoveries and, through encouragement, advances it's understanding of what has been discovered. Parents know the dangers in preventing a child from expressing itself, in preventing it from finding its own creative outlets. Parents are often amazed at the happy child who learns independence quickly, develops strong legs, and finds hands quickly doing what his brain tells them – all of which are the secret result of discovery. At an early age the child learns about the environment in which we live, activating its body and finding outlets in its expression through activity. The child moves into adolescence and continues to learn about its environment at an alarming rate.

This is good and is a part of life. However, on reaching adolescence, the discovery process is, by necessity, overtaken by the needs of academic knowledge. But I often ask myself whether, in our quest to gain knowledge from the billions of sources that exist today, such as advertising and other commercial publicity, we fail to exploit our ability to draw our own conclusions about the information we are given. Have the majority received so much misinformation that we now accept issues without thinking and or making our own conclusions? Have we become passive, governed and manipulated to the extent that we just accept what others tell us without constructive thought? If so, are we not in danger of failing to become activated in face of real personal or even world-changing crises.

Min found me in my corner of solitude and asked me what I thought of the final production. She had been involved in helping with costumes. "I wonder if these young people realize their good fortune in receiving such encouragement and a chance to gain insight into their potential," I said. "Yes, its true," replied Min, "but would they have had that chance in the first place, if their parents hadn't taken the risk in bringing them here, and then coming to support them in their presentation. It all starts here, doesn't it, with confidence building I mean. These young people have worked together to get this show on tonight, and it has been great. But think, too, that the majority probably came with pre-conceived ideas on what they were going to do. Then they met, made friendships with each other, and passed on those ideas and received some themselves. Those who came to play the actor, found themselves dabbling in the dance - even some of the boys. Those that wanted to play music, found they could express themselves in body rhythm. Those who only wanted to dance, suddenly found their voices. And what about the boy who struck up a friendship with a girl playing the flute, and then suddenly discovered a new world in music making. Or for that matter, the girl with all those complexes who came only to help out with the costume-making, and ended up as one of the players - with a leading role."

"Yes," I replied, "surely this is what education should be about.

Primarily self-discovery, then confidence building, and finally information-seeking. It seems to start off that way, but just when we reach the most complex stage of our life's development it all goes out the window. We get brainwashed into dumping our individuality and slotting into the machine, which is alright for some, but certainly not for all. Look at these young people, Min. Angelo's stretched each one beyond where he imagined he could go. Look how they all met that challenge, and think of how many avenues have now opened up in each mind as a result of their increased awareness."

Chris joined us. "They really pulled it together didn't they. Quite impressive. Well, in two weeks we'll be starting on our own 'Giamboree'." This name was Chris's Italian adaptation of the English word 'Jamboree,' and the name for his summer music festival of chamber music concerts at some of the mountain villages in the area. "We have fifteen musicians coming from England, plus Elizabetta, Antonio and myself, and yourself Stephen - if you still want to be involved with the dance". "I most certainly do," I replied, " if you think it will add a positive element to the concerts." "OK, perhaps Elizabetta and yourself, Stephen, could do something together." "Fine Chris, we need to get together and talk about it. When do your musicians start arriving?"

Chris's original intention behind the Giamboree was to create an outlet where a few select musicians could come together, and play chamber music in a relaxed atmosphere. To clarify how this intention became a reality, and evolved into a respected festival for players and public alike in the subsequent years, it is necessary to reveal the background to this inspiration. When Chris and Karen had finally decided to return to Tuscany in 1987, and settle there permanently in their rustic, converted sheep pen, it was a decision that recognised the sacrifices they were making. Chris would be leaving his secure and respected position as co-principal of the viola section with the Bournemouth Symphony Orchestra. He had no equivalent playing contract in Italy into which he could step. However, he did have a wealth of experience in every level necessary for his survival, and the motivation to put that experience into practice for new ideas and projects. His parents had seen to it that. As a young man growing-up in a small mining town in northern Ontario, Canada, he learned many practical trades; from carpentry to bricklaying, car mechanics to joinery, plumbing to gardening

Music was encouraged in the Redsell family of five brothers and sisters. His mother, Lucy, was born in England and played the piano in her hometown, Ringwood, near Bournemouth. Chris developed an ear for music at an early age, and began his musical education with the piano, moving gradually to the violin. Adolescence brought physical growth, together with an obvious natural talent for music, and his teacher suggested he change his studies from the violin to the larger viola. The reasoning behind this advice was that if Chris continued to grow, not only physically but also in musical ability, he would soon find his large hands and long arms a hindrance to progress with the violin. Chris was disillusioned by this advice, having set his heart on mastering the violin, but reality made it necessary for him to accept the advice. After re-adjusting to the new fingering and spacing on the larger fingerboard of the viola, he continued to exhibit encouraging signs of his ability.

Chris's growing passion for music on every level, plus his disciplined attitude towards study, ensured that the horizons of his professional musical career broadened through scholarships and introductions to new teachers. Notable among these was Andrew Dawes, who eventually became well known as first violin in the Orford String Quartet in Canada, which he founded and remained with for twenty seven years. Chris had remained in contact with

Andy even when his further studies took him away from Canada to Rome, and to an Italian maestro, Dino Asciola. Andy's achievements with the Orford String Quartet also became Chris' hidden dream, and with this focus he emerged from years of study into the real and not so dream-like world of the professional musician. He arrived in London ready for professional playing work.

At this point, Karen Honeyman, soon to become Karen Redsell, enters into Chris's life. In her early childhood, Karen was brought up by her maternal grandparents in rural Shropshire. The eldest of two girls, her introductions to life were ones that suited her character well. The affinity she developed with her natural and beautiful surroundings succeeded in igniting her imagination, and she learnt what it was to dance, what it meant to listen to the music of the wind, what it was to feel free and to belong to that freedom. Karen adored her guardians and was very responsive to the old-fashioned moral upbringing with which they weaned their two charges. She reveled in being part of a loving household with her sister, without the other distractions that deprive families of true bonding. Indeed her world might not have extended further had not she and her sister, at the ages of seven and five, been whisked from this idyllic environment by their mother, who was struggling alone to make her way professionally in the vast metropolis of London.

Karen and her younger sister found themselves suddenly in a very different situation to that in which they had, until that moment, been brought up. Their friendships with simple and uncomplicated farmer's children were exchanged for more involved relationships in the city. Their school life became a battleground for the complexities that arise in young people who are searching desperately to find security amidst confusion, alienation and humiliation. Karen pined for Shropshire and the love of her grandparents. She pined for the simple life that they had generously offered her. A 'fish out of water' in London, in her early adulthood she turned eventually to the only place left to go – to within herself. Just as I had done at the end of myself in Sweden, just as Anke had done at the end of herself in a mental institution, just as so many of us do when finally there is nowhere else to turn. She found a tiny seed of hope on which to cling, a glimmer of light, a faith that she was not alone. Throughout those formative years she sought in many different directions for self-worth, for a reason to her life.

Karen returned to Shropshire at the age of eighteen, trying to recapture the freedom of spirit with which she had danced in her early years. Finding her grandparents aging but unchanged in their love for her, she stayed and worked in a local stable where she had also the occasional opportunity to ride one of the many horses. Slowly Karen regained the inner peace that she lost when she left Shropshire for London. Her work at the stables gave way to more responsible employment as an auxiliary nurse at a nearby hospital, and it was in this direction that Karen felt ultimately that her life had a purpose that was worth pursuing. She found a way of caring for the sick as her grandparents had cared for her. She listened sympathetically to the stories of the dying. She personally rejoiced with those that recovered. Karen discovered that she really felt for those with whom she came into contact, and for whom she cared.

At the age of twenty-six, Karen thought she had found her niche. Being un-ambitious by nature, and gravitating naturally towards peace and tranquility, she was content with her uncomplicated role in life. However, destiny had other intentions for Karen. While visiting her mother in London she was introduced to Christopher Redsell, a Canadian of her age, single, and just embarking on his career as a musician. Her mother, Louise, was the manager for two leading, London-based orchestras: the London Mozart Players, and the London Bach Orchestra. Chris had met Louise when enquiring about positions for a young violist. He was invited to be an evening guest at Louise's house, with David Wilson her co-manager, when Karen made her chance appearance.

Karen's future was unalterably changed that evening when Chris asked to see her again. After a short courtship, Karen was whisked away once more. Not to London this time but to Canada, to a world of open spaces, open minds and open doors. She was welcomed with open arms by Chris' brothers and sisters, and found a warm friendship with Andy and Karen Dawes, and their two daughters, Deborah and Tammy - who became her bridesmaids at a wedding in Canada. It was a whirlwind romance, which swept them both off their feet until realities began to seep into their existence. A musical contract was offered by the Orchestra Nazionale di Santa Cecilia, which brought them to Europe and Chris back again to Rome. But the 'big city syndrome' that was already an unhappy part of Karen's personality, manifested itself again in Rome. Chris, with his honest and genuine personal integrity, found that he simply did not fit into the system of a large organisation.

While he was in Rome, Chris renewed contact with his former tutor, Dino Asciola, who invited him to participate in a summer festival of music taking place near Lucca. This was the event being organised in cooperation with Signora Consoli, at whose home Chris and his wife would reside during the festival. So it was that, in the summer of 1980, Chris and Karen discovered an area of Italy that was hitherto unknown to them, and found the sheep pen and adjoining land for sale near the village of Fiano. This, in turn, brought a move from a secure but stifling environment that was unsuited to both, to a place of their own where they started their entire life anew. Maria Gloria and Carlos entered eventually into their lives as did Elizabetta, Signora Consoli's daughter, and Chris and Karen embarked on a fresh and influential path together.

The downpayment for the Redsell's property was made with their tiny savings, leaving them with little more than their dream. As dreamers, however, they were both well equipped for the realities. Chris already spoke fluent Italian, and Karen knew enough Italian to get work at a popular restaurant in the nearby village of Loppeglia, which belonged to Atillio and Concetta. The restaurant attracted clients from a wide area due to Concetta's excellent cuisine, and charm and hospitality of both her and her husband. Karen was looked after and treated well while Chris was away in Florence, necessarily earning money by playing the viola.

Before any renovation work on the sheep pen could commence, the first project was to use a bulldozer to build-up the land that fell away steeply, directly in front of the ruined building. A track was hewn out of the clay hillside from the road that led up to the cemetery, down to the enclosure in which was nestled the building. When this was completed, the Redsell's moved onto their land in the spring of 1981, bought outright for the sum of 4,000,000 lire. They constructed a tent from donated canvas and, during that summer, from their makeshift shelter they worked on turning their dream into reality.

One might say that real motivation is needed to live in an improvised tent on bare soil through a hot Italian summer, building walls from stone collected from the hillside or forest, with no financial back-up other than what was saved by Karen or Chris in their work. Although the Redsell's did not lack motivation, they lacked almost everything else. But this is how it is done still in many countries. In our western civilisation we have become so complacent that it is difficult to imagine how a man and a woman can realise their dream through such hard endeavour and toil. We are so reliant on our system that we forget that there is an alternative.

When the villagers became aware of the conditions under which the Redsells were struggling, they came to their rescue with all manner of materials, food and offers of accommodation. When it was discovered that Karen was pregnant a few months later, with the house still nowhere near completion, the village women insisted that she must stop all physical labour. Help was given and the building work accelerated, so that a single room could be made habitable with light and water, while all around was rock and rubble, sand and cement, dust and dirt. Emily was born in August of 1982, and the house was completed eventually together with its garden. Soon afterwards Chris was offered the position of co-principal viola with the Bournemouth Symphony Orchestra. An opportunity that was too good for him to refuse, but which required the imminent departure from their newly realised dream to an urban living in the south of England.

It was now autumn 1983. I had not yet met Chris and Karen, and would not do so for a further two and a half years. Focus On Dance had been operating already as a performing and educational dance unit for over a year. One of its major sponsors invited our group to present a showcase for invited guests and interested parties at its central headquarters in London. Our sponsor had distributed over a thousand invitations to would-be buyers, promoters, funders and critics of our artistic product in the London area. We were elated at the confidence demonstrated by this magnificent gesture. The entire costs for the performance, including our expenses and fee, were covered by our sponsor and we expected great things to come of the event. As it turned out, however, only a handful of people accepted the invitations and the majority did not bother to reply. For myself, this was to be the first of many subsequent disappointments. I was to find out later that the people who organise the arts in England, and who are paid high salaries from public money, are mostly only interested in the prestige that big and famous names can bring them.

But included among the small number of guests, who stayed behind after our show to enquire about the activities of our group, was an elegant, middle aged lady. She ensured that she was the last to speak to me and introduced herself as Louise Honeyman, the manager of the London Mozart Players. This orchestra was also supported by our sponsor, for its work in music and education. Explaining that while not being a musician herself, or having any knowledge about dance, she was impressed with the quality and professionalism of our performance. She felt therefore that it could be mutually beneficial for her orchestra and my group to collaborate on a joint project for schools involving music and dance.

The project attracted the attention and interest of our sponsors, and evolved further one evening over dinner with Louise and her co-manager, David Wilson. The orchestra was in the second year of a three year sponsorship contract, which also involved some educational work with Essex Education Authority. It was proposed that there be five days of introductory dance workshops for middle-school pupils aged between nine and twelve, who would then attend a final production involving both the dance group and orchestra. Louise's conception was that the project trace the history and development of dance and music from the court period of the 17th century, through the classical and romantic eras, to late 20th century popular music and contemporary dance. The musical content would include four 17th century court dances, four dances taken from Tschaikowsky's Nutcracker ballet, and finally an adaptation of a Toccata and Fugue by Bach.

The dance content would include four authentically choreographed and costumed 17th century court dances, three solos from The Nutcracker: the Arabian, Russian and Sugar Plum Fairy, and conclude with a zany and energetic dance based on the sport of skiing. The choreography for our court dances was taught us by an

Historic Dance connoisseur and expert, Elizabeth Goodchild, who lived and worked in Dorset - our home area. She became eventually a good friend and staunch supporter of our company's educational work. The magnificent costumes, that were part of an enormous collection of handmade copies of authentically styled 17th and 18th century court dresses, were lent to us by Elizabeth's collaborator and beneficiary of the Historic Dance Company, Anne Hannay.

The dance education would take place during five days of workshops at different schools, and precede a final demonstration with the orchestra, which would involve over three hundred pupils from a total of fifteen schools. Each day, three schools were to be visited with a comprehensive, participatory workshop intended to instruct the pupils in the development of dance, during which pupils with a good sense of rhythm and movement coordination would be taken aside and taught a simple dance to the music. This, they would perform all together, with the orchestra, at the demonstration performance. The pupil's musical education would be completed with a conductor, noted for his lectures on music and music playing, taking the dancers, orchestra, and three hundred members of the young audience through the whole magical experience encompassing three hundred years of music and dance.

The workshops were well received. And at the conclusion of our final performance, when the euphoria of our young particiants had subsided, it became obvious that the principals and our sponsors were delighted at the outcome. The Education Authority asked the dancers and orchestra to repeat the project again in a year, and our sponsor immediately agreed. One month after our performance in Essex, Focus On Dance went off to Cardiff in Wales. There, in eight days, it visited twenty schools with the same workshops, culminating in a performance with the orchestra to over two thousand middle and secondary-school pupils at Cardiff's St.

David's Hall concert auditorium. It was by far the largest audience to which Focus On Dance had ever performed.

Later that same year, the administration of the Bournemouth Orchestras, comprising the Symphony Orchestra and the smaller Symphonietta, invited me to come to their office. They had learned of our successful collaboration with the London Mozart Players and, as their orchestras were about to introduce educational projects into their own activities, wondered if a similar collaboration was possible for schools in Dorset. However, it never got beyond the discussion stage. Too many complications arose with the project, and a sponsor could not be found. It says a lot for Louise Honeyman's undoubted talent for getting things done. Since that time she has not only demonstrated her business acumen by assuring her orchestra's future in bleak economic times for the performing arts, but has also given it great credibility as being one of the few British Orchestras to operate without a deficit. Louise was included in 1996 Honours List, when she retired from the active management of the London Mozart Players.

The major sponsor of our joint project continued to support Focus On Dance until I terminated its activities in 1986, unable to attract funding from one vital source - the Dorset Education Authorities. Shortly after making this decision, I met Louise Honeyman again under very different and rather amusing circumstances. In the summer of 1986, my company gave an open-air performance in the magnificent setting of the Beaulieu Abbey ruins in Hampshire. The event was a lavish occasion and attracted an elite audience from London and the south of England. Officiated by Lord Montague of Beaulieu, it was a fund-raising event in aid of an environmental charity operating from the Beaulieu Estate. For the occasion, Focus On Dance had been in rehearsal for four weeks to create a new work, 'Heartland.' The accompanying Gustav Mahler's music was to be played by a piano quartet comprising lead violin, viola and violoncello from the Bournemouth Symphony Orchestra, together with a guest pianist. The beautiful costumes created for our dancers were designed by Lord Montague's daughter, Mary Montague. The event attracted sponsorship from a leading British bank, and was a splendid occasion designed for the wealthy upper classes. It was my company's final performance.

As it was an elite occasion, I was able to entice the representatives from our major sponsors to attend, as well as a leading international funding organisation for whom we were also a client. Our own fund-raisers and Board of Directors, and members of the Dorset Education Authority were also in attendance. All agreed to sit around a table after the reception following the performance, to discuss the future of my company: the Focus On Dance Performing and Educational Company. In my eyes it was a formidable gathering of powerful people who held our continued activity in their hands. The two most obvious absentees who declined attendance were the dance officers for our area's Regional Arts Association, Southern Arts, and the Arts Council of Gt. Britain. Earlier in our short, four year history, these absentees had given us encouragement and hope in the funding for our projects, but latterly were being very quiet.

I left at the end of that meeting knowing that I could not continue with my company. I knew too that, after the experience of setting-up my own company and operating it on every level, that I could not go back to seeking work with the already established companies. With their belief in our work, British Petroleum, Marks and Spencer and the Gulbenkian Foundation had kept us afloat and moving forward for three years, and assuming that the local Education Authorities - together with Arts Council and Regional Arts support - would recognize our value to their community. At that meeting it was spelt-out clearly to all concerned that neither the Education Authority nor the County Council had any policy concerning annual funding for my dance group, and that this situation was unlikely to change in future years.

A few days after this depressing meeting, I spent an evening with the Redsells in Wimborne, Dorset, where I re-lived my earlier visit in May to their house in Tuscany, having been excited at the local street activity in Florence. I knew then that Focus On Dance was bound for a showdown at Beaulieu in June. If the decision went against me, I had already decided that I would close the company and set-off for Europe in my camper van, and to try some busking while I thought about my future.

At that time, I did not know the Redsells very well, although it was apparent that we had a lot in common. I with my camper van, windsurfer and caravan; they with their bright yellow ambulance, sailing dinghy and the history of their simple home in Tuscany. While I had yet to discover the pleasure of busking, I discovered that Chris too, in moments of dire need, had also taken his instrument to the streets of Italy and Switzerland.

Chris and Karen were talking about moving back to Italy and making a determined effort to live there once again. They were also thinking about organising a summer musical event, perhaps for the local people who would otherwise never hear live classical music. I casually added that four years of head banging against the arts bureaucracy in England might just see me out there too. "You think that four years is a long time. My mother has made a career out of head banging against this bureaucracy. But there again, she thrives on it. She's the manager for a couple of London orchestras," Karen said as she removed our dinner plates and replaced them with clean dessert bowls. From her tone, I gathered that she disassociated herself from her mother's actions. But I was intrigued, and continued "oh really, we were quite involved with a London orchestra on a schools' project a couple of years ago. It was one of the highlights of Focus On Dance's four years."

"Well, I know that one of mum's orchestras did a successful school's project with a dance group. I wonder if it could have been ....." "Us," I interjected, "Louise Honeyman. London Mozart Players. British Petroleum." I knew her mother could he no one else. "Well I'm blessed," Karen expostulated. "You mean you've worked with Louise. Focus On Dance with the London Mozart Players," Chris joined in the conversation. "Why yes, of course he has. I remember mum talking about it when we came from Italy to England. 'The best schools' project the orchestra had ever done,' she said. How very novel. I suppose she has no idea that you know us, does she." "I don't see how she can know," I replied. Karen looked mischievously at her husband, "Oh Chris, let's get her away from London for a weekend and down here. We'll surprise her with Stephen. We won't say anything to her."

And so it was that Louise and I met again, and reminisced about the collaboration between my dance group that had been forced out of existence, and her orchestra that was embarking on a new residency at Fairfield Hall in Croydon, its future secured in London. I see Louise quite often now when she comes to Italy. She bought a property in ruins, near to her daughter and son in law in Tuscany. It has been beautifully restored, mainly by Chris and Karen. Little could I have known that, during those active days with my dance company, the lady who stayed behind to speak to me after the Focus On Dance performance at British Petroleum's Britannic House in London, would one day become my neighbour in Italy.

'Giamboree 1990' was Chris Redsell's fourth summer festival of chamber music to be held in Apuanian mountain villages. The idea of offering live classical music on a professional level to the local people of Fiano and Loppeglia, in a simple and containable way, had been at the back of Chris' and Karen's minds since they completed their house eight years earlier. In particular, Karen was thinking about introducing music and craftwork not only into the local community, but also to the more isolated areas deeper into the mountains. Her childhood in Shropshire was firmly entrenched in her memory as she became familiar with the seasons and timelessness of the mountains, where minds can perhaps more readily respond to stimuli of the senses. Karen could see the creativity, and when she discussed her thoughts with her husband, they did not fall on deaf ears. And so it was that birth was given to the concept that would ultimately become 'Giamboree'.

At that time, however, the Redsells had no money, and no entrepreneurial instincts to realise their ideas. They knew no other professional musicians in the area apart from Elizabetta Fiorini, whom they had met in 1980 through her mother, Signora Consoli. When Chris was offered a contract with an English Orchestra, their ideas of bringing music to the mountains of northern Tuscany were exchanged for social outlets in suburban southern England. As a concept, 'Giamboree' was put on the shelf but by no means forgotten.

It was during my first visit to the Redsell's house, having started my new career as street dancer incognito three months after my debut in Lausanne, that Karen's concept was taken down from the shelf and dusted again. Following this debut, I had travelled to Italy and to Lucca, and had been invited to stay for Christmas at the Redsell's house where there was to be a big gathering which included Karen's mother, Louise Honeyman. It was during this festive time that Chris, intrigued to hear of my comparative success with street dancing, asked if we could both perform a 'dance with music' at the piazza of the nearby village of Loppeglia, "to see if anyone takes any interest at all". Encouraged by the reaction of people, who came out of their houses to watch, listen and applaud, the seed for Giamboree began to germinate within him.

Chris and Karen returned to England in the New Year, but they knew it would not be for long. In the summer they returned to their house, Croce, with four friends who were professional musicians. Ostensibly coming for a holiday, they agreed to play several concerts of chamber music in the piazza at Loppeglia, and Giamboree was born. Karen provided her guests with the very best in hospitality and caring and, in an ambience of excitement and stimulation, Chris' unique concept of a music festival was destined to grow. While lacking entrepreneurial experience, Chris had friends in the surrounding mountain villages who were creative, and whose motivation was to bring a little pleasure to the hearts of the local communities.

Over the four years since the group of five musicians gave their initial three concerts to the villagers, word circulated in British music circles about the extraordinary experience of playing chamber music to people in high mountain villages, where the only remuneration was the lavish Italian cuisine offered as an after-concert dinner by the villagers. Most of the musicians enjoyed the experience as a delightful alternative holiday, alone or with their families, and found the atmosphere relaxing after a stressful year working with large orchestras. Understandably, they wanted to return each year and, with an ever-widening circle of musicians offering their services, Chris had no difficulty in developing the music further. The numbers grew each year, and accommodation started to be a problem. The musicians brought with them sleeping bags, tents, mattresses and camper vans. Louise's now completed house, as well as the house of Piera and Marcello Barzanti - between my own and the Redsell's - were occupied, as well as Croce.

In August of 1990, eighteen musicians arrived from England, Italy and Canada, with their friends and families. During the rehearsal period prior to the commencement of the festival, all meals were taken at Croce. Karen worked hard in the kitchen in summer temperatures exceeding 35° C to feed everyone who, as they were on holiday and providing their services free, expected some sustenance. No profit was made from the festival, since no charge was made to the audience, and there was no sponsorship for the event. It was all a little chaotic from a management perspective. But it was a very popular and successful event and, for myself, one of the most rewarding experiences I have had in my diverse career. Elizabetta and I danced together in two choreographies, that were constructed in a matter of days and perfected while performing them to a receptive albeit uninformed audience. The quality of music and singing was of an exceptional standard and, in the interim years until the present time, has remained on this level of professionalism. While many of the venues have now changed from mountain village piazzas to city halls and wealthy villas, the mood has not changed and some of the original villages still claim a concert between the more prestigious ones.

I danced once again the following summer, but then declined further participation for two simple reasons. First, many of the villages started to invite musicians to play in their beautiful catholic churches, where dance was not permitted as it is considered unfitting for a place of worship. Second, the concerts gradually moved further from our area, requiring the participants to stay for up to a week in other parts of the mountains. La Casetta was developing in a way that prevented me from staying away for longer than a few days in the hot and dry summers. However, I continued to give my whole-hearted support for this innovative and original music festival and, as a result, have made lasting friendships among the many musicians who attended from both sides of the Atlantic.

At the back of Chris' mind, while being carried away by the sweep of the summers activities, had always been the person who was behind his inspiration for 'Giamboree,' namely Andy Dawes. He had often written to him, keeping Andy informed of the progress of his career. Early in 1992, Andy wrote to Chris from Canada explaining his decision to close the Orford String Quartet after twenty seven years. He wrote that he and his wife, Karen Dawes, would be coming to Europe. Initially, they would be going to Paris where he was to leave his precious violin with a master repairer, and then he would be touring Europe to study European music education and the teaching of string instruments, with the aid of a Canadian Government Grant. As they would be spending some time in Florence, they wondered if they might visit Chris and Karen in their home.

In the event, Chris and Karen convinced them to stay much longer, and the two musicians - teacher and pupil - combined their talents with flautist, Antonio Barzanti, to give a couple of quickly-organised concerts in Lucca. For Chris, this was the beginning to the realization of the dream to which he had clung since leaving Canada to continue his music studies in Rome. The dream was to reach fulfillment eighteen months after Andy's first visit to Italy, when Andy offered to participate in a 'Giamboree' and bring a second violinist and a violon cellist with him. He asked Chris to make up the quartet with his viola, a compliment paid by a master to his former pupil. The concerts, which played to packed houses in the summer of 1993 in Lucca's enormous church of St. John the Baptist, were a memorable occasion and difficult to improve on in future years.

Chris found himself moving down new and exciting avenues. With the increasing recognition of his work, two new orchestras of professional musicians in Lucca and Reggio nell' Emilia invited Chris to direct and conduct their concerts. Giamboree continued as a summer music festival in Tuscany, and has also begun to operate under this name in southern England and eastern U.S.A.

In parallel with Chris' activities, Karen converted an old wooden garage on the hillside above their house into a studio. Busts and bas-reliefs in terracotta adorn shelves that once housed spanners and screwdrivers, and she receives commissions for her sculptures. With a growing family, adolescent Emily and younger son Domenico, Karen is busy and sees Chris only rarely. But when she can steal a little quiet time, she disappears to her studio and - with the inspiration of the hills all around her - she reflects on life while moulding the clay with her hands.

The Redsell's chosen direction, romantic as it may seem when compared to the other directions they might have chosen, is not a bed of roses. Chris earns his money playing with an orchestra in Switzerland and, although not on a full contract, is away for many weeks of the year and home for only just a few days. However, their lives are full, unpredictable and challenging, bringing stimulation and strength to combat to living so individualistically,

Emily, their thirteen year old daughter was a four year old when I first knew her. She would dress-up, and present her family and friends with a performance complete with improvised dance, impersonations, and jokes picked up from her father. She has gone through the many stages that most young people healthily pass through before finding their own personalities. An undemanding child, Emily would content herself for hours in her own world and rarely needed the approval or commendation of her parents in her creativity.

It was inevitable that Emily should become intrigued by the all-encircling influence of music and dance on her young life. She began piano lessons with Signora Consoli, and dance classes with her daughter, Elizabetta. Her music studies extended to the violin, coached by an encouraging father, and to the flute, instructed by

Antonio Barzanti. However, music eventually gave way to dance and, in turn, after five years dance gave way to horse riding. It would seem that Emily has now found herself, incorporating her poise and deportment from dance, with rhythm from music, into her riding progress.

Domenico, now just turned three, is passing his early childhood in an ideal world. He steps from his front door into a freedom that few will know. He has the unrestricted wealth of creativity and expression in the nature, and natural sounds surround him all the time. While he knows the pain of separation from his father, who must be away for weeks at a time, he knows too that he can count on his father's undivided attention when they are together. He is developing a personality that is at once endearing, and with an added sense of caring for those around about him.

That summer, amid all the activity on both an artistic and social level, I put into practice my plan to produce large quantities of hot water from decomposing grass. My temporary bathroom and kitchen had been constructed. The bathroom and kitchen sinks were installed with ludicrously inadequate plastic-tube plumbing, which initially caused constant flooding. The freezer reservoir was positioned above the house and, within five days of inserting the cut grass around the boiler, the water was hot. I invited everyone I knew to come and see for themselves how efficiently my system worked, and I was congratulated by all.

The first practical use of the hot water generated was to have a hot bath, my first very own hot bath since I last lived in rented accommodation in Sweden sixteen years earlier. It was also my last very own hot bath, as I soon discovered that - once the grass around the boiler had decomposed and generated its heat - it was certainly not inclined to repeat the process. The water in the boiler, having run cold, did not re-heat again. Min was sceptical, but I was not to be beaten. On emptying the haystack to repeat the experiment with freshly cut grass, to my surprise I found that only a small proportion of its volume had lost its heat - that part where the boiler was situated. The hottest part was where there was most humidity. My newly acquired knowledge, gained by a combination of facts learnt through experience, was put to use again in a second attempt. I realized that the heating process would be more efficient if, first, smaller quantities of hot water were used and, second, if water was sprinkled on to fresh-cut grass as it went into the haystack. After five days of heating-up and being used only sporadically for showers and dishwashing, the water continued to remain piping-hot for a total of eight days. Whereupon it gradually cooled until an unexpected August summer rainstorm rendered it stone cold.

With insufficient quantities of cut grass to make a third haystack, further experimentation was put on hold for the remainder of the year. The next year, however, with enormous quantities of fresh-cut grass once again at my disposal, I experimented further but was unable to maintain the water at a reasonable temperature for longer than three weeks. But it was not until the subsequent year, in 1993, the fourth year of experimenting, that two more ideas were tested and proved to be of value, which enabled me to keep the water around 50°C from April to November. A second, smaller boiler was installed which could be moved manually from one place to another within the haystack. This fed the larger boiler with warm, if not hot, water so that the temperature in the larger container was not constantly changing with each small consumption of water. Also, when the temperature of the water began to drop, I removed the already decomposed grass from around the larger boiler and replaced it with fresh grass. In so doing I made sure that, as the haystack decomposed, the air pockets were forced out by compressing the grass and adding more fresh-cut grass. I found that I needed also to protect the stack from external changes in temperature, such as sudden rainfalls or early night frosts.

Now, by planning carefully when I cut my grass, and ensuring there is always an adequate reserve left untouched, a single haystack can keap generating heat for about ten weeks. By producing three haystacks a year, I can safely count on eight months of permanently warm water, and two of these months also produce hot water. I have also found that another advantage in maintaining the haystack as hot as possible is that the de-composing grass, which is destined for my vineyard or garden, breaks down into excellent manure far quicker than if it were not heated. While people in my village have to purchase supplies of animal manure, I have a self-sufficient source of ready-made organic compost for my land, which has also given me a valuable source of free energy.

The knowledge gained from this successful project has stimulated me to delve into other safe, free and natural sources of energy. After using gas lamps to provide my lighting for two years, I invested money into the purchase of a photoelectric solar panel that would convert the sun's rays into electricity, and charge a twelve volt car battery. Years of experience living in caravans and camper vans has taught me about wiring a twelve volt system, where a mistake is non-lethal due to the low voltages involved. The sun's rays have now successfully given maintenance-free, safe power to my house for four years, winter as well as summer. I invested in a second solar panel during 1995, which considerably augmented my supply of free electrical power.

With the rain-fed water system, heated by fresh-cut grass, and solar energy for lighting as well as the operation of some twelve volt domestic appliances, my house rapidly developed into a unique domicile where I was in total control of everything. On the rare occasions when something has gone wrong, I have always been able to remedy the problem instantly at no cost to myself, or any cost in someone else's time. But I have yet to discover an environmentally friendly method of heating my house during the short months of the Italian winter. When heating proves necessary, I consume small quantities of wood in my marvelously efficient wood-burning stove. In winter months, the stove provides not only heat, but also a permanent kitchen range, and hot water when the grass is not growing. I am nevertheless always exploring other ways to benefit from the sun's power and create heat in winter. Notwithstanding this, my fuel source is totally free, coming either from dead wood collected in the forest during the dry summer months, or from a nearby factory that discards enormous quantities of wood as a by-product of its manufacturing process.

Chapter 13

Puppy's Litter

Spring 1994

"I've looked into it," Stephen. "It's going to cost thousands of pounds to get the rights to use the recordings you want." "Then it seems that the only alternative is to try and sort out the music ourselves," I said in a depressed tone of voice. "Can't we go ahead and film using the recordings I dance to, and at a later stage dub our music once we've sorted it out." There was a long pause on the telephone. "It would make editing extremely difficult unless our sound tracks were identical to your recordings," was the reply. "It's better to wait and get our sound together first, and then film using it." "OK David" I said, "I'll have to think about this one."

I hung up the telephone, wondering how on earth I was going to come up with six good quality recordings of the music to which I performed on the street, that could be used on a video tape together with my dance. When I wrote to him in London that November 1993, David Ball had leapt at the opportunity of making a professional videotape of seven dances performed by myself, in locations of outstanding natural beauty in Switzerland and Italy. With the letter I had enclosed an amateur video of my dances, filmed by a friend in a studio in Switzerland. He wrote back immediately, agreeing to participate in the project.

I arranged to meet him for a day in London during January 1994, while I was on my way from Italy to Newcastle upon Tyne to visit my parents. I wanted to discuss the feasibility of my idea, weigh up the pros and cons, and establish a budget. It was also an opportunity for myself to see some of his work, and assess his creative ability as a new professional just out of college, for a project that I would be financing personally.

Now, into February and only three weeks later, it seemed we had met our first major stumbling block after a very positive start to the proceedings. All going well, we had intended to commence filming in April, meeting up initially in Switzerland and slowly descending into Italy. I had a few projected locations in mind but nothing certain. David, of course, would have to vet each location for suitability.

At our meeting in January, I had already expressed my concern to David that the conditions under which we would be travelling, working and sleeping may not meet with his approval. I went to great pains to make it clear to him that the entire project needed to be done on a very minimal budget. In order to keep the costs down, we would be obliged to live in my converted mini-bus when we stayed at the locations until filming was completed. Having previously left my two dogs in a makeshift enclosure on my land before travelling to England, I was not prepared to leave them again in April, perhaps for three to four weeks. It also seemed likely that Puppy, my bitch, would be pregnant considering the constant activity in the New Year between her and Hector, my dog. This being the case, her pups could be expected early March. I intended finding homes for all but one of them in Switzerland at six weeks old, and I might not be able to guarantee they would all be gone by the time David and I met up again in mid-April. In any case, there would be at least two dogs and one very young pup with him and myself in the mini-van.

David laughingly dismissed this as not being a problem. Later, when April finally arrived, I saw how fortunate it was that our film had had to be put on the shelf for some time. What seemed to be a small potential inconvenience in January, could have developed into a catastrophe if our project had gone ahead with what turned out to be a litter of eight pups, all of which had grown to quite a size by April. The making of our film eventually got under way in August that year, thanks to the handful of professional musicians who came to participate in Chris Redsell's 'Giamboree' musical festival that summer.

Puppy's whelping duly began on schedule in early March. I had run out of firewood and had moved from my house to the caravan for the rest of the winter. I planned to leave towards the end of March, with the dogs and however many pups arrived, to commence a dancing tour of Switzerland. Money was very short and I wanted to be dancing and earning as soon as possible. I thought that the pups, who would be three weeks old, could survive the trip. This turned out to be true. But it was myself, not them, who nearly became a 'cropper.'

My old and now defunct camper van, which was positioned directly in front of the caravan, would be an ideal nest for Puppy and her first newly born pups. She would be almost twenty months old when her litter arrived. She had had her first season uneventfully in June of the previous year, while separated from Hector for ten days. I had also been told that, because of her young age, a pregnancy from her second season was unlikely to produce more than five pups. Certainly, as March crept in and her whelping drew close, she did not appear to be carrying any more than this number.

I was well prepared for the event. Min, who experienced a 'merry time' keeping Hector away from Puppy during her first season in June 1993 while I abandoned ship to visit my parents and brothers in England, had jokingly sent me a book on dog care. Included in this book was a chapter on every stage of whelping and its complications. All the evidence indicated that everything was progressing normally. But curiously, Hector deliberately avoided Puppy immediately prior to her giving birth to his offspring, until quite a number of weeks afterwards. During her season earlier, her scent was so enticing that he would not let her out of his sight for a moment, day or night for six days. Fortunately, he was not presented with any competition, and so I did not have to deal with any contests over what he obviously considered as his property. Now, as the time approached, I settled Puppy in the camper with adequate blankets and heating , leaving Hector alone in the caravan.

On the second day of March, Puppy's anxiety was quite obvious. I took this as a sign she was already into her first stage of labour and that the birth of her pups was imminent. All day she was restless and could not settle. I too became restless, behaving more like the father than Hecter, who contentedly slept through the drama that reached its peak just after midnight. I had already set up my bed in the camper for that night, surrounded by various items that my book suggested should be to hand for the birth of pups. I anticipated a busy night and was not wrong. The first tiny bundle arrived at the same time as the village clock struck one o'clock in the bell tower of the church, just metres away from the camper van. Puppy then went into action, and I marveled at her frantic instinct to break the protective membrane that contained her first living pup. She fussed and licked her firstborn until it squirmed and gasped, and she knew it was breathing. She then cut the umbilical cord with her teeth, nuzzling and pushing the pup to her side where it began to suckle. I witnessed, for the first time in my life, the un-ending miracle of procreation - its complexities, its hidden secrets, its tremendous variation in all forms of life. Then I sank into slumber, Puppy calm by my side, with her pup attached to one of her ten swollen teats.

In a semi-conscious state I wondered whether she would only have the one pup. Then, there was a flurry of further activity and I found that I had been ridiculously naive. I stared at three tiny new presences, already out of their protective membranes, and being licked over simultaneously by their mother. So far, I had served no practical or useful purpose whatsoever. Neither, fortunately, was I required to do so, as it was unlikely that I would have known what to do despite studying all the information contained in Min's book.

Puppy settled again, investigating the four appendages now attached to her breast, and I closed my eyes again. Suddenly, Puppy separated herself from her litter, leaving them floundering, as she delivered a fifth pup and promptly repeated the same after-birth attention that she had given the others. When she again settled with her pups, I felt around her abdomen with my hands and then went to sleep with a satisfied smile, convinced that she had given birth to her last pup.

It was starting to get light when I heard the church bell strike six o'clock. Puppy was contented and quite settled. I was amused by the scuffling and sucking sounds coming from underneath her. However, on lifting her back leg I counted not five, but eight bundles of flesh, each no bigger than a small hand. I had slept through the remaining three births. Puppy had needed no assistance from myself, no encouragement, and none of the accessories that I had carefully acquired beforehand. She had done everything by instinct, and had done it all perfectly. She was to go on doing it perfectly until all eight normal and healthy pups were weaned. Puppy was a wonderful mother. Her success endeared her to me, and gave me a respect and love for her that I had previously had some difficulty in developing.

Four years earlier, when I had witnessed Hector's extraordinary behaviour with Meep in Amsterdam, Jo, Ineke and myself had resolved that we would allow our dogs to mate and and that I should keep one of the pups. I returned three times to Amsterdam and, although Hector and Meep acted out the same instinctive play with one another, we despaired as Meep was never in season.

I lost touch with the Kelly Family after my fourth visit to Amsterdam. By then it was two years after Dan Kelly's stroke, and he had made a miraculous recovery, regaining the use of every moveable part of his body except for one hand. With his family, he decided to sail their boat up the North Sea and into one of the rivers in Germany, where all of their concerts were now taking place. They left me no forwarding address, and it was three years before I heard from them again, by which time their already successful family act was well on the way to international recognition.

As Hector and Meep did not mate, my thoughts turned to securing a bitch for Hector. I wanted to have a bitch who would live with us permanently, thereby creating a complete family, and to allow her to keep one of her pups that she herself would rear, together with Hector and myself. It was Elizabetta Fiorini who, during her summer multi-media course for young performing artists in July 1992, asked if I would rescue a beautiful, five week old puppy. One male and one female, cross-bred between a golden retriever and a collie, were all that remained alive of an un-planned litter of seven pups - five being put-down at birth. The young owner of the retriever bitch, a student of Elizabetta, was desperately seeking homes for the two pups, convinced his enraged father would not allow them to live. Would I, she wanted to know, perhaps take the young bitch, as she knew I was intending to find a mate for Hector.

I replied that I would go and see the pups, but my real intention was to find an abandoned bitch, already mature, and in need of a good home. Nevertheless, I arranged to meet the seventeen year old boy, whose father had stipulated that the two remaining pups would follow the same path as the others when they were eight weeks old. It was a sensitive and desperate young Italian who endeavoured, with all of his honest charm, to get me to take both of the pups. They were now nearly six weeks old. Their golden retriever mother was a stunningly beautiful animal and, against what seemed then to be my better judgment, I took the young bitch - waiving aside the young man's further pleas by saying that I already had a mature dog at home. On arrival at La Casetta with the puppy, henceforth to be known as 'Puppy,' Hector's immediate reaction - after an inquisitive sniff - was to reprove my idiocy at introducing a foreigner into the household. Puppy's reaction was to squeeze into a space beneath the kitchen sink, where I could not retrieve her, and simply refuse to come out.

Five days after this frustrating introduction, during which time I became convinced of my folly in bringing home a five week old pup, Puppy suffered a traumatic experience that nearly killed her and left me guilty over my in-attention. By this time Puppy was becoming inquisitive about her new surroundings and, with increased confidence, would wander out of the house and into the vineyard. One hot day in August, I was working by the road below La Casetta and had inadvertently left the front gate open, unaware that Puppy had gone through it and was on the road. In the summer, teenage boys from the village use the road as a practice ground for motorcycles and scooters, descending around its steeply inclined curves at alarming speeds. My reaction to a squeal of brakes on road was immediate, and I saw that his rear wheel had pinned my screaming pup to the road where he had come to a halt.

"Ho fate male, ho fato male," the young boy gasped in Italian, looking around to discover from where the screaming was coming. I rushed to Puppy, sure she must be squashed, as I lifted his rear wheel clear in a super-human display of strength, unconcerned for anything but her welfare. Five minutes later, Puppy was in shock, and in a coma that lasted three days. Paulo, the veterinary surgeon, said she would probably come out of the coma without any adverse effects. But I was to observe her carefully every hour, and keep her quiet and away from noise or any activity, and allow nature to take its course.

In my guilt, I felt I was being punished with a physically handicapped dog, that would prove to be a useless mate for Hector. It was a miracle that Puppy recovered fully from this awful incident and that, one week after waking from her coma, she seemed none the worse for the experience. However, she developed an annoying habit of squatting and urinating whenever she was caressed or scolded, as if the shock had affected the nervous control of her bladder. Subsequently, I avoided showing any emotion for her while in the house, friendly or otherwise, in order to save my carpets. My patience became exhausted in those initial months when, for example, with the door to my house open in the August heat, Puppy came in and defecated on my living room floor - rather than in the great outdoors. I was usually unaware of this until I realized I had stepped in something, whereupon I would uncontrollably give vent to a curse directed at Puppy. She, in turn, would instantly squat and add insult to injury by also urinating on the carpet. When I then lunged at her, intending to throw her out of the house, she rushed for her safe space under the kitchen sink and would remain there for the rest of the day.

Hector did not make the situation any easier. He refused even to acknowledge the presence of Puppy, except when she approached him in her inquisitiveness, whereupon he would growl warningly deep within his throat. If she persisted, his eyes would flit from her to me and the growl noticeably rose in pitch. Occasionally the end result of these confrontations would be a reprimand to Hector, after he had frightened Puppy to the security of her safe hiding place. More often, he would simply move from where he was lying to a safer distance away. However, Hector never chose to be near Puppy, and this became cause for concern when I couldn't find him and had to go down to the village and search for him.

I began to regret forcing such a young concubine onto Hector. The intention to create a similar situation to that which existed between Hector and Meep in Amsterdam, rapidly dissipated as I despaired at driving my friend and companion away from his own home territory. I imagined that Hector might eventually prefer to find a new home, rather than tolerate this new presence, leaving me with a bitch that tried my patience and for whom I was developing no attachment whatsoever. I began to worry that in September, when I needed to leave La Casetta and go north of the Alps for my autumn dancing tour, the two animals in my cramped camper van would cause major disruption in my otherwise tranquil life. I was desperate for Hector to call a truce, and make an attempt to co-habit with Puppy.

Puppy was nine weeks old when we left for Switzerland and later Germany, and she was still hypersensitive to any positive or negative emotions. By then, it was becoming a squeeze for her to get into her safe space under the kitchen sink, and exiting required a 'super-pup' effort on her behalf. She became confounded by this new situation, and would hesitate momentarily before diving for safe cover. However, some progress was made in modifying Hector's adverse social behaviour. Provided there were no advances from Puppy, he now wandered occasionally to where she was lying and searched for information with a sniff at her rear-end. A week into our tour, he had concluded that her scent was friendly, possibly feminine, and that all that was required was a little patience - with which he was, in fact, well-rewarded fifteen months later.

Hector loved to travel in the camper van and reacted excitedly to the impending signs of a journey. Puppy has always been reluctant to enter the camper van at La Casetta. She preferred to remain behind in the vineyard until I either insisted loudly that she come, or went and brought her unwillingly. That first time, at just nine weeks old, with no prior experience but sensing our departure, Puppy went to her place of security and no amount of coaxing would convince her to come out. I physically extricated her, made no easier by her ability to make herself larger at will. Her pitiful squeals caused a mixed reaction of remorse and rage within me, as I realized the entry to her hideaway should have been blocked beforehand. Fortunately, on returning to La Casetta a month later, her new size denied further access to her haven and she failed to find another place safe from my grasp.

Once inside the camper van, Puppy settled by my side with her head against the engine cover, and slept during the whole time that I drove. Since this first introduction to travelling four years ago, her place has remained unchanged when we are travelling. It is as though the noise and vibration of the engine block-outs the reality of what is happening, enabling her to tolerate being in a mobile and limited space. Her perspective of this changes quite dramatically, when I stop or apply the brake. She rouses at once and becomes excited. Often it is a false alarm whereupon, as the camper van again accelerates, she will resume the same position, head and one ear suffering an intolerable ordeal on the engine cover. Eighteen months later, when travelling with her three week old pups, she would only allow them to suckle her from this exact same position.

On the other hand, Hector has always been alert whenever the camper van is in motion, rarely settling or sleeping, his nose at the open window in summer or the air vent in winter. Occasionally, the necessity of long motorway drives means hours of non-stop travelling. To alleviate his boredom, Hector would change his stance at the passenger-seat window and ask, with his paw against my leg, if he could move onto my lap and look out of the other window thereby getting smells from the other side. In so doing, I was aware that I was driving illegally with a big dog on my knees, even though his hind legs on the floor bore a large proportion of his weight. However, in this position he did not stir, and was never a source of potential danger or distraction to my driving. Now, as an older dog with severely restricted eyesight, this is his preferred position since he can remain there without over-balancing.

With two dogs in the limited space of the vehicle, albeit on better terms with each other than before, new changes were inevitable. Hector became very protective, not only of his food, but also of his bowl even when empty. He had never been wolfish in his eating habits, although he obviously enjoyed his food. On the other hand, Puppy was positively passionate about hers and, given a chance, would be about everyone else's too. This was naturally unacceptable to Hector who, from the start, needed to assert his authority over this young upstart in the exuberance of her youth. This action was not carried out overly aggressively by the elder dog. He simply gave her plenty of warning which, if not heeded, would be followed by a snap and a high-pitched wail from the culprit. Hector would then glance at myself with an expression of remorse as I, acting as peacemaker, would need to scold both animals. As time went on, though, Puppy would learn to wait patiently until Hector had finished his meal, whereupon he would allow her to consume the remaining crumbs that he had left. With this major breakthrough we passed the remainder of our mealtimes in comparative peace and politeness.

Sleeping arrangements were less complex although Puppy, once she felt more confident with me, developed a trait which as first frustrated, then intrigued me, and which I now relish with delight. This trait has been refined and adapted by her over the years, adjusting herself to my response and, once she knows that her action has not irritated me, building it to a point where one of us must eventually back off. Each morning at my bedside, Puppy would carefully and gently insert her nose into my face at my first semi-conscious stirrings. If my responses were positive, she would then massage the whole of my head and shoulders forcibly with her muzzle while discretely clambering onto the bed. Once on the bed, she would pin me down with her legs and squirm all over my head and neck. Then, minutes later, she would settle her twenty-five kilo body on my chest and happily continue slumber if I did not complain or remove her to another part of my bed.

Mossy now joins in this early morning activity, although he is more sensitive to my needs, making sure first that he is invited onto the bed after I have made the necessary space available. He then simply turns himself over on his back, thrusts his paws in the air in a choreographically contemporary position, and lays the back of his head in my arms while I stroke his chest. Hector normally remains curled-up on the driver's seat until I have risen and dressed, and am ready to let all three dogs out of the van. He suffers from extremes of temperature, particularly the cold, and often will want to spend the night under my covers. I will allow him to do this on very cold nights, either at the lower corner next to my feet, or the upper one next to my head. Hector has the ability, which Puppy and Mossy lack, to remain tightly curled-up in one place all night, therefore causing no disturbance to my sleep.

The two younger dogs, on the contrary, like to occupy as much space as possible in the comfort and warmth of the bed. This invariably results in my being pushed unconsciously to the edge of the bed, where the covers cease to serve any practical purpose.

Puppy and Mossy are therefore not allowed to sleep on the bed when I am occupying it. However, this does not preclude subtle attempts during the night, until I awake in discomfort with an agonising pain in a leg deprived of blood circulation, and shout to Puppy or Mossy to desist. Their reactions at being ejected from such warm and comfortable positions are inevitably slow, but I always win and, at least until morning, am assured of a peaceful rest.

Slowly, Hector and I began to accept our newly adopted 'child,' who was now growing rapidly. Puppy's muzzle appeared to grow the fastest, undoubtedly under the influence of her collie genes. The gangling legs were a close second. Her droopy ears folded in a non-conventional way and, from the front, gave her a look that resembled an old-fashioned French policeman in his comical hat. Her physical attributes did not endear her to me in those early days, whereas I always found Hector to be a very handsome dog. Eventually, I realized that I should not judge her solely on her appearance. Although her face lacked the character of Hector, which Mossy has inherited, she developed into a very beautiful, blond animal with her own attributes. I became deeply attached to her, both as a mother and faithful companion.

With Puppy's introduction to the family, my games of hide-and-seek with Hector were superseded and have never returned. Puppy would never leave me out of her sight for long enough to enable me to hide and, with her continual presence, Hector became disinterested in continuing the game. My earlier fears that Hector, at some point on the tour, might leave us and fail to return were to prove unfounded. A sort of 'friendship at a distance' developed between him and the obviously intelligent Puppy, and a new game replaced hide-and-seek. Throw-and-fetch became the order of the day, and has remained the dominant amusement on our country walks ever since. Mossy also now involves himself in this activity, although his mother definitely has the edge having developed a high standard in her retrieving skills. This game gives all three of us a never-ending source of amusement, and infinite pleasure and laughter to myself as an individual. Hector, his activities limited by advancing years, is content to play at his own pace and find his own interests.

As the tour continued, Hector became increasingly protective towards his potential young spouse, approaching at a run when other dogs showed an interest in Puppy, and warning them off should any harassment continue. Puppy seemed comparatively disinterested in any other dogs, and would often run away, squealing, arousing Hector's protective instincts but not to the point of a dog fight. Encouraged by these signs, I felt that Puppy would integrate successfully into our small community, and eventually produce Hector's pups to pave the way for the third and final addition to my odd family.

Everything continued to run smoothly while we were on the road. Puppy adapted well to the new situation and her earlier puppy-hood habits improved gradually. By the time we returned from the first tour in early October, she was already larger than Hector although carrying a fraction of his bulk. Unable to creep into her safe space beneath the kitchen sink, she was content to lie outside on the vineyard terraces, or inside on the sofa, always near to me. As the summer ended, my previous impatience with her cooled and was now well under control. Puppy had no further need of her hiding place, and her increased bonding with myself meant that she would not allow me out of her sight for one moment.

I remained fairly detached from Puppy initially, enjoying the new game of 'fetch' on our walks, but failing to nurture that special empathy with her that I enjoyed with Hector. His independence of me, in a way, mirrored my own desire to be independent of the system in society, which is forced on us. This new, young and vulnerable presence, who would never leave my side, and who seemed so desperate to please, only succeeded in irritating me. It forced me to question within myself why I found it so difficult to give her the same affection and respect that I had given so easily to Hector. I was not at peace with that side of me which favoured one dog more than the other. It was as though I was being shown, through these two dogs and my reactions to them, that I needed to learn a new tolerance to help me in my life with people. Perhaps a compromise between independence and dependence, from someone like myself who, in his life, had never seemed able to compromise.

Inevitably, this new idea manifested itself in my dance and so became much clearer to me. During ten years of street dancing, I had been confronted by some fairly big issues within myself, which always needed resolving before I could move forward, both in my life but more particularly in my dancing. When I started out in Lausanne, my perspective on where I could go with my street dancing was quite limited. I know now that I will never reach the point where I feel I am at the top of the mountain. Whenever I sense that I can take my dance no further, a new door appears and opens, leaving me constantly in awe of life and what can be learnt from it. For many years, I carried a burden in my street performances that held me back despite the strength, conviction and confidence I had gained. When I had a large and responsive public around me, my dance would reach extraordinary heights of liberation, fluidity and expression. There was a two-way energy flowing, a feeding, and a building between my public and myself.

In more recent years this has become the realization of a three-way energy, rebounding from and binding us all together with a force outside our own dimension. At such moments I sensed strongly that I was not dancing in my own consciousness, but that I was being taken. Not pushed, for I would go with it joyously and willingly. Not reticent or even wanting the attention to be on me, for it was clear to me that without this third presence I was nothing and going nowhere. However, on those occasions when there was not a good audience for my dance, or when people preferred to look the other way, I would feel this third and vital energy force had deserted me. Anger manifested itself in me as I tried to try to draw attention to myself, unable to understand how one day everything could be so right, and the next day so wrong. At these occasions I was vulnerable to injury if I did not get myself and my emotions under control.

At this time in my life I was not yet reconciled to my own performance, suppressing the necessity within me to impress others, and suppressing my anger at failing to capture the people's attention from other enticements. I wondered whether I was not just another enticement, trying to manipulate people into parting with a little of their money. A battle within me was being fought and won. I began to feel, more strongly than ever, a divergence from the technical cleverness and impressive, choreographic wizardry in my dance, which experience showed attracted a good audience and kept the money flowing into my collecting box. I needed to find a level within myself, together with this inspiring and expressive force, where my dance did not change in quality or motivation through lack of an attentive audience.

My opposing feeling about the two dogs, also found expression in the reactions to my audience. Favourable on good days, when my public were in accord with my dance, unfavourable on bad days, when I became frustrated at people on whom I was dependent but who were unsympathetic to my dancing. These feelings finally reached a climax one afternoon, at a performance in the south of France. Seeing no reaction, I lost control and vented my anger at the shoppers in the street, who were attending to their own business, oblivious to mine. Almost immediately I suffered a debilitating injury to my knee, and later took out my continued anger on Puppy.

I reflected later as all my mixed feelings about Puppy, and my performances before the lack of an audience, came to the surface. I reprimanded myself. What right had I to require that everyone in the street take an interest in what I was doing? In any case, was it not unconventional in a still conventional world to be dancing in the street in the first place. What audacity on my part to reproach anyone who chose not to watch or even be curious.

When observing shoppers in later years, and because of the chosen direction in my life, I have often felt sorrow and compassion for people whose main objective is the acquisition of money, and the convenience and passiveness it brings into their lives. Purchases in the shops mirror our lessening ability to be creative as we buy presents for our friends, family or children. Has it become unacceptable to receive a gift made by someone, with his own hands, because of imperfections? I have often thought of the part shopkeepers play in the production of the products that they sell. Do they have any sense of satisfaction at the end of a day either spent waiting for the customer, or in non-stop activity to make endlessly flowing money?

It slowly became apparent to myself that I needed to change my own sense of purpose, before attempting to change other peoples. I no longer wondered whether my dance had the power to move people. I knew without doubt that an inner force was using me to send a message to those willing to open their eyes and minds. I began to think less about dancing for people and more about expressing what was going on within me while I danced. It excited me tremendously, this new power that was creeping into my expression. I was not sure, then, where the force came from but I was certainly happy to go in its direction. I told myself that people would react if it were right for them to do so, the purpose was no longer to make them react.

This change brought with it a marked improvement in my feelings towards Puppy. The desire to depend totally on the new energy infiltrating into my work, helped my attitude towards her, allowing me to gain a strength of purpose through being gentle and more adaptable. Yet again I found myself on a new rung of my emotional ladder, and I liked the view better from my higher outlook on everything.

Regrettably, Hector became increasingly detached from me, preferring solitude and sleep to his past romps and tumbles. His own youth had passed, and another young life - with its abundant energy - was just beginning. However, Hector still took an ardent interest in Puppy's smells, sensing no doubt that something exciting and arousing would eventually happen. And finally it did, Puppy came into her first season in late June 1993. It was very bad timing on my part, as I had to leave both my dogs in the hands of their guardian angel, Min, who was spending part of the summer at La Casetta. I had previously arranged flights to visit my parents and family in England, and had to leave just as Puppy's season started. As I was leaving, I advised Min to keep them apart during this period as I felt Puppy was too young at only fifteen months to have her first litter.

I was not present for the ritual that developed, but the following extract from Min's diary on Puppy and the demented dog not allowed access to her, is worth recording.

Extract for Min Stewart's diary, Wednesday 9 June to Saturday 26 June 1993.

'Wednesday 9 June'

'Well, we survived the first night here alone. Even though it was quite late when Stephen eventually left, I still awoke at my usual time of 6am. Hector and Puppy gave me their usual early morning greetings. We all feel good and eager to get on with the day. With my apple and the dogs, I set off for the woods. Puppy tried her hardest to play with Hector, but he's too busy sniffing and smelling, not only the early morning aromas on the air, but probably more so Puppy's own scent. The cuckoo was singing. It reminded me of England. The perfume along the woodland track is quite delicious, it must be the acacia. Plenty of wild strawberries to be picked.'

'After our return, while the dogs slept, I gathered some lemon balm and, crushing it, rubbed it all over Puppy's lower and upper back legs. I am told this is a good deterrent against dogs when bitches are in season. She gave me a puzzled look, then she licked herself I could tell instantly that it was not one of her favourite flavours. Hector also gave me a funny look. I must watch them closely as Hector is definitely interested.'

'Thursday 10th June.'

'A wonderful night's sleep, accompanied by a cool breeze

this morning, has helped me to adapt quickly to being at La Casetta on my own. I decided, after breakfast, to take the fresh drinking water bottles up as far as the tap outside the cemetery. I used the old pushchair to hold the water containers, what a sight I must have looked with the pushchair, water bottles and two dogs. We had not gone very far from the cottage - maybe ten yards -when we saw a snake on the road, It was not moving. Puppy, of course, decided to investigate. I tried to run and grab her but the pushchair and water bottles decided to part company, not a helpful thing when you are half way up a 'helter-skelter' hill. Thankfully for us the snake was dead. It was about eighteen inches long, silver and black, with a very flat head. Poor thing looked as if it had been caught in a strimmer.'

'Yesterday, I had heard a pathetic dog crying, up a small track off the lane, so this morning I decided to investigate. Hector, Puppy and I cautiously went towards the poor creature, still crying. It was tied up on a short rope, with a tin hut as a shelter. Our hearts were saddened. He is guarding what looks like a place for shearing or slaughtering sheep. I wanted to get close enough to see if he had water, but he became more and more agitated, and the three of us retreated hastily when the rope looked as if it might snap. Puppy was not too thrilled with this experience, and our Hector was trembling all over. He is not terribly brave, our Hector. It is extremely hot with no sign of the rain promised yesterday. Hector's interest in Puppy's smells is increasing by the hour, it seems.'

'Friday, 11th June.'

'The heat is intense. I worked in the garden for two hours and then retreated into the house for an hour. This morning, after covering Puppy in the lemon balm, I decided to use, on myself, the watermelon sun protection cream that my friend Janet had given me for my birthday. Well,.I attracted vast numbers of insects, including a huge buzzing thing that would not leave me alone. I swear I caught Hector smiling. The dogs and I had a beautiful late evening walk after which we settled in the house, leaving the door open.'

'Saturday, 12th June.'

'It was very grey and misty this morning. I thought perhaps we might have some rain, the ground certainly needs it. At half past seven we took off for our walk in the forest. On the main track there is a newly 'fenced-off' section of the wood, complete with large wooden gates, padlock, bolts, etc. This arrangement was new to me. As I stood looking at it, trying to imagine what purpose it served, I became aware of a rustling and something moving within the compound. Guess what, there before me was the cutest cinghiale (Italian for wild boar), quite young and with a yellow tag in its ear. The dogs went haywire. Hector, of course, wanted to retreat as fast as possible, whilst Puppy was more curious. I knelt down to reassure the dogs. The little cinghiale remained where it was. I shortly became aware that there were in fact two, the second, and slightly larger animal, kept himself half-hidden. I plucked up the courage to put my hand through the fence, and they had a good sniff. I must bring them an apple tomorrow.'

'Puppy has stopped a great deal to attend to her rear-end, and Hector has tried to mount her. I think she imagines he wants to play for she then tears off after a stone or a fir cone.'

'Sunday 13th June.'

'We had a very disturbed night. Hector was constantly growling, barking and trying to get out of the house. I kept getting up to see if anything was outside, but whatever it was seemed to disappear whenever I opened the door, it's most unnerving. Perhaps it's another dog after Puppy. Help. Help.'

'We started out on our usual early-morning trek, but Hector soon became a real problem. Puppy must be in 'full-flow' now. He became more and more insistent in his attempts to mount her. I was equally insistent that he should not, hence a real battle emerged. Puppy became quite fed-up and cross with him also, and showed her annoyance by giving him a nip. This morning he has become quite deranged. I kept him on the lead and he spent most of the walk on his hind legs. I prayed that my arm socket and the lead would take the continual tug-of-war that is now developing.'

'I decided not to return through the village, as normal, in case Puppy attracted all the local dogs. So we came back along the track. It started to rain halfway back and I quickened my pace, but it was only a shower. As the day has progressed, the battle with Hector has become more intense. He is like some poor creature in torment, tearing around the house and sniffing wherever Puppy has lain or passed-by. I tried to keep them apart and in different areas. It's not straightforward though. It's hot and humid, and the battle with the lead this morning has ruptured a large blood vessel in my hand. I do hope the entire month will not be like this. I spent some time simply sitting with, and stroking, Hector. I must say that Puppy is being amazingly good, and I have had no trouble with her whatsoever. She is obedient and certainly does not encourage Hector, in fact she seems fairly fed up with him. She is incredibly loving towards me.'

'Monday, 14th June.'

'Last evening we moved to the caravan where it is a little cooler at night, but to try to sleep, with both dogs together, was impossible. First of all, I put Puppy in the house and had Hector with me. Hector would not settle at all. He was either scratching at the door, or trying to get out of the window, or simply crying and howling. So I brought him up to the house and down came Puppy with me. I imagined I had made sure that there was no way that Hector could get out of the house, or damage anything within it and, with a very big prayer, I left him.'

'I had just settled into bed when the rain started. As the water situation is now critical I threw my clothes on and rushed around the vineyard in the dim twilight, making sure every collector was in position to catch every drop. Of course, this started Hector off again. I am trying very hard to keep my attitude sweet. It rained quite a lot and it should keep everything going for a few days at least. Hector was very pleased to see me this morning, but it soon became obvious that he was even more delighted, in fact ecstatic, to see Puppy. Please, not another day of battles.'

'Hector is doing everything possible to get at Puppy, no matter where I put her. I don't want either of them to spend their days shut away in the cellar, but it seems that it may be the only answer.'

'Tuesday, 15th June.'

'I awoke this morning to the sound of a dog vomiting, it was Puppy. She seems very off-colour. During this morning she has vomited bile several times and is constantly chewing grass. I hope this does not mean that she is in fact already pregnant. She certainly does not want Hector's attentions, I guess only time will tell. Hector is now tied up permanently and very miserable. I have spent some time fussing him and trying to get through to him that this time its just 'not on.' He is so sweet, pops his paw onto my arm and looks so pathetic and pleading. He has a permanent erection. I wonder if he is in pain. Puppy is, at this moment, howling like a wolf. Its something in the sound of the bells in the church tower that sets her off. Did I really expect to have peace and quiet while Stephen was away.'

'Wednesday, 16th June.'

'It was not easy to get to sleep last night amidst Hector's

pitiful cries from the house. As soon as Puppy and I came up from the caravan this morning, Hector tried to 'mate' her head. It seems he is quite demented. Puppy is staying well clear of him. It's a tug-of-war during walks. Unfortunately, they are quite exhausting.'

'Just past the cemetery and into the woods, we were ambling along the track when, out of the corner of the eye that was not permanently on Hector, I noticed something move. There, directly before us, in our pathway, was a very, very large grey and black snake. Very much alive and only about two yards ahead of us, its head raised. Puppy was running straight for it.'

'I managed to grab her. Hector, who was already being held firmly on the lead, took full advantage of this situation. By the time I had disentangled his lower region from Puppy's head, the snake had gone, but where. 'On which side of the track was it lurking,' I asked myself. The other question was, do we run like mad past where it was, or try to 'magic' ourselves to where we wanted to be. We did neither. In frozen, fairy footsteps, I edged myself and the dogs past the spot, my eyes fully dilated, my senses acutely alert. There it was, on the grass verge looking as intently at me as I was looking at it. I am not sure what the snake did next, but we ran, with Hector still trying to mount Puppy throughout this potentially life-threatening moment. Life certainly is not dull.'

'It's the close of day now. We have survived yet again. At this moment both dogs seem fairly settled, mainly because I have given them a huge chicken dinner. They are lying either side of me. Brahm's Violin Concerto playing softly in the background. As a final big blessing its raining. Not quite 'A Year In Provence'. Perhaps more a 'Finale in Fiano'.'

'Thursday, 17th June.'

'Last night I shut Hector in the house. The glass doors were firm1y closed, Stephen's green wicker chair pushed right up against them. Hector was still howling and barking at 2.45am. By 3.30am he was outside the caravan, scratching at the door to come in. How he managed to get out of the cottage is beyond me. I feel that I have not slept for days.'

'I took a large stick with me on our walk, this morning, just to show a bit of authority. However, nothing, but nothing, deters this dog. Not even when Puppy gives him a good nip. I kept Hector on the lead for half of the walk, and Puppy on the lead for the return half, the idea being to give to both, the chance to have a good run. The only exercise that Hector got was his perpetual dance around Puppy. I have had to tie him up for most of the day, down near the cellar. Puppy has been in the house. I have made a temporary gate out of old clothes airers that I found in the cellar, which succeed in keeping her inside, yet which allow the glass doors to remain open for air. Stephen's windows in the house do not open and it gets quite stifling in there during the day.'

'Today I have managed to get quite a lot of gardening done. Planted over thirty-three young aubergine plants, having dug tons of manure into the ground, yesterday. Also planted out basil and harvested peas. Tonight I will have to fetch water again.'

'Friday, 18th June.'

'Hector obviously hates being separated from us, so last night I tied him up outside the caravan with Puppy inside. This was fine until 3.30am, then another two hours of scratching, howling, barking, crying. As this day has progressed it has become worse. Hector is now mounting everything that is stationary, including the couch on which Puppy is presently lying. I tried tying him up near the front gate. At least here he can choose to stay in the cellar where it is cooler, or lie out on the lower terrace. However, he chewed through his lead so he was put back in the house again. Here he just went 'bananas', jumping up on the windowsill and knocking everything for six. I am at my wits' end to know what to do for the best.'

'Stephen had fenced in an area around the fig tree as a future enclosure for some chickens. Thinking this might be a safe place to put Puppy while I got on with a project of my own, I put her in there. After a while, I glanced over to see if she was all right. I could not see her so I went over, looking and calling. She was nowhere to be seen. During the entire period of her season until now, she has been no trouble at all, has made no attempt to go off on her own, and has certainly discouraged Hector's advances in every way.'

'I searched everywhere for her. Oh my God, I thought to myself, after all the battles to keep her and Hector apart and she's gone. I ran down to the woodmen. Had they seen her. No. Up to Chris and Karen at Croce. No, they had not seen her either. Chris said he would be driving down the valley shortly and would keep his eyes open for her. My mind was full of anxieties, visions of hundreds of dogs pursuing and mating her.'

'Well, Chris and I arrived the same time at La Casetta and there, lo and behold, was Puppy - inside the gate. I really let out a prayer of thanks. She was covered in brambles and, on investigating the enclosure, I drew the conclusion that she had slipped down into thick blackberry bushes and had been momentarily trapped between the thicket and the fence.'

'Saturday, 19th June.'

'Last night I felt so exhausted, that I decided to put Hector in Stephen's old camper van next to the caravan. With his water and food in there, plus a cool temperature, he would be all right, I thought. Puppy and I slept soundly until the morning in the caravan. He had howled and barked for some time before settling, but it was at least a relief this morning to see that he had not escaped.'

'Puppy is, again, a bit off-colour, with occasional vomiting. We now have another little chap on the scene, a coloured beagle. This has made poor Hector even more demented, especially as this dog has taken to sitting outside the gate and howling. This vacation, Stephen Ward, wherever you are, will need another vacation for me to recover.'

'Because of the little beagle, and the chicken-coop drama yesterday, Puppy is now confined to the house once again. I feel so sorry for her, she is quite fed-up. Hector stays within my sight at all times.'

'Sunday 20th June.'

'Today it is very hot and humid. The beagle has plagued our walk this morning. He stays just a little out of reach. I had to keep both Hector and Puppy on their leads. The former would most certainly have taken off after the beagle. Back at the house, the scamp of a beagle tried to get under the gate, and then appeared on the top terrace. Hector is positively choking himself to get at it.'

'If our Hector does not die of frustration, and Puppy does not 'pressure cook' in the house, and I do not die of exhaustion pushing the water containers up and down this wretched mountain, we will have a modern day miracle happening around here.'

'Monday, 21st June.'

'As last night became quite cool, I put Hector in the camper van, Puppy in the caravan, and allowed a friend to take me for a pizza. I was gone for but two hours and worried myself silly throughout the meal. However, when I arrived back the dogs were fine. Hector was settled in the camper van and had eaten his dinner, which he has not been doing lately, and Puppy welcomed me with a great show of affection. I took them for a late night walk. Hector behaved so well that I let him sleep in the caravan with Puppy and I. In the early hours of the morning there was a lot of disturbance outside the caravan. Eventually, looking fearfully out of the window, I saw the beagle making a hasty retreat.'

'Tuesday, 22nd June.'

'There has been no rain now since the last fall eight days ago. The cistern is dry, as are all the other water containers. It will break my heart to watch everything in the garden die. Last night, Hector was, yet again, behaving like a demented bull towards Puppy I regretted my decision to let him sleep in the caravan, but this morning he has started to play a little too. It has been incredibly hot today, and the camper van is like an oven this evening, so I am going to risk allowing Hector in the caravan again for tonight.'

'Wednesday 23rd June.'

'Last night I was just drifting into a deep sleep, with the upper part of the caravan door open, when Hector decided to throw himself out of the door and chase off whatever was out there. I, of course, had to give chase too, to get him back before he took off inevitably for the village. Eventually, having dragged him back, we settled down with the door closed and the window half open. At 5.30am Hector woke me by nibbling the bed cover. I put Puppy down on the floor and Hector came up for a cuddle which he really enjoyed. There is a hint of the old Hector in him this morning. He ran free during our walk this morning. I kept Puppy on the lead. Every now and again he would come tearing back, not to mount Puppy, it seems, but more so to bound up to me and rest against my legs for a pat and a bit of love. I swear there was almost a smile, as if to say 'It's me, the old Hector'.'

'We walked for nearly two hours. Since getting back, the dogs have simply wanted to hide from the sun and to sleep. A friend came up from Lucca with a truck to help me bring water down from the cemetery, a mammoth task. At the moment he is also crashed-out in the house. It looks as if he has had too much sun. However, I will line up all the water-carriers in the hope that we can get started as soon as he comes to.'

'Thursday, 24th June.'

'Yesterday evening, we finished watering the garden quite late. Today I have to make a decision on what to try to keep going in the garden and what to allow to die. The artichokes have died already. I was praying that the much promised storm would have come by now, but its even hotter. The ground is so parched, plants are wilting before my eyes. I have bottled some courgettes, I hope they stay good so that Stephen and I can enjoy some of the fruits of our labours when he returns, and before I leave.'

'Friday, 25th June.'

'The dogs and I slept together in the caravan again last night. Puppy's season must have finished, her rear-end is normal again, and she is better in herself. Hector is now showing little or no interest in her, and this morning's walk was a good free run for both of them. In fact, it was Puppy this morning who became very excited when we got out of the gate, leaping onto Hector. Hector yelped, came to me and held up his paw. I knelt and rubbed it better, and pretty soon he was bounding along as normal. We saw the cinghiale again, I whistle to them and they nearly always come.'

'They love the apples. Puppy can't resist barking at them, but always looks at me sheepishly, afterwards. 'Sorry, I just can't help it,' she says with her expression.'

'Saturday, 26th June.'

'Today, I made four trips up to the cemetery with the water containers on the pushchair which now, with every trip, is disintegrating under the weight. It was muggy and very humid. Hector decided he would not make a fourth ascent. He had simply had enough. We sat out on the terrace until late into the night.'

'In the caravan, at 2.30am, I was awoken by the sound of a real shower. The dogs must think I am mad as I tear out of bed and race around the terraces, just to make sure that all the water collectors are ready for the 'big storm.' They look at me, then at one another, as if to say 'funny things, humans'.'

'I left the door open, after returning to bed, to let the fresh air in. It drizzled on and off throughout the night. I woke up once, about 4.30am at what I thought was the sound of thunder, it turned out to be Hector snoring. I think we have, at last, returned to normal.'

Min Stewart, La Casetta, June 1993.

After giving birth to her litter of eight puppies, Puppy naturally would not leave them for a moment, needing constantly to clean and feed them. Hector and I, therefore, went alone on our twice-daily walks in the woods behind the house. On these occasions, Hector seemed more than happy just to be with me and away from the alarming smells of the eight new arrivals, which were kept near the caravan where Hector and I were then sleeping and living. He regained a little of his youthful behaviour and our old game of 'hide-and-seek' was rekindled from the ashes. However, the walks became long, drawn-out affairs as I found that Hector was extremely loathe to go back to the house, trying every tactic to delay our return. I began to see his new version of the game as a very sly way of finding an opportunity of escaping my presence. When he returned eventually, he would not go to the caravan, since he knew that he would first have to pass the camper van from which escaped some strange sounds and very odd smells. He would, instead, wait outside the closed-up house, higher up the hillside, until I discovered his whereabouts and dragged him back to the caravan.

Anticipating our departure - two dogs, eight puppies and myself - towards the end of the month, I was desperate for Hector to react more sensibly with his offspring while I could still keep them in a place separate from himself. Once we were underway in the camper van, this would no longer be possible. However, my efforts at calling a truce were seriously hampered by Puppy who clearly indicated, by her snarling growls, that father was not welcome when I attempted to introduce Hector into the nest. Hector needed no convincing at all. He suffered not the slightest sentiment of rejection, being desperate to remove himself from the scene of activity at all costs. When the young puppies' eyes had opened, I introduced them one at a time into the caravan, hoping that Hector would allow his curiosity to overcome his terror. Every day I removed a puppy from a very concerned mother and introduce them into his presence. His tolerance was nil. His curiosity, if possible, was even less and I despaired. On 24 March, exactly three weeks after the births, I could delay no longer. I had only sufficient money to get us all to Switzerland where I would need to dance daily, and not just once a week as I had been doing in Lucca.

The content of my performance had not changed sufficiently, in the six years I had been dancing in Lucca, to warrant the continued support and interest from the townsfolk. It seemed as though the bottom had dropped-out of the street dancing market for myself in Lucca. As tolerance by the police could not guaranteed in other

Italian cities, I felt there was no alternative but to travel to Switzerland, where street entertaining was permitted in practically every city. Besides this, I had decided to find good homes for seven of the puppies and was loathe to attempt this in Italy. My experience and observations showed that Italy did not have a very good a record in protecting animal rights. In contrast, the Swiss are well known as a nation of animal lovers, and legislation protects animals from abuse. As soon as the pups were weaned, my plan was to take one or two of them with me each day into a city, and display a notice "free to a good home" by my dance floor. In this way I hoped to place five bitches and two male puppies. I would keep one male and hope Hector would adapt to it in a peaceful and tolerant fashion.

I left La Casetta prepared for the onslaught. People who know me, and had experience of dogs and puppies, donated old covers, used blankets and torn curtains. Initially, I failed to recognise how real was their concern, and left half of the donations behind - which I later regretted. I created a makeshift separation in a cupboard in the camper van, that divided the sleeping and living quarters from the driving and entrance areas. At first, there was adequate space for Puppy and her litter in the front area, allowing Hector and myself the remainder of the van. But it was not long before eight curious and active puppies, eager to expand their spatial horizons, encroached upon our area.

By this time, a long-suffering Hector had finally decided he would not be risking life and limb in allowing the puppies to approach him. He drew the line if they attempted to climb over or suckle him, when he would panic and go out of control if I did not let him out of the camper van immediately. From his bed in the rear, he leapt clear of the separation, alighting for a split-second at the entrance before exiting with great relief to freedom. His return was not so self-accomplished, and the only way I could get him to the rear of the camper van was to carry his thirty-five kilo body on my shoulders, over the seething mass of puppies below. His only place of safety was the bed onto which the four week old puppies could not climb. Eventually, and just before they left for new homes, even this respite for Hector was forfeited. Sharp-clawed paws found the strength to climb the draped covers as their curiosity of this strange, aloof, black dog got the better of them.

I can only imagine it must have been purgatory for Hector, when a return to severe winter conditions in southern Germany forced us to remain imprisoned inside the camper van for six days, all windows closed against the freezing blizzards. It was also a testing period for myself. Until that time, I felt that I had coped extremely well. The journey from Lucca to Lugano in southern Switzerland, and then over the Alps to St. Gallen in north-east Switzerland, and on to Lindau, Oberstdorf and Fussen in Bavaria, reaching Augsburg near Munich, had gone comparatively smoothly. The weather was good, as was my dancing. Puppy was a doting mother and kept her brood under control, exercising discipline when necessary, and love and affection constantly. The demands of eight energetic puppies were colossal, but she met the challenge instinctively and the litter thrived on her attention.

I did not take a back seat in all this activity. For everyone to survive in such cramped confines, I adopted necessarily a policy of stringent discipline. This applied not only to Hector and his boisterous, demanding off-spring, but also to myself, as I realized that the situation with eight quickly growing puppies could quickly get out of control.

Initially, Puppy cleaned up the puppies' mess with her mouth, as is natural in breast feeding bitches. Once we were travelling and the puppies took solid food, she refused understandably to do this and, inevitably, the covers for the litter quickly became soiled. With no washing facilities, I realised why I had been advised to take as many old covers as I could accommodate. Within a week it seemed we were living in a permanent public toilet. This was extremely unpleasant for myself, and the week of imprisonment due to winter weather nearly brought me to the end of my tether. Eventually, some progress was made with makeshift toilet facilities in the form of low cardboard boxes, in which were layers of newspaper that I could wrap-up and discard. Most puppies got the idea that this was for their toilet. But their aim was not always inside the box, which I positioned underneath the steering wheel, with the result that I needed to clean the area regularly and thoroughly.

With the winter weather there was nothing else I could do but grin and bear the over-powering smell that seemed to permeate everything. Whereas previously I had been able to let the dogs out of the camper van to exercise at least twice-a-day, it was out of the question to exit the camper van, which at least had the luxury of warmth in the winter conditions. Then during one particularly cold night, the heater in the camper van gave a final flicker and extinguished itself, the gas bottle being empty. On that occasion I was grateful for the warmth that Hector and Puppy, who by this time was tiring of her pups, gave me under the covers in my bed. In sub-zero temperatures in Augsburg the following day, it took six hours on my bicycle to find a place that would refill the two gas bottles, one Italian and one Swiss, both of which had non-standard fittings for use in Germany.

With the camper van heated once more, I counted my blessings and was somehow able to bear the inconvenience of my temporary living quarters. Indeed, I almost regretted the moment when I would have to give away these endearing, affectionate, tiny, vulnerable creatures, who had so intimately shared their first five weeks of life with me.

Only two of the eight puppies appeared to be identical, the others being noticeably different and therefore easily identifiable. I had already decided which one of the three males I would keep. Physically, each puppy had its own characteristics. One was lean and completely blonde, which I felt was too identical to Puppy. Another, dark brown, did not catch my eye as much as the third - a stunning, robust, tri-coloured puppy. He was white, black and light brown with extraordinary markings on his face, and I thought that this was the puppy who would make-up our trio of dogs at La Casetta. He was also the strongest of Puppy's litter, growing faster and eating more than the others, although all of her litter were healthy and active –I had no concern about finding a home for any of them.

Just as a mother and father marvel at their child's ability to learn about its new environment through its senses, so I marveled how quickly the puppies gained independence as they became stronger, and how rapidly their individual characters developed.

When the puppies were out of the camper van, it was always the same individuals that would rush into new discoveries. They would form a team to find and surprise other family members. Two bitches were quite fearful of straying, and would whine constantly until Puppy reassured them with her presence and a gratifying lick.

On such excursions, which did not extend too far, Puppy would be busy ensuring that there was no cause for concern when a puppy whined or squealed. She was always available to extricate any of her brood from danger and them bring back to the fold. Hector, under my watchful eye, understood he was not to wander at these moments and they were not part of his own daily walks. He normally remained seated at a safe distance and, when discovered with glee by a wandering youngster, now began to allow himself to be investigated. I wondered if he drew any conclusions about the heredity of the eight bundles of energy now constantly surrounding him. His behaviour had calmed down dramatically since we started our journey two weeks earlier, and we were all living a comparatively peaceful existence.

I was constantly intrigued by what I observed, making many comparisons with human situations. Behaviour patterns in humans had always aroused my curiosity, as I sought to learn about myself through them. I now found that canine situations were not far removed from those of homo sapiens, knowing what I was observing was pure instinct, trial and error, rather than education and conditioning. Watching the interaction between all eight puppies, and in particular the three males, I began to see the tri-coloured puppy was unsuitable for the environment at La Casetta. Harmony between the three dogs was very important as, of necessity, they would be confined to a small space for hours during my absence, while I was dancing. If I chose to keep a male puppy, it must be of a docile nature to avoid usurping Hector and causing friction.

But the intended tri-coloured addition to our community was developing anything but a docile nature. It started to take control when the communal platter of food was put on the floor. Dominating its allotted space, it would push aside its neighbours on either side, with warning growls if another pup came too close. When I gently disciplined it, there were signs that this might lead to a scuffle, even though none of the other seven puppies showed signs of undue aggression. This particular individual was not only a loner, a characteristic I would have accepted happily, but was also positively anti-social – always seeking to possess improvised playthings when it saw another pup with one of the many I had provided. It never played with the others and was badly behaved with its two brothers. Clearly dominant, I could not risk a challenge to Hector's position as head of the dog family once this puppy had matured.

At the same time, I gradually noticed an endearing character developing in the dark-haired male, at whom I had only previously glanced. In contrast to his larger brother, he played gently with all of his brothers and sisters, enjoying the food without being unduly possessive about his space at the communal platter. When I played with him to see if there was empathy between us, he responded in a wonderfully charming way, rolling his eyes while cocking his head and almost grinning at me. Our relationship developed and deepened, and I knew in my heart that I had found Hector's successor in this little charmer who matched Hector's own attributes exactly.

I had made this decision during that week of confinement during the severe winter weather. I knew it was the correct one. I knew too that the tri-coloured puppy should go to a home that had no other dog, other than perhaps a bitch, and that the owners must be young and prepared for a disciplining period. But at six weeks old, he was developing into a magnificent dog, and I had no difficulty ultimately in finding the perfect owners for him.

Mossy, as my ultimate choice for La Casetta came to be called, has never given me cause to regret my last-minute change of heart. He seems to understand his position in the family perfectly. He is a healthy and happy dog who, unbeknown to me earlier, has developed many of Hector's physical attributes as well as those of his mother, Puppy. But, and perhaps best of all, he fits perfectly into our unconventional lifestyle. He adapts to every situation, whether it be city constraints or rural freedom, responds to my discipline, and respects totally his mother and a considerably older father. He has taught me a great deal and no doubt I will go on learning from him. He and Puppy are inseparable, be it an amicable rough-and-tumble on my settee, a flying chase over the fields nearby, or a competitive dash after a thrown stick. Hector has retained his characteristic trait of loner, that I have always enjoyed in him, while adapting well to our increased community. At night-time, he can often be found curled-up on the settee, which now rarely seems to accommodate a human being, between two warm heads draped across his neck and his rump. It is the harmony that I prayed for during that fascinating time in Switzerland and Germany.

Puppy's milk began to dry-up. Her eight puppies, who were now quite large, became simply too much to cope with in our cramped quarters. Not just for myself, but also for Puppy who was tiring of their constant demands, and more so for Hector - who by now had resigned himself to what probably seemed like eternal purgatory. There was no safe place left for him where the puppies could not explore, and several would clamber over him, nibbling his ears, his jowls, his paws and his tail. Finally, it would be too much to bear and Hector would remove himself to another temporary respite, leaving behind his tormentors who quickly turned to other amusements.

By this time I was having greater success with the puppies' toilet facilities. Most of the covers I had brought with me were already dumped, soiled beyond restitution, and had been replaced by newspapers that I had picked up in Switzerland while they were awaiting collection. My thoughts turned to reducing the numbers in the camper van, and increasing the available space in order to return to a normal existence again. It was mid-April and the weather, although still cool, had a feeling of Spring that encouraged me to get on with the task at hand. I did not relish the prospect of finding homes for seven puppies but, due to their increasingly rapid growth, this had to be done urgently and quickly. I decided to go to St Gallen where my dance always enjoyed success, and stay there until all seven puppies had gone. I told myself that if it proved impossible to find homes for every puppy, then I would bring the remainder back to La Casetta and rear them myself.

As these final days passed, I was torn with emotion between the now desperate need to reduce the numbers in the camper van, and my affection for every one of the puppies who were now each displaying their own individual personalities. A dress rehearsal was planned at Lindau, on the northern shore of Lake Constance. Riding my bicycle, with its trailer containing the dance floor and accessories, I attached a small pack to the front of my chest. Inside it were three puppies, their heads exposed to the air, but with warm bodies snug in the interior from which they were unable to escape. In order to prevent their wandering off while I was giving my performance, I had also bought three tiny collars for miniature dogs as well as a length of cord.

It was Sunday afternoon and normally there would be a throng of day-trippers on this attractive island town, from Switzerland and Austria nearby, as well as the Bavarian Germans. However, the unpredictable weather had reduced the number of visitors considerably. Those braving the cold, lakeside breezes were diminished even further, when we arrived on the scene accompanied by a sudden, heavy downpour of rain that soaked the dance floor and myself. I pushed the three puppy heads down into my pack and zipped it closed.

Drenched, I packed-up my stage and returned to the camper van depressed and disillusioned, my determination having waned considerably in the interim. I looked around the litter in the camper van and felt very discouraged. The vehicle was alive with sound and activity, and I wept, not out of self pity or frustration, but with love and peace. I took each of the puppies into my arms and prayed. My hopes and intentions went beyond the welfare of these vulnerable, tiny creatures, to the welfare of all unprotected and innocent life, human or animal, in a world seething with the miracle and wonder of life.

The following Monday morning was bright and sunny, and I danced in St. Gallen. A large crowd soon gathered around me, mainly to watch the antics of two puppies enacting their own dance, as they entwined themselves around the cord that prevented them from straying onto the dancefloor. Photographs and a notice surrounded my collecting box by the floor. The crowd's curiosity encouraged me as, between my dances, I answered questions, gave information, and passed the two puppies around the audience. I had written out notices in advance that stated clearly the responsibility involved in accepting a six week old puppy as a gift, that was about to embark on a habit of gnawing everything in sight. I wanted potential owners to realize that a living puppy was not a plaything, to be discarded when no longer required, but represented a 12-15 year commitment. Undoubtedly a source of great pleasure, but also quite an expensive investment with no financial return.

Within the hour I had given the two pups to their new owners, sufficiently assured that they would be looked after and had found good homes. As I returned to the camper van with my pack empty and weightless, I felt a gratitude seep into my spirit as I reflected over the last weeks. I thought of all the rich privileges granted to myself, and of the many new, intriguing lessons learnt as a result of my own increasing awareness.

The weather brought everyone out of doors that week to enjoy the sounds and aromas of Spring. I brought the last of the seven puppies to the town centre on Friday, having kept the tri-colour puppy until the end, as I knew he was special. Although he gave me no reason to change my earlier decision, he certainly captured the eye as a strikingly handsome young dog. I knew he would immediately draw attention to himself but, on the day, he stole the limelight entirely.

The intervening days of the week had not been straightforward. On Tuesday, after giving the third puppy into the hands of a gleeful young girl standing by her smiling parents, I had taken my bicycle trailer with the dance floor and attached it to a park bench, in a quiet area near the centre. I intended to leave it there overnight, as I was finding the long cycle ride from the car park to the town centre rather difficult, with all of my paraphernalia and two large puppies at my chest. I frequently left the trailer padlocked to some object, when I found the distance too large between the camper van and where I performed. The floor weighed seventy kilos and my strength, after a day of dancing, could be very limited.

Over seven years, I had always been able to retrieve my equipment from where I had left it. But on this Wednesday morning, with the next two puppies for adoption at my chest, I spent an hour trying to find the place where I had left the trailer the night before. Had I been too tired to remember the exact location? It was certainly not where I thought I had left it. I cycled frantically around the town, searching all the places I had left the trailer on previous visits to St. Gallen. By midday, I was convinced that the trailer and my floor had been removed, although I did not know why. They were of little value and, while I could not believe they had been stolen, I needed them to work and they were not simple to replace.

At the police station, they were sympathetic but not helpful. I believed that I had left the trailer and floor in front of the Public Library, and enquiries there gave a more positive lead. Early that morning, the park caretaker had mentioned to the library supervisor that he had removed an odd-looking contraption from underneath the bench nearest to the entrance. He was not contactable until Thursday afternoon, when I was able to speak to him and fortunately retrieve my floor and trailer from the rubbish dump outside the town centre. While making these enquiries, I thought it advisable to take the puppies back to the camper van, and I returned later in the day, unable to dance, but with the two puppies and my notices. With no street performance to attract an audience, and direct them towards the puppies, I wondered whether I would be successful. However, no sooner had I taken them out of the pack on my chest than, once again, I found a large crowd around me. Maybe, I thought whimsically, if I could only dance with a permanent circus of puppies to accompany me, I would be assured of greater attention from the public than if it were the other way around.

One puppy had already gone when an older couple enquired about the second puppy, a blond and white smooth-haired bitch. Initially, I thought they were too old to take-on a young puppy. But when they both showed their affection for her, and explained that their doctor had advised the husband to get a dog to ensure his daily exercise, my heart melted and I succumbed. They asked if I could wait fifteen minutes with the puppy while they finished some business in town, pressing a fifty Swiss franc note into my hand, and assuring me that they would return. I remonstrated that I was not selling dogs and I could not therefore accept the money. They said it was an assurance for them that they would get this particular puppy, and I could repay the note on their return if I so desired.

Five minutes after their departure, with a crowd still around me enquiring about the puppy I was holding, I was confronted by two men who pushed their way through the crowd. Thrusting police identification cards in my face, they demanded that the puppy and myself accompany them immediately to the police station. Explaining that I was awaiting the return of the couple to whom I had promised the puppy, others in the crowd demonstrated against this interruption. Sensing a possible scuffle, the two plain clothed policemen bustled me into a waiting car without further ado, and drove me a few hundred metres to the central city police station.

After many confrontations with police during my career as street dancer, I was very aware that my present activities were out of the ordinary, and that police were often called upon to act in cases of suspicion. During the short journey to the police station, I asked if I were breaking the law in attempting to find - in the only way that I knew how - good homes for my puppies. I was informed that they had seen me making transactions with live animals for three days and, on this day, had witnessed me receiving cash for such a transaction.

I was interrogated at the police station. What was my business? Where was I living? Where was my camper van parked? How many dogs did I have? My answers to their questions must have amused my interrogators. After two hours my forfeited passport was returned with a smile and an apology, and I was assured that could continue to find homes for my puppies in St. Gallen with the full authority of the police. Enquiring why I was treated with so much suspicion, the police replied that live animals were being sold to Switzerland for illegal experimentation, and that I was suspected of involvement.

The elderly couple who had given me the 'retaining fee' for their puppy had come to the police station, after being advised on their return that I had been arrested. By this time my camper van had been traced and examined, while the police concluded my story was accurate. The couple had been given details of the camper van's whereabouts and, on finding it, had left a message asking me to contact them regarding the puppy. The following day, they were duly re-united with both their puppy and their fifty franc note, and two further puppies were found homes.

My dance floor was retrieved that afternoon. I gave the park caretaker my opinion of the council employee who throws something onto a rubbish tip, that obviously has value since it was secured by a lock and chain, without thought for the person who clearly intends to return and retrieve it. Had I left it for longer than twelve hours I may have been more understanding. But, in the light of what happened later in Montpellier, I finally learned an important lesson - to keep my property with me at all times. Its value, uniquely to myself, is too great to take the risk.

On that final day, with just three dogs in the van and one here with myself, as I set up the dance floor I wondered how things would turn out for the tri-coloured puppy. By then, I had made a pact with myself not to keep any contact with the people who had adopted the puppies. Although each one had been part of my life for six weeks, for which I was enormously grateful, we had arrived now at the point where one short episode in their life ends, and another begins.

The town centre was full of pre-weekend shoppers and, as I danced, my eye caught a man photographing myself. He asked me later if I spoke French and, on hearing my reply, enquired in his own language whether I would like copies of what he had captured on film. He asked if I would still be in the town the next day, and I confirmed that I would while taking the tri-coloured puppy form the arms of some admiring young children.

"Ah, il est beau! Il est à vous?" "Yes", I replied, "he's mine. He's the last of seven pups that I've had to give away this week". "Mais il est magnifique, ce petit chien. Combien vous en voulez pour lui." I agreed he was indeed magnificent but did not cost anything. He was free to go to a good home.

The man asked if he might photograph the puppy and said that he was interested in taking it. Would I come to his house around the corner with the puppy and meet his wife. I explained briefly that I was looking for someone special for this puppy, that he may grow up to be anti-social to other dogs and therefore somewhat of a problem. The man told me that he and his German wife were moving shortly to the south of France, near Aix en Provence. They had bought a small-holding with an adequate space for a young dog to exhaust his energy, and that they would often be riding when they would like to take the dog. He felt sure his wife would fall in love with the puppy and would like myself to show her the puppy after I had finished dancing. I said that I would go with him straightaway, and he patiently waited while I packed up.

At their home, just a few minutes walk from the square, his wife indeed was charmed by the little visitor. She suggested that, as I was staying in St. Gallen until Saturday night, they keep the pup overnight to see how they felt notwithstanding my warning of his character. I agreed, feeling that they were taking the proposition seriously, but intuitively believed that I had found the right owners for the seventh and final one of Puppy's litter.

Back at the camper van, our family was reduced to the number with which it would continue into the future. I took little Mossy in my hands and he looked at me with that comical expression which has now become so familiar. "Well, Moss the boss!", I exclaimed, without taking stock of what I was saying, "I wonder how bossy you are going to be". The nickname has rather stupidly stuck with me, though its significance is not real. There is no boss among us since Mossy, as the newcomer and the youngest, has learnt his place easily and well, contributing to the superb amicability between the four of us.

Two months later I had Puppy spayed, after being subjected to pressure from my friends and neighbours. Something deep inside me regretted my ability, as a human, to enforce my will upon an innocent creature simply because of the inconvenience to myself if I did not act. It is arguable, when the world is over-run by human life, whether we are morally justified in manipulating nature where domestic animals and wildlife are concerned. Nature has always taken good care of the world and ensured its continuation and control of life, until man learned a few of its secrets and decided he would change the course of events. As I am a product of the present, I carry my own share of guilt in assuming that I can 'humanise' animals to fit into my lifestyle. But in trying to eradicate one form of natural suffering such as hunger and sickness, and the cruelty involved in the selection of the strongest, we inadvertently impose sufferings of a different nature. Among these are physical and mental sicknesses that our natural defences are not equipped to handle. And in our newly found inadequacies, we degenerate our animals through abuse, intensive farming, and hunting - not through necessity, but as entertainment to alleviate boredom.

We would do well to elevate our thoughts and consider animals' behaviour, their instinctive knowledge, and the natural relations between species. In so doing, we would learn more about ourselves.

Three Dogs and a Dancer by Stephen Ward

Chapter 14

An Introduction to a Journey

Summer 1994

"The best summer for a good few years. It should be a good year for the wine", people in the village were saying. Indeed the black and white grapes, already fat and swollen with their delectable juice by mid-August, were positively bursting on their trusses. In five years, I had not seen my vineyard looking so beautiful. The fruit maturing on the pergola above the stone patio outside my kitchen, was hanging so low under its weight that one had to stoop when standing to avoid collision. Another older pergola, higher up on the land, had collapsed under so much weight. In order to avoid losing the grapes, which already were dropping off, I had left them suspended on an odd sculpture of crossing lines and foliage. Only after all the fruit was removed in late September, was I able to carry out repairs to restore it.

The summer in Tuscany had begun in early May, with a sudden and fierce heat after almost a month of constant rain. After returning from Switzerland in April, I had ensured that I collected as much rainwater as possible in order to see myself - and my now flourishing gardens - through a normally dry, Italian summer. However, it could almost be guaranteed that the summer heat would be broken sometime, with a refreshing and usually much-needed summer rainstorm. This would often be in the middle of the night. Any nocturnal eyes would see the strange sight of me, rushing naked around my vineyard, setting up rain collectors in every corner.

But, by mid-August, the long-awaited rainstorm had not materialised. The land had not seen a drop of rain since early May and all the collectors were empty, including six ponds in the Japanese garden, where most of the water had evaporated under daytime temperatures of over 40° C. Even the enormous cistern was dry, which gave me the first opportunity for many years, of cleaning out all the detritus that had gathered at its bottom.

For two weeks I had brought quantities of water to La Casetta and its gardens from a ground spring lower down in the valley, prior to David Ball's arrival from London to start work on our proposed video project. Now, ten days later, another guest had arrived from Augsburg in Bavaria.

When I had casually invited Frau Gertrud to spend a holiday at La Casetta I had not, in all honesty, expected her to accept my invitation. The invitation had been extended in June, following a letter from her in which was enclosed a beautiful poem she had written. It had been inspired by my performance in Augsburg during a cold and windy afternoon, which preceded the week of severe winter weather in Germany when I had to cope with two dogs and eight puppies in my camper van.

Gertrud, a spinster in her early sixties, was an authoress of poetry, fairy tales and fables for adults as well as children. My first impression, when she timidly approached and begged me to spend a moment in her company, with a look of urgency in her suffering eyes, was that I sensed within her a spirit beyond the normal aura surrounding curious observers of my performance. She endeared herself to me immediately. We sat together later in the plush luxury and warmth of a nearby Bavarian tea room, fluster and shy embarrassment mingled with formality. Gertrud desperately needed to tell myself, a total stranger, what had happened to her while watching the performance. She had scribbled the poem on a piece of paper prior to approaching me, and now wanted me to read it.

Gertrud spoke no other language than German and, although I could communicate quite well in the language, its use in poetic form was much too complex for me to follow. I could not understand most of what she had written. However, moved by her courage in approaching a foreign artist dancing on the street, and her obvious difficulty in trying to tell me her feelings on what she had seen, I asked if she would kindly type her poem and send it to me in Italy. I explained that I had two German friends, who spent each summer in their house near mine in Tuscany, and they would translate her poem for me.

The reply by return-of-post from Gertrude in June, accepting my invitation to come to Italy, came as a bit of a shock. I realized that I had 'jumped the gun' in asking someone I did not know, and who appeared to lead a sheltered life with a certain standard of living, to come to my simple and incomplete home in the hills. I immediately sent a further letter, letting her know what to expect when she would arrive in mid-August. I explained that my house, although reasonably comfortable, had no modern conveniences and that the bathroom facilities were limited with lighting restricted to dim, solar-powered, twelve volt appliances. Finally, I added the time I could spend with her was limited, as there would also be another guest with whom I was to make a film of my dance.

I had anticipated that, under the circumstances, Gertrud would now decline my invitation. I was therefore perturbed when she wrote again, saying that she would still like to come, and that she was willing to stay in a nearby hotel if we found her visit inconvenient. David and I made extra trips to fetch water prior to Gertrud's arrival, expecting our consumption to be considerable - which turned out to be the case. My reunion with Gertrud on the train station at Lucca was a little strained, as I fought with my German, and anticipated a rather complex time ahead with the three of us at La Casetta.

David and I were already in the throes of the most important project of my life. As David and Gertrud could not communicate, I had to ensure that I was always available as interpreter. This can be tiring and confusing when one is not in total command of all the languages one is translating. The situation became extreme later in August, when my Italian friends and neighbours, Piera and Marcello Barzanti, invited us all for dinner at their house just up the hill from La Casetta. It was an amusing evening, by the end of which the three languages were so mixed up as to be incomprehensible. My efforts as interpreter became so confused that I often translated the wrong language, inevitably causing much laughter and expressions of sympathy over my taxing role of interpreter.

Gertrud came to La Casetta on the understanding she would stay for one week, whereupon the situation would be reviewed. Prior to her arrival, David moved from the house to the caravan so that Gertrud might have more comfortable accommodation, with direct access to the bathroom. For some time previously, I had been following my usual custom of sleeping in a tent erected on the dance terrace at the top of the land. The house had no roof insulation and could be uncomfortably warm at night, but this was not a problem for Gertrud. David and I were comparatively cool in our respective sleeping quarters, so the arrangement suited everyone.

By this time Mossy was nearly six months old, and had grown into a handsome dog who complemented our community considerably. His nature and character were all that I could have desired, and he had developed a bonding relationship with myself that was respectful, if sometimes playfully boisterous.

All three dogs were an immediate success with David. Although overwhelmed initially, Gertrud soon accepted them to her heart, and quickly developed an empathy with Hector and his charming gentleness. The dogs were not to be seen in the daytime heat, disappearing into the darkest and coolest recesses of the house. But as soon as the summer sun started to edge below the hilltops, they appeared like spirits rising out of the ground, ready for action. The look of expectancy in three pairs of brown eyes burning into my conscience, until a loud "come on then, walkies" sent them in a flurry of excitement to the front gate, tails destroying any object left in their path.

The summer evening walks through the forest were magic times for myself, with my three companions lost in their own worlds of smells, sights, play and freedom. It was never quite the same again with Hector, after the incident in January of the following year, but during that special summer of 1994 nothing was yet on the horizon to mar my experience of a lifetime.

During the six week duration of the project, seven dances were video-taped, in seven contrasting locations, with five pieces of music being played and recorded by high calibre professional musicians. On reflection, it seems to me that David and I were quite naive and blind to the problems at the outset of our work. The final two pieces of music were recorded eighteen months later, due to a number of problems, causing a delay in the final editing and completion of the film. Oblivious of these future setbacks, we stepped out that summer into an exquisite experience that was, I could only conclude, a 'guided mission'. Experience of theatre and television taught me that nothing is possible without money. But my own experience in founding Focus on Dance, and in ten subsequent years of street dancing, had also shown me that anything can be possible given sufficient desire and will-power. Indeed, achievement is likely to be a more rich and rewarding experience if money is not always available.

Min has been a focal point in my later life. It was through her that I met David Ball, through her that I came to know the Redsells, and through her that I discovered a new direction in my dance that ultimately brought me the realization of where to go with it. Without Min, my story would never have happened.

In the latter period of my work with Focus On Dance, I had begun weekly, adult dance classes in Bournemouth with a simple style suitable for participants with little experience. The style developed during school workshops when careful prior analysis of dance movement was necessary for untrained bodies. My theory was that everyone uses some form of coordinated movement all the time, whether consciously or unconsciously, and therefore we express ourselves through what we do with our bodies. My thinking was that dance is the thought, feeling or stimulus before we move, which manifests itself in how we move. My teaching sought to implant this thought or stimulus into my participants' minds, using movements that were already familiar and which automatically resulted in coordinated movement.

With strong but simple rhythm as an aid, most individuals found that in only a short time they were essentially dancing. By using their own imaginations, they also found they could express themselves through their bodies in ways that they had never thought about. Far from being the physically painful discipline that we normally associate with dance training, they found the experience pleasant and mentally stimulating. For the first time, individuals began to think and concentrate on how their minds controlled their movements. I found it a fascinating experience to observe the individuality and differing rates of progress in each of my students. Their self-awareness was evident as they mastered a movement through their own understanding of where it came from, a source unique to each person.

One particular evening, a student remained behind to speak to me after the class. She explained that she was a member of a Christian dance group that comprised ten ladies who developed dances to present to the church congregation at Sunday worship. She had spoken to her group about my dance class. They would like me to give them an introductory class, with perhaps a further separate course to help broaden their movement vocabulary. I replied that I was not a Christian, although I approved of most Christian teachings, and asked why her group did not join our secular evening classes as she herself had done. Given a rather dubious and unclear answer to my question, I agreed to give an experimental class to her group.

So it was that I first met Min, a member of this lively and spirited group of women who possessed only limited rhythm and body coordination, but with unlimited desires to broaden their potential for their faith. It was at the third of the ten weekly classes at their evangelical church outside Bournemouth that Min invited me to meet two friends of hers, Florence Mary Ball and Paula Dowthett. They were part of an ecumenical Christian community in Dorset, from where they led The Sacred Dance Group Ministries with which Min herself had been involved, until recently. The Group's activities had a considerably broader aspect to those of the church dance group. It functioned on an international as well as a national level, taking its teachings to every corner of the world where a need was expressed, through dance performance and workshop participation. Its operations were financed entirely by donation. It received no secure or regular income for its administration, the upkeep of a large property in rural Dorset, or for the welfare of an international community of Christians - whose numbers approached twenty people on occasions.

At the time, it seemed strange to me that I should bring my style of teaching to Christian dance groups, when my thoughts and philosophies seemed worlds apart from theirs. One advantage in teaching Christians became clear while working with the group from the church: their intense concentration and reliability was extremely gratifying, and our progress was therefore relatively good. Other factors caused me to look a little deeper within myself when I started teaching the Sacred Dance Group, who were largely a nucleus of young people from all walks of life committed to their faith. Dance presented itself as the sincere expression of that faith. It was therefore a means to that end, and not an end in itself - which is exactly what dance has come to mean now to myself. My dance takes me forward down new avenues in my life, and has ceased to be the purpose of my life. Knowing this helps me face a future when I can no longer physically dance, but will certainly continue to discover the dance within me. I am therefore assured of continuing to learn from life through the dance, and for myself this is a joyful and reassuring thought that guides me onwards towards new and enlightening experiences.

Aware that I did not belong to this community spiritually, I prepared myself for when I was invited to remain for a communal meal after the class, or watch a rehearsal, or attend a birthday celebration. I felt that I would be under pressure to reconsider my beliefs. But, if anything, it was I who instigated the discussions into what I was sub-consciously seeking. These individuals were already well on the way to finding the secrets within their lives.

So I began to find myself at ease in this atmosphere and looking forward to my twice weekly classes. I began to relish the in-depth conversations and discussions with the members of the community, many of who were there in a different capacity to that of dancer. There would often be other guests at the meals, and I found myself intrigued by the honesty, sincerity and clarity of community members in relating to these guests as well as to each other. I discovered that I also wanted these same qualities within my own life, and that surely they could help me find the way forward in my life and my work.

Florence Mary Ball's husband, Denis Ball, a Doctor of Theology, would rejoin the community when not on some foreign mission. He and Florence Mary, together with Bill and Paula Dowthett, had started the community a number of years ago with a small group of dancers who had been touring Europe. In England at that time, their dance intentions brought controversy and challenge as they confronted the stubbornness with which religious organisations clung tenaciously to old doctrines. Theirs seemed a daunting task for which only commitment and a strong faith could help them. But the individuals branched-out from the community, taking dance to Australia and America, as well as into Europe, and continued the work in new communities. This resulted in a source of never-ending new blood, which flooded into the old farmhouse in rural Dorset. Any outsider such as myself, could only draw the conclusion that in this place, and with these people, was a unique and very special spirit that could not be simply labeled as enthusiasm.

Something began to dawn in me as I sensed, through these young people, as well as in the older leaders, Florence Mary and Paula, that the dance could bring a deeper joy and satisfaction than I was finding on the surface. Although in position of teacher, I began to ask whether I was being taught indirectly to open myself up to an alternative way of looking at my dance - how I taught it as well as performed it. It was preparation for the revelation that presented itself a year later - when the time and circumstances were right. Every decision, every meaningful friendship, every path, had each brought me closer to understanding what 'to have faith' really meant, and to what heights one could aspire with this wisdom.

I had always believed in my dance, but never dreamt it was the key to a new world that I was entering, just like a baby making its first step in life - falling over, then trying again. The revelation came one sunny afternoon in April 1987. I was sitting on a stonewall at Montreux, Switzerland, gazing over the azure-blue Lake Leman at the snow-covered French Alps. For two weeks I had been psychologically fighting an injury to my hip and knee, which had developed following an Easter dance course in which I had taught.

By this time I had been an itinerant dancer for six months and, providing my body held out, was satisfied that I could continue as a busking performer indefinitely. During the past months I had visited local dance companies in Switzerland and Italy, and participated in the daily training classes that are a professional dancer's life. I enjoying the stimulus of working again with other dancers and, at the age of thirty-six, being able to maintain a standard in classical ballet training comparable to younger dancers. But I was not inclined to start another term in the professional theatre, and in my heart I knew that one career had terminated, while another was just beginning that was far more exciting and challenging.

At the end of the four day dance course, I gave a spontaneous studio performance of my dance on the street at that time. The organiser of the course asked my permission to video-tape the performance. We watched the video later that evening while I nursed a nagging pain in my right knee and hip, which had begun during that final presentation. This was the first time I had seen myself on video, since leaving Focus On Dance for the streets of Europe with my new, improvised dance style. Floods of tears came to my eyes, catching my colleague unprepared. We watched the video again when I was more in control of my emotions, understanding what had moved me so emotionally the first time. It was a mixture of frustration at my wounded body's limitations, and awe at seeing how an unchained spirit had been set free in my dancing in those first six months since leaving England.

Following that Easter, I carried these emotions for ten weeks while I waited for my injury to heal. I was faced with a decision on whether to return to England from Switzerland, where I had funds to tide me over a non-active period, or remain in Europe and hope my injury was not so serious as to leave me destitute. I had no means of drawing on any money from my present location, nor did I have much with me other than that earned during those four days in Lausanne.

I decided to remain in Switzerland for the time being. My injury had become quite disabling in the two weeks since the dance course, and I could barely walk at times. Sleep was something of a luxury. I descended out of higher alpine areas, where I had gone to find peace, in search of a warmth following a heavy Spring snowfall. I had earlier reached frantic levels of anger as I panicked over my future, but this was now subsiding with a quiet acceptance of what had happened. Alongside these contrasting emotions was the memory of my feelings on seeing the video, and the message that my dance had burnt into my brain. Looking at the majestic scenery, I reflected and listened to music on my recorder, closing my eyes with gratitude for the gentle Spring air.

At a certain point in the music, I felt unable to open my eyes, my being whisked away into space as a sudden air current can whisk a bird in flight. In that limitless dimension I danced, not with a body, but as a spirit. I have often tried since to re-enact that moment, when I saw my vision of really being free to dance. I remember seeing and feeling the magic of what was happening, yet being unable to open my eyes until long after the experience was over, when I once more became aware of reality.

Eventually, I looked away from the lake, mountains and sky towards my two hands. "What on earth was all that about," I asked myself. The constant pain in my hip had ceased momentarily and I felt filled with peace, with the knowledge that all would be well. That the problem was out of my hands, and that I must simply go forward 'in faith'. I could not help but recall my decision, some years back when all had seemed similarly black and futureless, to hitch-hike to Scotland in search of peace of mind among the hills and heathers. What I experienced there was incomparable to anything in my life before or since. Anything, that is, other than this present phenomenon and what ultimately developed from it.

I left Switzerland with two images in my mind, one real and tangible on video, the other an unclear but a far richer vision of dance. My plan was to head for the Mediterranean and the caressing, therapeutic healing powers of the sun and sea. I did not know then that it was to be a further seven weeks before I could dance again. During those weeks I went through many periods of self-questioning, remembering my experiences at Lausanne and Montreux. They were my saving grace as I entered a period that, to me, seemed comparable to Christ's temptation in the wilderness.

I decided that the little money I possessed would be kept for petrol, so at least I would remain mobile. I was fortunate in finding a gloriously beautiful and wild area between Toulon and Six-Fours Les Plages, on the south coast of France, where I was free to park my camper van. It was a haven amid the turmoil of industrial ports and tourist resorts, with access to the sea one and a half miles distance from the craggy, cliffy coastline. What the region lacked, in terms of restaurants and hotels, was more than compensated by its wondrous, unspoilt beauty and wealth of wild food - that I lived on for seven weeks. I started to keep a diary following my experience at Montreux, and continued with it during this period and until I returned to England in July. This was an unprecedented action for myself, but one which I appreciate as I look back at what was a milestone in my development.

Every Saturday, I went to Toulon for the basic essentials and to charge up the camper van's batteries. Slowly, I depleted my limited funds and began to fear that I would run out of money altogether. What I was gleaning from the wild food around me constituted seventy percent of my daily intake. I longed for the nutritional delights of a supermarket until I discovered that, at the Saturday street market in Toulon, the stall-owners throw away all the fruit and vegetables that were too bruised to keep until the Monday. All I needed was the courage to go around the stalls, as the stall-owners were packing up, and pick up what had being thrown away from the rubbish bins. This may sound easy for someone who is desperate, but it is a great deal harder for someone who has never had to do it. Fighting against pride, I joined the ranks of the poor, the aged, the alcoholics, the street urchins, and turned a blind eye to the disdaining looks of the shoppers and stall-owners,

I returned to the camper van with enough partly rotting food to feed me for a week, and I felt rich beyond all measure. Was it because I had obtained something for nothing. Was it because I had overcome my pride. Or was it mental relief at not having to eat wild roots and herbs for a week that I rejoiced in this newly found and renewable abundance. Despite feelings of guilt at not having earned this reward, it was nevertheless a rich blessing. After this discovery, my daily walks amongst the shrubs and conifers to look for food ceased to have the same enticement and excitement of self-survival.

Now I began to wonder whether my mental attitude towards my injury, which was quite dark and bleak at times, was actually preventing its healing. I knew that, if I was to emerge from this enduring economic predicament, I needed a strong mind with which I could dominate and overrule my physical disability. I began to exercise carefully, using my arms, head and upper back to express what I felt within me. Slowly I was reassured that the disability would be overcome, just as my back problem gradually dwindled and disappeared in Scotland. It was now ten weeks since that Easter in Switzerland. I convinced myself that, at last, I would be able to step forward in the future and re-live the emotions I had felt then through my dance.

The first attempts at dance were made just over the border into Italy, where I was literally spending the last of my money on petrol. They were understandably restrained, but nevertheless profitable, under intense physical suffering. Encouraged, I gradually danced my way back through Switzerland again, on to Germany, and finally to England, where I immediately sought specialist advice on my hip and knee. Nothing adverse was diagnosed, and nothing was prescribed. The pain had virtually ceased by this time and I was impatiently planning my next tour. My dance had changed and I had also changed. I never forgot, or will ever forget, what had caused the changes.

A year later, in June 1988, I sat again at the dinner table at Longmead, the farmhouse which housed The Sacred Dance Ministries. There were some familiar faces but quite a number of new ones. As usual, the conversation was animated while eating and I found myself talking to David Ball, the twenty-eight year old son of Dr. Dennis and Florence Mary Ball. I was spending summer in England, while preparing a one-man show for the Edinburgh

Fringe - the outrageously popular and successful alternative arts festival, that takes place in late-summer alongside its world-famous parent, The Edinburgh Festival. In my performance, called 'I am a Dancer', I wanted to express the different stages of development and maturity I had undergone during my career to date. In particular, my approach to dance, and culminating in the newly found passion of freedom for my dance on the streets.

David agreed to photograph me at the studio of the Dorchester Ballet Club, which Elizabeth Goodchild had generously offered for me to prepare my performance. We discussed how best to use his photographs in the publicity for my show. I asked him innocently whether being surrounded by dancers at Longmead had ever given him the desire to try dance himself. His face changed and assumed a far-away look, and I noticed his eyes were moist. As he got up to leave I put my hand on to his shoulder to deter him, and asked if we could talk about whatever had suddenly upset him. But he left me and, as I caught up with him, he gave vent to his emotions, telling me he had always longed to dance but lacked the courage to join the community dance classes,

Putting both hands on his shoulders, I smiled and looked into his eyes. Next time he came to Dorchester with his camera, he was to bring some loose clothing with him. I would then give him an assessment class and tell him whether or not he should start dancing at twenty-eight years of age. Overcoming his initial awkwardness in the studio, David gradually gained confidence and I saw him daily after finishing my own rehearsals. Within six weeks he had the semblance of a dancer. I was astounded at his application, at his progress, at his sincerity of purpose. I took photographs with his camera and showed him the results.

My rehearsals were finished in late August, and I gave a pre-festival performance at the reception in Dorchester, organised by Elizabeth

Goodchild and Anne Hannay. I introduced David to them, saying I would be unable to continue teaching him but felt he was ready to join the more advanced classes at the studio. I did not see David again for five years. Elizabeth took him under her wing, and involved him in her Historic Dance Group as well as her own classes. Eventually, he entered the Laban Centre for Dance in London as a mature student . In just two short years, David had accomplished what other dancers took seven years to achieve. At the age of thirty, he now began a professional course in dance and all that surrounds the profession - choreography, stage production, stage lighting, design, and collaboration with musicians, photographers, artists of every description. In short, he was fulfilling his dream.

I kept track of David's progress through Min, who was in touch with Dennis and Florence Mary. I renewed our contact in 1993 from Italy after learning that, in his third and final year at the Laban Centre, his enthusiasm and determination had persuaded the directors of the Centre to provide facilities for a new specialist direction. On his own initiative, video-tape techniques for dance had been the subject of his third year and comprised the major contribution to his final degree. Having seen his will-power in realising what seemed an impossible dream five years earlier, my intuition told me David was the right person to help me realise my own impossible dream.

The idea to make a video-tape of my street performance was first suggested by Johnny Kelly, eldest brother of the nine strong Kelly Family. During one of my teaching visits to Amsterdam, I had asked him to video my dance so that I could compare my performance then with the short film that shocked me in Lausanne four years earlier. Johnny offered to make the arrangements for the video-tape and also a video-cassette, that would be offered for sale during my performances. I lost contact with the Family in 1991 when they moved from Amsterdam to Germany, and the idea remained, but with no possibility of being realized until David came into view. When contact with the Family was resumed four years later, through a telegram in August 1995, my dance was already video-taped and most of the music recorded.

In the period between the Kelly Family's disappearance and David's achievements, I had often thought of making a film but it seemed an impossible dream. I did not have the money necessary to finance such a project, and had lost contact with anyone in theatre who might have offered me help or advice. I fantasized that my video would be a dance tribute to nature, and all the inspiration that nature had given me, since my dark days in the Scottish winter-wonderland when I did not know if I could ever dance again. Later, on tours with Hector and Puppy in the camper van, I stopped at places far from anywhere - high in the Alps, deep in the forests, along gorges of fast-running melting snow. I imagined how perfect it would be to give my dance back to the very source from which it came, in these settings where there was so much movement and expression.

I wrote to David from Switzerland, enclosing a stunning photograph of an alpine scene, asking how he would like to film dance in such a setting, with such a backdrop. I received his reply at La Casetta. He wrote that such an idea was not only feasible, but challenging and original. And so, eventually in the summer of 1994, we embarked on 'the impossible dream.' We had no music, no money, and no plan. But with enormous motivation, and in just six short weeks, it came together in a way that neither of us forecasted - even if we had had an unlimited budget and a shooting script from which to work.

Three Dogs and a Dancer by Stephen Ward

Chapter 15

A Dancer's Journey

August - September 1994

Chris Redsell gave me permission to speak to the half-dozen musicians who had gathered for rehearsal in the kitchen of Louise Honeyman's renovated Italian house, just beneath the Redsell's house in Fiano. Amid the sounds of tuning instruments, musical scales, odd passages of music and animated conversation, he coughed and smilingly introduced me as a friend and neighbour, who wanted to ask them something.

Giamboree, Chris' summer music festival, was shortly to begin, the eighth in the annual series of concerts for the town of Lucca and its surrounding countryside. High calibre soloist musicians from both sides of the Atlantic had gathered at Croce, the Redsell's home, and were preparing for the concerts that embraced every epoch in classical music history.

I was nervous, for I had a big favour to ask of them. These talented men and women were here on holiday and received no fee for their contributions to Chris' unique festival, entering entirely into the spirit of the festival with only their goodwill. I wondered whether my request smacked of the profiteer in an already charitable situation. Would they feel taken advantage of simply because they were here on that goodwill.

I explained my dilemma. That without music, my dance video project could not get underway. David and I had three manuscript copies of music with us. We asked for an extension of their already considerable goodwill in order to play the music and have it recorded. While no fee could be offered for their services, I would ensure a percentage of the profit from the video sales went to each participant, once the film was completed and edited.

It sounded a very risky proposition to my ears, and I would have understood if the musicians declined my request. However, after enquiring which three pieces of music required to be played, all the musicians agreed to find time on the following day to rehearse and record them. Two further dances required a contralto singer and an oboist, neither of whom were available that summer at the Giamboree. It would be a further eighteen months before the artists and facilities were found in England to record these pieces of music. The sixth dance was performed to music from a single instrument. Debussy wrote a mystical piece of music for the solo flute that was entitled 'Syrinx', and to which I danced four years earlier at Giamboree. Later, Antonio Barzanti played this same music during a performance by myself at one of the Giamboree concerts. When asked, he readily agreed to play Syrinx for the video project.

The music for my seventh and final dance on the video was undecided at this time. It had not at all been predetermined for the film. It emerged later from a spark in my memory, that took me back ten years to 1986, and to an experiment that four artists - the two jazz musicians, Mike Trim and Helen Hurden, the painter Anke Petersen and myself - had undertaken at the studio in Dorchester, using improvisation. This experiment was the forerunner of my new style of dance that eventually became my sole form of movement expression.

While attending a Giamboree jazz concert amid summer perfumes in the gardens of a villa outside Lucca, my eyes widened as I listining and watched a harmonica player, accompanied by four other jazz musicians. He played his tiny instrument as though he were dancing with it. His movements intrigued me and, with my trained eyes, I could see they were not awkward or ill prepared. There was a supreme partnership between the artist and his tool, as well as with the music being played. My mind soared with an idea for a new dance on the video, an improvisation for two dancers and a harmonica player - who would also be one of the dancers.

When I explained my excited thoughts to David during the interval, he smiled and said the same thought had also crossed his mind. He observed that it would also be a good contrast to the other, more classical, pieces of music and serve to balance the content of the video. He suggested that the dance terrace, at the top of my vineyard at La Casetta, was the ideal spot location for this dance and it was obvious that more than a single thought had crossed his mind. I could not concentrate during the second half of the concert. My mind was on other things, rather than the music being played. The harmonica player then returned and played some virtuoso music to an appreciative audience, and I could barely remain in my seat. I reacted to his music, he was a master and a very animated one at that.

The lighting conditions were perfect on the following morning, with visibility excellent to as far as the distant hills above Pisa. I hastily removed my 'summer residence' from the terrace. The tent was full of paraphernalia necessary to my night time well-being, and the evidence had to be out of sight. David was comparing camera angles, judging the light, and experimenting with a hand-held camera. Charlie, the Italian-American harmonica player of the evening before, had accepted the challenge of playing his harmonica in an improvised dance with myself, when I approached him after the concert. He had never done anything like this before, and was unsure whether he would be sufficiently inspired for the video. But he was willing to try. As he and his family were leaving almost immediately for Sicily, to visit the place of his birth and childhood, the recording would have to be done the next day.

Charlie arrived two hours late. It was already midday when we started, and the heat was intense. My dance floor, with terra-cotta tiles underneath it, seemed ready to melt underfoot. We did our first 'take' blind, without any preparation. I suggested to Charlie that he follow the rhythm on his harmonica only when there was a definite rhythm in dance movement, and we allow the spontaneity between us to be the source of our inspiration, rather than the sound of the music.

With dance in the 1970s, came a new idea entitled 'Contact Improvisation' that swept into European New Dance circles from America. Often performed without music, but sometimes with improvised live sound from a player who gained his inspiration from the dance movement. It was a duet that used physical contact and any combination of the sexes. During my years with Focus On Dance, I have seen some dancers take this concept to a very high standard in their performances. To the point where one was convinced they had spent months preparing every movement in which two bodies essentially became one. However, the idea of creating an improvisation between dancer and musician, who would play and interact with the performance, was one that needed little explanation to Charlie. He understood at the outset and, with just two simple guidelines on how to start together and finish together, we performed and recorded our improvisation, David moving around us with video-camera in hand.

At the end of the first 'take', which lasted no longer than four minutes, David said there was only one point where he lost us. There was one more 'take', naturally totally different to the first, and we descended out of the blistering sun into my house, to look at the recordings on David's monitor. Charlie was amazed as we looked at the two rushes, as were David and myself. I felt we had been guided to commence the project in this way. The first dance, totally improvised, was to a very high professional level. It was an excellent omen for all that would develop from this beginning.

Three Dogs and a Dancer by Stephen Ward

When Gertrud arrived from Augsburg, she found herself with two men wildly excited about the video recording they were making together, one of whom bordered on the fanatical. It must be remembered that, at this time, Gertrud knew neither David nor myself – although she had spent an hour with myself after that chilly street performance in Augsburg, four months earlier. Although sensing each others deeper spirit then, we had not really considered the differences in our lifestyles. Thus, there was potential for a tense and complex period of adaptation to these differences when we eventually came together. I was trying therefore to look after Gertrud's welfare and well-being while, at the same time, being only too well-aware that David had come from England to achieve what was a 'one-off' opportunity for my project.

What I had not considered initially, was Gertrud's ability to adjust and enter into the spirit of the adventure in which she found herself now involved. Both being sensitive people, we found ourselves trying hard to make an out-of-the-ordinary situation more ordinary, neither of us wanting to give the impression that she was an inconvenience. However, once I understood that Gertrud was really more than happy to be just herself in such an informal environment, I began to see her visit as yet another blessing in disguise.

In contrast, David's nature was such that anxieties over unimportant issues had no place in his thoughts. His lack of reaction to my own tensions made me see that, instead of simply allowing circumstances to unfold and conclude naturally, I was attempting to control and manipulate them. In so doing, I was making them far more complex than they were, my mind was constantly finding solutions to problems that did not exist. I felt Gertrud would not be able to cope with La Casetta, three energetic dogs, and two eccentric Englishmen rushing around the countryside to find locations for the recording. I wanted to find a way to include her in our activities, bearing in mind her age and limitations. But it turned out that Gertrud was happy just to be left in peace in the glorious natural setting that is La Casetta's heritage. She was content to participate on the periphery of our project, but on her own level, and not where I was attempting to take her.

When we embarked on the second dance, Gertrud therefore accompanied us in the capacity of stagehand. She was content to busy herself with small jobs that gave her a sense of contribution, without interfering in the task in hand of making a dance video, and I was grateful for her presence and her intense interest.

While I no longer needed to have an audience around me, to provide the intensity that is the essence of my street performance, I found myself unprepared for the camera, and concerned at my awareness of it while performing. I reasoned that it represented the reason for my dancing in these out-of-the-ordinary circumstances, and took the place of an audience that would normally be around me. During the shooting of the later dances, I would learn to turn to another source for the strength for conviction in communicating my dance, and let the environmental setting become my inspiration. But now it was Gertrud, in these first days of shooting, who made me realise that this was not a time simply to let the actor and performer in me take over.

I thought back to the times in my life when I wanted desperately to dance with nature's splendour, but was unable because of physical disabilities. At those times I had dreamt that I was dancing, and on one occasion was transported out of my injured body to experience a freedom I had never realized or before contemplated. It gave me a new understanding of what the dance was for and from where it came. I wondered now whether such moments were a preparation for this present moment, but then concluded that everything is a preparation. In our lives we reach conclusions for which we have been endlessly preparing, only to find we go on preparing for the next conclusion with experience gained from the last. When the video recording was finished in late-September, my feelings were so poignant and magical, that I realized again this was not a conclusion but merely preparation for the next higher rung in my ladder of experience. Where my dance was to be enriched again, bringing new thoughts, stronger convictions and greater energies.

At the end of the video recording, I had not imagined the development in expression, inner-conviction and communication that this new experience would give me through the dance. It has been an extraordinary journey that will continue, provided I move forward at my own pace and not force it, and that I follow the signs to new adventures and into new understandings. Everything is a preparation, not only for what we might do, but for the wisdom we gain in doing it.

We had a location on our doorstep again for the second dance. At the end of the road that ascends to the village cemetery past my house, chestnut and acacia woods take over from the olive groves. Bulldozers cleared a wooded hilltop five years ago, with the intention of creating a football pitch for the village of Fiano. For months, machines pushed trees, roots and mud down the banks on all sides. Then, after a particularly heavy rainstorm, a landslip occurred that threatened to engulf the Redsell's house which was situated immediately below the work area. An appeal to the local council produced quick results, and caged boulders were placed on the land below the mud slide to halt its flow.

All work on the football pitch ceased, and the massive blot on the landscape has since been left to lick its wounds. I pass the site every day with my three dogs, and observe how nature slowly repairs man's thoughtless intervention. Since its scalping, the hilltop has served a number of purposes. First as an illicit but handy waste tip, until the local council discovered the presence of dangerous chemicals in watercourses lower down the valley. Second, as a motor-cross course for young bikers, until the area was fenced off as being too dangerous. Now, the site is a store for countless tree trunks that are destined to become roof beams, waiting for re-birth in a new form that is practical to man and his shelters. Use of this white elephant as the site for a cultural video on dance was not anticipated by the villagers. No one therefore witnessed the early morning activities of David and myself, as we started recording at 5.30am in order to capture the magic of a summer morning in Italy - hazy dawn, with the warm orange light from the sun, as it rose over nearby treetops.

The baked clay surface was strewn with acacia seedlings and briars, and was ideal for my roll-out dance floor where the beige floor molded perfectly with the colour of the earth. For David, the recording was straightforward and completed in three mornings, each identical in lighting and scenario. Gertrud helped ensure that the three dogs accompanying us did not inadvertently appear on the video, and she was also at hand with towels and water for myself.

Although this dance was an integral part of the video, the simplicity of its recording contributed to the feeling that it was a dress rehearsal for the challenges that were yet to come. Often, the out-of-the-ordinary conditions warranted considerable thought and preparation on how best to record the superb natural effects that became available. These effects were sometimes transitory, and therefore required quick decisions to complete the recording before changes made continuity impossible.

I look back with a smile when I recall the discovery of our third location. I wonder what made me wander up that stone track, to find such an original and contrasting location to those that we were to use. I pondered over which dance to perform there. I have an affinity with natural stone and rock, which is particularly evident when I visit the quarries of famous Carrara marble found high up in the Apuanian Alps. The area is littered with active abandoned quarries, with huge slices of solid mountain sawn away and transported as enormous cubes to the Mediterranean port of Carrara, on lorries that defy the massive weight of their loads. Seeing the long and precarious tracks these lorries travel, one wonders at the ingenuity and tenacity of man to profit from his environment. While I find marble extremely attractive in its polished state, I question the extent to which this beautiful range of mountains has been desecrated.

I have travelled with friends on the coastal motorway between Carrara and Viareggio, where this dramatic mountain range commands attention in an otherwise bland, urban area. "Is that snow on those mountain peaks, at this time of year?" my summer passengers would incredulously ask. "No, it's marble rock, rubble and dust from the quarries", would be my reply. And the rivers and streams, that are very low during the summer months, would reinforce my point as we passed over their white water carrying the dust towards the sea. When practically every peak over a twenty mile distance gives the visitor an impression of being snow-covered, the extent of this lucrative industry can be imagined in an area designated a protected nature reserve.

Gertrud, David, myself and the three dogs had come from La Casetta on a dual-purpose excursion. The primary intention was to find a location in which to record the improvisation to Debussey's 'Syrinx' for solo flute, with Antonio Barzanti. For this dance we sought a location preferably near the sea, and ideally with nothing else in the scene but the sky. A secondary consideration was that I wanted also to show Gertrud the natural beauty of northern Tuscany. Costa di Versilia in August is in the high tourist season, and our search along the coast for a location was in vain - unless we were prepared to tolerate others in our backdrop of sea and sky.

Eventually we drove over the mountain pass that connected the coast with the valley on the other side of the Apuanian Alps. We travelled at a slow pace, taking in the scenery and natural beauty of the landscape after the fraught journey along the coastal motorway. A suitable location for Syrinx had not presented itself and, high up in the mountains, there was no water of any description. However, I felt sure the mountains would provide an inspiration for the next of my five remaining dances. But, as the afternoon waned, David and I were increasingly frustrated and it seemed that only Gertrud and the dogs had enjoyed their day out.

We returned to La Casetta feeling that a more detailed reconnaissance of the mountain pass would eventually yield a suitable location. We decided therefore to return, and spend more time there with less distractions, for the dogs insisted on being included in everything we did. Gertrud suggested that she stay at La Casetta with Hector, Puppy and Mossy - who had come to accept her as one of the family by this time - saying that she would enjoy the space and peace of being alone, with a clear conscience. We left her with her three protectors, as David and I went back to the pass to seek a location, being prepared to stay for a few days. David shared my renewed enthusiasm as we set forth again, on the day after our previous excursion. My idea now was to dance with my beloved mountains as a backdrop. When I wandered casually up a rough stone track, high on the pass, to look at the splendid vista of mountain and Mediterranean, I was unaware that the track would lead me to an experience that has haunted my memory in the years that were to come.

I was excited when I saw the extent of the huge marble quarry, which was on three levels. The view from the quarry was everything that I dreamed of, and the vast expanse of the forty by forty metre flat, marble stage was overwhelming. I thought it a perfect setting, providing the summer heat-haze did not fade out the distant backdrop. In my thoughts, all I could envisage was the view of the mountains and sea, a view I had seen and related to countless times in a number of different places.

When David arrived fifteen minutes later, I ran to him in elation and showed him what I had discovered - the view, the backdrop, the space, the huge, flat, marble stage. "Have you looked the other way," he said. "We are inside a marble mountain. The most surrealistic stage set I have ever seen". I looked at him, aghast. It was true that the blue-streaked white walls and stage of this quarry were imposing, but the area was littered with bits of rusting machinery and strewn with odd-shaped, elephant-sized pieces of sawn marble. My vision was limited, all I could see was the view. I wondered later what Anke Petersen, my German friend in Dorset, would have seen. She had shown me how to fantasize through my eyes, in order to stimulate the senses and increase the pleasure in my mind. Now David was telling me to turn my eyes from this enticing view, and look the other way into the heart of a mountain. Into the wall of blue-streaked, smooth white marble, that rose fifty metres high towards an azure-blue sky, and which rose perpendicularly from three horizontal levels - each about five metres in height.

It was true that the weird, symmetrical boulders lent a superb atmosphere to an already majestic setting. I began to see what David saw, what Anke would have seen, what no-one would have seen had it not been for man's desire for marble. This indeed was fantasy, and on a real level. It was the stage set of the century, and it was ours, free, a gift. For myself it was the most perfect stage that I ever dreamt I could dance on. A stage of white stone, inadvertently created by man, and superbly lit. Had he seen it, Wagner would have abandoned plans for a dedicated theatre to stage his extraordinary operas, and today's technological wizardry could transform this ethereal space into something out of this world

Although our humble production was limited in funding and lacked theatrical effects, we now had a most original and dramatic location for our video recording. However, the location did not come without challenges. First, it was immediately obvious that we could only record early in the morning until 1100am, in the shadow without direct sunlight. After that time, the sun's rays would stream over the top of the marble wall and into the quarry. Alternatively, we could record for two hours in the late evening, when the setting sun cast an orange glow directly into the quarry. At any other time, the intense sunlight and reflections from the white marble were blinding - unless the sky was overcast. Additionally, the concentrated heat from the sun in the afternoon made dance impossible, due to the unsightly perspiration that would be all too evident in the recording.

That afternoon, between frequent liquid refreshment breaks, David studied camera angles, lighting contrasts, and shooting plans. I selected and cleaned a space where I would dance, at the front of the first floor level of marble. Using a broom , borrowed from an obliging but curious proprietress of a mountain inn further up the pass, I removed the marble dust and small stones from a weathered stone surface. David had said uncompromisingly that I must dance directly on the marble, since putting a brown dance floor on a white marble surface would not only look out of place, but also be sacrilegious.

As the evening approached, I saw that dancing before 7.00am was going to be difficult due to the angle of the sunlight. As my eyes were very sensitive to bright light, the better of the two options was to work in the morning when the sunlight would be diffuse rather than direct. An added advantage was that I would also be fresher than in the evening and, with four to five hours in which to work, we would probably only need two sessions for the recording.

Despite David's insistence that I get a good night's sleep in the only proper bed in the camper van, I awoke early in the morning, feeling restless and unrested. I had been unable to switch-off my mind, that was overactive with excitement and anticipation. The dance I originally planned for the quarry was superseded by another that, dramatically, I considered would be a stronger dance in the quarry environment. The dance is a prayer for a sinner. It is also my prayer, for it relates so closely to my life and myself:

> Amazing Grace, how sweet the sound,
> That saved a wretch like me.
> I once was lost but now I'm found,
> Was blind, but now I see.
> 'Twas grace that taught my heart to fear
> And grace my fears relieved.
> A precious gift did grace appear
> The hour I first believed.

Long before the dawn appeared, I was already on my marble stage, in spirit if not in body. As the music requires an exceptional singer, it was one of the two pieces that we had not been able to record in Fiano. I would therefore be dancing to the original sound track used for my street performances, and the correct accompaniment would be added later. I had already played the music a hundred times over in my mind, envisaging how I would fit my dance into the dramatic setting of the location. By the time that David's alarm clock went off at 5.00am, I felt as though I had danced all through the night.

By 7.30am we were ready. My body was exercised, and David's camera angle decided for the first take. As I knelt on the cool marble surface, head bowed, hands crossed behind like a prisoner locked in his mental cell, I felt the privilege that accompanies humbling in the presence of a mighty energy. On that first take, the prayer from the sound track reverberated off the walls and seemed to penetrate my body, so intense was its message:

> Through many dangerous toils and snares
> I have already come.
> 'Twas grace that brought me safe thus far
> And grace will lead me home.

Had I ever really listened to what these words were actually saying? Had my dance that portrayed this prayer ever truly expressed the heart of the man who wrote it, a slave trader en-route from Africa to America with his live cargo. After a revelation, he persuaded the captain of the ship to turn around. It was the turning point in his life. Why was his revelation so strong that it made him react in that fashion? Why, I wondered, had this prayer become part of my performance and rooted a part of my mind, when I had not really studied what it was saying?

A vision of an anguished and desperate man arose suddenly in my mind's eye. I recalled a character I had portrayed in dance while working in the Ballet Rambert. Glen Tetley's poignant masterpiece, 'Rag Dances', created earlier by this same company, was revised and given a new voice. It is a ballet dedicated to the afflicted of our world, physically, mentally or otherwise. It is a depressing piece of work, originally choreographed to music by a Jewish composer living in a German concentration camp, during the last war. By some stroke of fortune, he survived his internment unlike the other musicians with whom he had rehearsed and performed the piece in the camp.

In contrast, Glen became aware of his own concentration camp through living in the city of New York. He created the characters in Rag Dances around the people he knew there who, for various reasons, were each serving their own sentences. The character I performed was called 'The Flier'. Glen told me he based this dance on a socially respected man he had known who, overnight, decided to become a 'street person'. He opted-out from normal, day-to-day human existence, deeming it to be dead-end and without point. Eventually, he became convinced that he could fly and did so, for one brief moment in his earthly life, before crashing onto the pavement from a multi-storey building in the city centre.

Amid the remarkable dances in the ballet, I had taken the interpretation of this weird character very seriously, knowing it was based on fact not fantasy. Such was the intensity of my portrayal, I found I could actually get inside the character and feel the frustration of his limitations, live the sensation of realizing his ultimate dream. The conclusion to the dance was finite. The end result was death, no doubt leaving the audience in a quandary over the futility of such a life. When I became aware this character was included in my interpretation of the prayer, Amazing Grace, I knew too its destiny would not to be that of 'The Flier.' Here in this stone sanctuary, I would become a lost soul who found salvation through hope, through prayer, through belief

David too, in his own quiet and rational way, was also excited. I could feel his intensity radiating towards me as he repositioned the camera to the edge of the quarry, and adjusted the tripod for the next 'take'. As I took up my position again, I reflected on my original idea for using the dramatic view to the sea as a backdrop, which would have meant David shooting from inside the quarry towards the horizon. My 'front' would have been the sheer wall of marble directly in front of me, and I would have been aware of the camera focusing on me. Now, I realised, the camera faced the other way and my 'front' was a magnificent open space - I was hardly aware of the camera, lost in the vastness of the horizon.

Two hours into the shooting on that first morning, we had to postpone our work after the fourth 'take' while a coach-load of German tourists ascended, inspected and photographed the quarry with their cameras. No one enquired why we were there, and we offered no information. They left after an hour, and we got ready to resume our work, but after a short while further voices heralded the arrival of more visitors. From then on a steady flow of tourists of different nationalities made the short pilgrimage to this shrine and, as the sun reached its full intensity, we knew our work for that day had reached its end.

After packing-up and moving the camper van to a quieter place, David set up the monitor and we watched the results of our morning's work. It is disturbing, but at the same time enlightening, watching oneself in a role intended to communicate a particular message, only to discover that the message is visually different when performed in a different setting. Such was my feeling on watching the rushes. I was not content with my portrayal of this profound, but simple prayer. I found the uniqueness of the setting to be awe inspiring, and my physical presence within it fitting, but I was not at ease with the interpretation conveyed by my dance.

I was pleased to discover this while there was still time to modify my rather over-stylised movements and expressions in favour of more honest and genuine ones. My inner feelings were real in the dance, but were not convincingly reaching the outer extremities of my body. As dance communication relies totally on the body to convey its message, I felt if I was to be audacious in portraying - through dance - this age-old prayer, it needed to be exact and to the point. Above all, I needed to feel that my dance related perfectly to what I was feeling while dancing.

That evening, as the heat began to leave the sun's rays, David suggested we return to the quarry and make some recordings to gain more experience of the setting. The recording would be of little use, as the lighting was very different to that in the morning, but I saw his suggestion as an opportunity for correcting the interpretation in my dance following my disappointment with the morning's rushes. After telephoning my neighbours to check on Gertrud's welfare at La Casetta, I drove back to the quarry where I had left David previously to set up his camera and prepare himself. The evening sun, shining almost horizontally into the quarry, gave it an ethereal, rose-pink effect on white marble. It was very beautiful, but short-lived as the sun sank lower in the sky. Neither was the same effect guaranteed on further evenings, as proved the following morning when clouds gathered in the sky, threatening a summer storm with rumblings of thunder.

By this time, however, we had returned to La Casetta and a warm welcome from Gertrud and three exuberant dogs. David was very pleased with his recordings, and I looked forward to seeing the rushes and the modified interpretation in my dance. Anticipating a heavy rainfall, I had travelled home quickly so as not to miss an opportunity to collect the rainwater - there had been no rain for fourteen weeks. But the rain did not materialize at Fiano, although, we passed frustratingly through heavy rain on our journey. The storms were confined to the centre of the mountains and did not arrive at our southern location. Next morning was as beautiful as the others, and the ground was still parched at La Casetta. The cistern remained empty.

After bringing water to the house from a spring lower down the valley, I settled into an easy chair with a glass of my own wine, and told Gertrud of the marble quarry and the 'amazing grace' we discovered there over the three days. David set up the monitor in the house, and we all looked at the material that he had recorded. When he switched off the monitor, we looked at each other in awe-stricken silence. It was a magic moment, a pearl in a shell. How, I wondered, could anything we do in the future compare with what we had just seen? Gertrud said with a quiet voice in German, "you have been blessed. You have truly been blessed with this treasure." David bowed his head, and a tear came to my eyes.

Three days later, Gertrud departed from Lucca train station for Germany and her home. As her connection to Florence came into the platform, her parting wish was that we continue to be blessed in making the recording – and that it would equally bless those who saw it. As her eyes looked into mine, she whispered that something had changed in her since coming to La Casetta. Never in her life had she experienced such truly found joy. Contrary to what I had anticipated, it seemed her stay was a blessing, not only for her but also for me.

Gertrud has returned twice to La Casetta since her initial visit. Her first return was in the summer of the following year, 1995, when I was not pre-occupied by any projects apart from writing my book. There was adequate water for the garden, kitchen and bathroom, and we had a wonderful time together. We laughed, talked and prayed. Our age difference was no difference as, in friendship, we related on a far deeper level than in most friendships. Gertrude and other friends such as Min and my neighbours, Chris and Karen, are surely dropped from heaven, from whom we learn about ourselves and how to give unconditionally, thereby contributing towards a better world.

During the three days left with Gertrud, I went with her and David to dance in the Piazza San Michele at Lucca, where I had danced so often before. I think of it as my 'home theatre.' For eight years I have given regular performances to the local people, as well as to tourists who come to this ancient, medieval town at all times of the year. Few people ever approach me to enquire who I am or where I am from, yet I must have become a common sight to its inhabitants - as the Piazza's street vendors have become to myself. I have wondered often what the people of this merchant town think, in their minds, about the eccentricity of the 'Ballerino di Piazza San Michele,' who is obviously not Italian. Some acquaintances have been made during this period, however, and I have spoken with them about my life, my dance and my simple home in the hills above the town. Perhaps, through them, word has spread to other curious locals who must, by now, have drawn the conclusion that I am human and part of their human community.

Gertrud sat on a stone step beneath the towering grandeur of St. Michele, and watched my late-evening performance. The air was balmy and windless. There were few people in the piazza, or indeed in the town itself. The inland towns of Italy virtually close during August, and particularly those within a reasonable distance of the coast. With so few people, most shops and normal services close down for the entire month. On this evening the piazza was quiet, and even the pigeons were inactive as no vendor was selling feed-corn for children to give them. A sprinkling of visitors had gathered in the space outside the church, and curiously joined Gertrud on the steps, perhaps twenty people in all. They were my audience from the beginning to the end of my forty minute performance. What else could a town that was closed offer to its visitors? Who else but me would delight in performing to this small but appreciative group, receiving satisfaction when they began to talk to one another, formality and language ceasing to be a barrier. Gertrud was in her element and when I finished my last dance, exhausted, she proudly brought the group to my dance floor and introduced me.

This was my world, and this was what I gave up the theatre to do. This was the reason I suffered nearly three years of depression, two years of disability, and a year struggling to find my way out and back into the light. Why I had suffered rejection at school through my desire to be a ballet dancer, an out-of-the-ordinary activity for a man in a society where men play sports such as football and rugby, to demonstrate their strength and courage. Surely, such attributes are not found in dance.

Recalling my days with Ballet Rambert, I remembered another solo performance that also prepared me for the controversial decision to leave the professional theatre and take my dance to the streets. Christopher Bruce's powerful choreography, 'Cruel Garden,' was produced in the 1970's in collaboration with Lindsay Kemp. A masterpiece of theatrical dance drama based on the contemplative and courageous life of the Spanish poet, Garcia Lorca. During the latter part of his life, before returning to Spain and a bloody death at the hands of his enemies, he had spent a period in North America during the terrible depression of the 1930s.

My solo dance was called 'the Negro,' and depicted this sorry time in America's 20th century history. My character was a performer, a tap dancer who, in his desperation to survive, had swallowed his pride and performed his heart-rending show on the streets for an occasional two cents, in his rags and tattered clothes. Like 'the Flier', it was a character, a person, that I knew and understood deep inside me. In my character interpretation in 'Amazing Grace,' I sought to show that even in the direst predicament there is always hope of salvation, and felt psychologically there was a remnant of 'the Negro' in my subconscious saying 'Do it, Stephen, do it, and make it a success and not a failure.'

Well, I did do it. Not with the intention of gaining fame and fortune. After ten years of experience, I can say it has enabled me to put aside all my burdens and I have progressed like the pilgrim who, at the end of his road, found all that he had been seeking.

Sometimes, I ask if a mere street performer like myself can claim such an inheritance, or whether I am simply living my life in a dream. But I have not yet awoken from this dream, or stopped trying to convince myself that I should. I do not know the source of the message within me, or if it has even a place or a purpose in the performances that I give. Whether it has all come together by chance from a thousand different experiences, or whether it was pre-destined, I hope will one day be clear. Certainly the people with whom I come in contact, and who encourage me, are of a like mind. I believe that, through being spiritually aware, we are able to understand what we are told by signs and messages, and in communication that expresses itself creatively through the soul - not in words

Antonio Barzanti, the flautist, led David and myself across an old stone bridge and over the narrow gorge. The bright sunlight, reflecting off leaves on trees clinging precariously to rocky sides, prevented one from seeing into the black depths below. We went along a well-worn footpath, descending gradually until reaching a deep green, crystal clear stretch of water. "This is the place" he said in Italian.

We climbed further down the limestone rocks to a point above the emerald water, where I thought of my early childhood and picture books with elves, fairies and goblins. The midday sun was just peeping over the highest rocks of the gorge, and casting a spray of filigree light to the lower depths where we stood. It was ethereal. Looking back up the gorge, the sun's heat caused vapours of humidity to rise between the rocks and trees, creating rays of shimmering light. The only sound in such an eerie and magical place, soon to be the location for 'Syrinx,' was the song of the birds.

Looking downstream to where the water filtered through the gorse, the sheer rock abruptly changed into the broader aspect of an open valley. The gorge broadened and the running water rushed over smooth, rounded boulders, to be carried further away. This, too, was another location for 'Syrinx.' "There is another spot, a little higher up-stream, beyond the bridge and the gorge," Antonio called to us, his voice echoing in the confined silence. A hundred metres beyond the bridge lay our third and final location for 'Syrinx.' Here the river tumbled between massive boulders, that had fallen there long ago, and which now blocked its progress to form deep pools before the water spilled to a lower basin. This was the driest time of the year, and there had been no rain for almost four months, yet lush vegetation grew around the banks and in the crevices of this humid, limestone landscape.

If our marble quarry was the perfect stage for 'Amazing Grace,' then these three contrasting paradises compared equally as the perfect location for my next dance, 'Syrinx.' I had earlier explained to Antonio my concept of creating a mystical dance for the video where he, representing Pan, and I would mold into the nature, becoming one with the sounds, shapes and light. Antonio immediately thought of this place as the ideal location. Every direction, every angle, every surface gave my concept perfect expression, and I decided that I would put myself totally in David's hands and rely on his skill in capturing this wonderful imagery.

The following morning was again hot and sunny, and we collected Antonio from his home and we drove to the gorge in a state of anticipation. Recording at each of the three locations was governed by the available light, which varied widely according to the time of day. The valley had the longest period of direct sunlight, the gorge the shortest with one hour, and the place of the cascading waterfalls and pools three hours in the mid-afternoon. Although Antonio would be recorded playing his flute live in each of the three locations, the music subsequently used in the video was later recorded separately in a studio. But his presence on location was vital for portraying an image of music and mobility within the natural surroundings. We hoped that the action of playing the flute, with the movements of my dance, would capture the spirit of this strange and wonderful solo, so evocative in its mood. And so it was. Our day of creativity ended in the evening with an invitation by Antonio's family to their lovely home, situated on a hilltop overlooking the valley separating the Apuanian Alps from the Apenine Mountains. By contrast, the next evening saw the same company gathered in my tiny, humble one room dwelling to watch the rushes on David's monitor.

Five days later, on the first day of September, my camper van was packed and ready to travel. It would accommodate three dogs, a dancer and cameraman, together with all our equipment, for a period of three weeks in Switzerland. There, we hoped to find three more locations where we could film the remaining three dances. We also intended to stop off en route, first at the gorge to complete the filming of 'Syrinx,' then by the marble quarry for some further video-taping to provide additional background scenes.

The dogs were left to their own devices at the gorge. A mistake on my part as in the heat of the afternoon Hector, who has an aversion to cooling water, had sought to escape the heat and could not be found. I was concerned that he may have wandered on to the nearby busy mountain road, and be a danger not only to himself but also to the passing motorists. We postponed our recording to go and look for him, putting the other two dogs in the camper van. Three hours later, I returned from an unsuccessful search worried and tense. I met David, who had been looking in an opposite direction, with Hector at the end of his lead. "where on earth was he," I shouted, more at Hector than at David. Laughing to ease my tension, David replied "he was fast asleep, curled up inside that old derelict barn. The coolest spot he could find, no doubt." The derelict barn was just one metre from the parked camper van. The only entrance for a dog was through a narrow hole in its wooden walls, which was one metre above ground level. Hector had jumped through the hole to find respite from the heat and, oblivious to our calls, had slept through the afternoon in sublime tranquility.

By this time it was quite late, and we had completed all the recordings except for myself in the water. These were reserved until the end of the day, since my hair and costume would get wet. We decided that the pools upstream were ideal for recording my dramatic emergence from the water, which would be slowed down in the editing studio. The water was limpid and fresh, and I looked forward in anticipation to this part of our work. However, it was not to be. At the moment of my reunion with Hector, the heavens suddenly opened, depositing three months' accumulation of humidity in a short and severe burst of rain. Summer had finally broken - the day I left home, after fourteen weeks of severe drought.

The storm had passed in half an hour, and we returned to the location. The crystal-clear water that had looked so enticing and so perfect for our purpose, had undergone a metamorphosis. An angry, raging torrent now usurped its gentle predecessor, forcing its way between boulders. It was now highly dangerous to even risk approaching the water, let alone to enter it. We postponed finishing the recording for a further three weeks, until we returned from Switzerland at the end of September.

That night, our first with the full entourage of dogs, we stopped at the pass near the quarry in the comparative luxury of cool, fresh air. Conditions inside the van, however, were not so luxurious. Three large dogs and two humans take up rather a lot of space, in a van where most of the vacant space was already occupied by equipment. The dogs found themselves a low priority in the allotment of their sleeping quarters. In their search to find a space large enough to spread out, in the balmy night, each moved about restlessly within their own confines. The result was that David, being six feet in height and therefore stretched out on the floor, was walked-over unceremoniously all night. I was at pains to keep them from leaping onto my narrow single bed. Neither of us slept well, and it took almost another week before we found a more satisfactory solution.

Cloud covered the sky the next day, which meant the recording time at the quarry was unlimited. Only the sporadic groups of tourists interrupted progress, and a considerable amount of background recording was added to the previous rushes. It was a good feeling at this location again, although the coolness in the air stole a little from the magical atmosphere of our first visit. The ballet shoes used at the outset of filming in the quarry were now in a diabolical condition. Sliding and turning on the stone surface, no matter how smooth it appeared, played havoc with them. My toes were now more in contact with the marble than the canvas, and in danger of similar annihilation. However, I was prohibited from playing safe with a new pair because of the need for continuity. The style of my dancing requires that a large proportion of the dance is spent on my knees, for which I am obliged to wear protective pads. While David thought the loose baggy trousers, that were my only covering, were an authentic feature and in keeping with the dance, I was becoming shoddily dressed. I was determined that the trousers would soon go the same way as the shoes.

With the video-taping of three dances finished, and one almost complete, we left one range of mountains for another terrain quite different from the Apuanian Alps. At two thousand metres, on the Lukmanier Pass connecting Ticino in Southern Switzerland to

Graubunden in the east, we pulled into a car park and contemplated the panorama that encircled us. While I have crossed many Alpine passes in the last ten years, and although it lacks the height of its neighbours, I consider this particular pass to be the most beautiful. From the south, one ascends quite steeply to its entrance until a broad valley is reached, whereupon the gradient of the road lessens considerably. The valley extends north-west for about eight miles, with the road rising gradually to its highest point overlooking a lake, before steeply descending along the northern side to a small town called Disentis, which is in another valley. The pass is closed between November and April, like most of the other passes. But in early September it abounds with the biggest and most succulent blueberries to be found anywhere.

Besides this major attraction, the valley has a quality not easily found elsewhere. In the lower, southern part, it is like a huge, landscaped garden with sweeping meadows that rise in a uniform and uninterrupted curve until giving way to enormous conifers - which, in turn, submit to lofty, pinnacled heights of over three thousand metres. The low-lying blueberry bushes abound everywhere on the valley slopes. At the time of our visit, these were beginning to show their autumn colours, lending a ruddy tint to an otherwise emerald-green landscape. As though some giant had taken a paintbrush to a vast canvas and, with a sweeping hand, coloured-in entire hillsides. The terrain changes towards the lake and highest point of the pass, as the unsheltered and exposed ground precludes most types of vegetation. Here we are above the tree line, and wild, untamed scenery leads the eye to bare mountains and permanent snow.

I brought David to the pass uncertain whether we could find a location, but feeling that there must be a setting somewhere along its eight mile length, where we might capture the inspiring landscape around us. We found not one, but two locations - two miles apart from one another. There could not have been a starker contrast between them, despite their being found in the same pass and the same mountains, but not at the same time. The first location being found two weeks before the second, during which time the Season's changing colours had brought about a remarkable transformation in the scenery.

The fifth dance was recorded in the upper reaches of the pass, with the haunting adagio from Handel's opera, Berenice, as the music. While still possessing the same improvised quality as when it was added to my repertory, the dance has been inevitably choreographed over the nine years as a result of countless repetitions. On arriving at the car park early in the evening, we took the dogs with us on a reconnaissance along the meandering stream at the bottom of the valley. David, suitably impressed with the scenic backdrop, was already in photographic mood, judging, comparing and imagining the possibilities. It was a great challenge for him in his comparative inexperience, but I had faith in him. I knew of no-one else who would be prepared to meet such a challenge within the scope of our limited facilities. For four nights he had not slept well due to the dogs, but he had not complained, and did not show any frustration with our adventure to date. A quiet, calm and unassuming man, David was a perfectionist down to the last detail within his capabilities, and I respected him for it.

It was a beautiful evening, and the cool, high-altitude air lent an invigorating energy to our steps. Hector dawdled as usual, completely lost in the scents and messages hidden from our meager senses. The two younger dogs, lost not in scents, but in the wonder of the vast freedom before them, were off before I was able to restrain them. They chased each other over the short alpine meadow grass, and down to the stream into where they plunged, shook, then again plunged again. The sun's rays had just left the highest peaks and an expectancy of night seeped into the valley. I prayed we would find the right place to dance and record among this splendour, which never failed to uplift my spirits.

Rushing back towards us, drenched, the dogs looked expectantly for an object in my hand that would be thrown for them to retrieve. But here on the meadow, there were no sticks or pine cones to be seen. No loose object after which they could scamper. I walked towards the stream, where I could be reasonably sure of finding some object for their pleasure. My attention was caught by what seemed, from a distance, a patch of bare earth next to the water, on a perfectly flat stretch of land. "What do you suppose that is," I asked David, who was still juxtaposing angles with distances, trees with mountains.

David shrugged, and I walked straight towards it, hoping that it would be solid and smooth. It was sand, hard-packed sand, and solid and smooth. An area just large enough to hold my dance floor of four by five metres. Around the sand was soft, uneven earth and meadow. I looked up, and then looked around me smiling. "Is this all chance, or is someone trying to tell us something," I called out. David's wry face answered my question. Throughout the full circle of our vision, only one angle to the north would preclude our recording. A barn, large and modern, spoilt what was otherwise a completely natural vista. Even the road was invisible, although some pylons situated higher-up the hillside might present problems. Otherwise the location seemed perfect for 'Berenice',

With our next location found, we returned to the camper van and discussed how and when we would record. The location, with its superb scenery in every direction, warranted our using the full scope of possible camera angles. For this purpose it was estimated that we would need five days of identical weather, so that each 'take' in a particular direction would have the correct angle of sunlight. The calculations were complex, requiring careful study and thought. I suggested that David and I change places for sleeping that night, arguing the dogs would settle better with myself on the floor and him in the bed. He would not entertain the idea, his own argument being that I needed the better night's sleep.

We recorded for three glorious days, between romps with the dogs and blueberry picking, when I was warned politely that the deep purple stain on my fingers would show on the recording. By now, I was beginning to understand how to summon the power of inspiration without the aid of an audience around me. Simply trying to recall how I felt while dancing on the street was not enough, neither was staring at the views and attempting to transfer the beauty and grandeur into my movement.

The key to my understanding was a deep self-interrogation of why I was making this recording, in the type of locations we were using. The realization that everything appeared to be provided, whenever we required it, led me to invoke help. This took the form of a simple moment of quiet contemplation of where I was, what I was doing, and why I was doing it, which brought inner strength and the all-important feeling of conviction before each 'take'. On occasions, I saw Gertrud's face and knew that she had been part of the plan. That my meeting her, and her subsequent visit to La Casetta, were just as important a part in this whole project as was my own dance contribution. Through this understanding I found myself finally in control of my dancing and knew, without any doubt, where it was leading.

During the second night on the pass, I left Puppy and Mossy outside, attached by their leads to the camper van. Hector remained inside on the driver's seat. David slept well and was duly appreciative, so we repeated this arrangement on the following two nights. By the evening of the fourth day, three days of recording were completed with only the hand-held camera shots still remaining. Heavy rain precluded the dogs being left outside that night. I insisted that I sleep on the floor, as I was concerned about David's welfare and considered the dogs to be my responsibility. Hector remained all night on the driver's seat, and Puppy and Mossy, content to be close by me, curled up together in the small space by my head and slept right through the night. And so it was for the remaining duration of our tour. David was unfortunately a little tall for my made-to-measure bed, but adapted his sleeping position accordingly.

Rain prevented our continuing with recording for the next two days. I became concerned that the weather had set-in for a period,

Three Dogs and a Dancer by Stephen Ward

as I was running out of supplies both for dogs and humans. More rain on the sixth day left us with no alternative but to descend from the Alps, and I suggested that we go on to St. Gallen. There I had some good friends who could offer us showers, and perhaps a proper bed for David. My suggestion was met with immediate approval.

David was a little dejected over the lack of progress. When I asked if he had enough recordings to edit into a good dance for 'Berenice,' in case the weather prevented our return to the pass, he was non-committal. I telephoned my friends Jiolia and Daniel on the road to St. Gallen, explaining the situation, and asked if it were possible to stay a few days with then until the weather cleared again. Jiolia answered. "You won't be bringing ten dogs with you, will you," she asked, laughing down the receiver. "No. Only three this time" I replied.

I enjoyed Jiolia's exuberent personality. She was Greek, spoke three languages fluently, and we had something in common - we were both solo dancers. I had met her several years ago while dancing on St. Gallen's pedestrian shopping street. At the end of my performance, she asked if she could perform a dance on my floor, adding that she had some Greek music on a cassette tape and could dance barefoot. On these occasions, when young people - mainly break-dancers - request politely to use the floor, I am always happy to oblige them once I have finished. But when I saw Jiolia dance, it was like a 'breath of fresh air,' and made me feel I was not so isolated in my street dance improvisation. Afterwards she told me that she always improvised the dance in her solo performances but, until then, had never had the opportunity or the desire to do this on the street.

After that first meeting, I spent some time with Jiolia. She had recently divorced from her Swiss husband and, left with a young child, had to take up teaching between solo performances so they could both remain in Switzerland. After a little experimentation in a studio, we attempted a contact improvisation together in St. Gallon's town centre. At the end of our ten minute show, we counted over two hundred Swiss francs in my collection, almost £100.

During dinner one evening with Jiolia and some of her friends, I picked up a record of the music for 'The Mission,' a film that I had seen a short time before. The musical score was composed by an Italian, Ennio Morricone, and had moved me greatly. "Do you think I could listen to this record," I asked. "Oh, it's beautiful music, so inspiring," Jiolia said in her charming way, with slightly-accented, theatrical English. "Do you know it?" I replied I had seen the film, and recalled being moved to tears.

From the moment the music started, I could not re-enter, socially, into the conversation of the evening, so great was the effect the music had on me. When the record-player finally switched itself off, I asked Jiolia if I could get into a studio the next day for half-an-hour, with that same music. By the end of that half-an-hour, I knew I had found a piece of music that was to become an integral part of my street performance. Called 'Gabriel's Oboe,' it has become music that haunts and fills me spiritually with overwhelming joy, and releases this emotion within me whenever I dance to it. It was the music for my next dance in the project, to be recorded at the Rhine Falls, near Schaffhausen in northern Switzerland - a place with a similar setting to that used in the film of 'The Mission' in South America.

After that first encounter with Jiolia, I was always happy to include St. Gallen on my tours, assured of a warm welcome, good cooking, and some animated conversation with this eccentric, profound, Greek lady – who was a few years younger than myself. She and her daughter, Lara, grew enormously fond of Hector and he seemed to be the highlight of my visit. They would take him for long walks in the woods near her home at Herisau, a short distance to the west of St. Gallen. An incident arose one day which emphasized Hector's natural aversion to water, including rain puddles, which unfortunately he can no longer avoid due to his failing eye-sight.

It was a fine late-autumn afternoon, and we were on the footpath skirting a small lake with several other people also on the path. A strong breeze from the lake had gathered the leaves and blown them onto the surface of the water, where they were then trapped by the confines of the bank. Hector thought this was solid land, for he jumped from the path onto the leaves, and promptly disappeared beneath them. Jiolia let escape an uncontrollable peal of laughter, but I knew the shock Hector would feel when he surfaced eventually through the leaves. When he did surface, Hector thought he could clamber on the leaves but, when he did not succeed, he made for the bank. Unfortunately for Hector, the place he found to exit from this nightmare was beneath a small bridge where the bank receded sharply. I lay on my stomache and peered under the bridge at a pitiful, shivering dog, clinging to a tiny piece of land inches below the wooden construction, the only respite that he could find. There was absolutely no way that I, from the bridge, could entice him to leave his haven and return into the water, so that he might be pulled out to safety.

A group of walkers stopped, curious to observe the outcome of this dilemma. Their eyes widened as I removed my shoes, socks and trousers, and then entered the water myself in order to reach Hector. In the struggle that ensued, I also lost my footing, going up to my neck in the water and soaking the remaining clothes on my body. Now becoming single-minded and determined, I tore Hector from the piece of land under the bridge, and thrust him into the water – following him to ensure he would not return. Hector swam to a bank beyond the bridge, where he was helped out by a couple of young men who had removed their jackets and rolled-up their sleeves. As soon as he was out of the water and on dry land again, the crowd near him dispersed like feathers from a hole in a beaten pillow, as Hector shook the excess water from his fur.

Cold and starting to shiver, I pulled the trousers back onto my wet legs, removed my soaking shirt and jumper, and put my jacket onto a naked and wet torso. Lara went to comfort Hector. Jiolia, with wide eyes, and a tense mouth that was doing everything in its power to prevent the escape of hysterical laughter, came to comfort myself. But when I saw her comical expression it set off a 'time bomb,' and we both laughed uncontrollably together. We often now recall this incident when we meet and Hector, oblivious to the subject of our conversation, will receive a pat on the head and a biscuit from Jiolia's larder.

Jiolia and Daniel, a brilliant musician with his own modern jazz group, had formed a lasting relationship after their collaboration on a joint jazz music-dance project. He stepped into the role of father to Jiolia's teenage daughter, and they have all remained together since. In October, 1994, after our recording was finished, Jiolia and Daniel spent a week with myself at La Casetta to help with winemaking. "What will you do with five hundred litres of wine?" Daniel asked, when the harvest was in the barrels, and bubbling and fermenting, to form a delectable organic wine. "Will you sell it?" "Why no, you clot," was my friendly response, "I'll drink it, every last drop." And this I have done each year since, once the wine has been left for six months to clear and mature.

Once he was seated in a comfortable chair, a glass of wine in his hand, and hair drying after a long, hot shower, I could tell that David was beginning to feel human again. I began to see the experience in completing the project was challenging him in more than one aspect. At the same time, however, I felt it also important for David to undergo these hardships to which he was unaccustomed. By recalling them, they would help him to recreate the true essence of what we were attempting to do in this project, in the editing studio.

Jiolia recounted her version of the story of my last visit to St Gallen, with eight puppies in tow. She was a wonderfully animated performer, and soon had David laughing uproariously as he imagined that week with my ten dogs in the same camper van that was presently our home. The weather, such an important element in determining our actions, remained cool, cloudy and changeable over the following days. I danced in St. Gallen, half expecting the owner of one of the pups I had given away five months earlier, to approach and speak to me. It didn't happen, and I could not help but wonder how they were all faring.

After four days of comparative inactivity, David and I were keen to return to the project, knowing that time was slipping by and he had to return soon to London. With two dances still to begin, and two to complete, the pressure was on - exacerbated by the continuing poor weather. I told David earlier about the Rhine Falls and my hope that it would provide a suitable location for 'Gabriel's Oboe', as one of the two dances still to be recorded. At this place the waters of the Rhine River cascade over a rift in the river bed, to crash forty metres below, before starting their journey to the North Sea five hundred miles away. From my previous visit, I recalled the area was already a tourist spot with hotels, restaurants and viewing platforms for Europe's most dramatic waterfall.

The two hour drive from St. Gallen to the Falls was done in silence. Before our departure, Jiolia informed us that the weather forecast for Switzerland was poor for the coming days. The thought crossed my mind that perhaps we should return to Italy for our last two locations. Certainly it did not seem we would find the impeccable weather again, needed to complete 'Berenice,' that we enjoyed during our earlier three days in the Alps. The misty rain continued all day and finally stopped when we arrived at the Falls. We parked the camper van in a car park and stepped into cold, wet air that was alive with drops of water falling from the leaves. Heard above everything else was the distant roar of the Falls, about half-a-mile away. It was late on Sunday evening. Dusk was falling rapidly in the poor light, and all the visitors had gone, leaving the place with an eerie, empty feel.

Dramatic though the Falls were, now floodlit with the advancing evening, I began to lose heart that this would be the location for 'Gabriel's Oboe'. Apart from numerous tourist facilities, directly behind the Falls was an unsightly metal bridge that carried the railway across the river. The only possible place to put the dance floor, where the view of the Falls would not be obstructed, was on the main access road facing the Falls at three hundred metres distance. Although the road was closed to vehicles, it would undoubtedly teem with tourists. For the recording, it would be necessary therefore to stop the flow of pedestrian traffic in both directions, a prospect that seemed very unlikely - given the presence of a large tourist centre on the other side of the road.

Even if permission were granted to use the location for a period of four hours on the following day, it seemed ludicrous to record a dance about the celebration of nature and its wonders, when there was such a human intrusion all around. Also, in the dull and cloudy conditions, the Falls would lose their dramatic quality. The technical problems seemed insurmountable. In the interim, David returned from his own survey, and drew a different conclusion. "Well, for a start," he said, "we would not find a better natural phenomenon than this. I think the place you identified is the best location, and maybe the only one. The distance to the Falls, with my lenses, won't be a problem if I can set up the camera as far away from you as possible. The restaurant though, by the road, doesn't allow me too much space. I can probably bring the Falls to just behind your head, or take them away so they are barely seen. The river and its single focal point doesn't give much scope on camera angles. So, from the right or left of you, or straight in front of you, my work would be fairly straightforward with cloudy lighting."

"Of course," he looked at me, "if it were sunny, very much would depend on the sun's direction. If it were behind you, we couldn't do it. Personally, I think the viewing platforms, flags and bridge would barely be seen. Anyone engrossed in watching the video would not notice them at all. The ferry trips to that massive rock in the centre of the falls, would need to be avoided, but I don't foresee a problem providing they are not running continuously. I've been right round to the base of the Falls, and there are some excellent viewpoints from where I can get some recordings. I think you should go as early as possible tomorrow morning and ask permission to close the road, if its not raining, while we are recording each 'take.' If it's cloudy in the morning we'll wait until the afternoon in case, by some chance, the sun comes out. I'll do some close-up footage of the Falls by myself in the morning. In short, Stephen," his mouth curled up at the edges, feigning a smile, "we'll go for it." There was nothing feigned about my expression as David finished. My heart was pounding. I was already praying, deep within, for another remarkable miracle,

Early at dawn on Monday morning, I left David and slipped quietly from the camper van to walk to the Falls with my dogs. It was dull and misty, and I reached the Falls and looked into the river, I saw nothing but greyness. Only the closest objects were visible - trees, the river, the road - and only the sound of the Falls penetrated the mist.

In low spirits, I slowly realised I must simply accept what was given with gratitude, we had already received so much in the way of ideal conditions. We had no control over the lighting, and it had been my idea to record the video out-of-doors. An ambitious decision, considering my financial inability to control anything. But my own time was unlimited. Provided that I could dance and therefore earn some money, I could stay here indefinitely until the perfect opportunity arose. However, David did not live in my world, and even though he had had to adapt to it for a period of time, he could not claim it for his own. I walked along the river, deep in my thoughts. Was I really being honest in making this video, or was it just a hair-brained scheme to justify my dancing on the street to the world? Perhaps even an excuse to make more money, so that I may live in a world of comfort and security like everyone else. In short, was I a contradiction of myself and all my beliefs?

Puppy brought me a stick to throw, and she and Mossy scampered after it. I looked in the direction of the sound coming from the Falls, and stopped. "God willing, we will film 'Gabriel's Oboe' here today," I shouted, tears coming to my eyes. Puppy returned with the stick, closely followed by Mossy, and brought me back to reality. I looked around to see if anyone had heard my cry. Hector had heard and, in his instinctive way, sat down in front of me and lifted his paw for me to take, looking into my face. I laughed, taking it in one hand while blowing my nose with the other. Puppy waited in anticipation of another retrieval.

How I loved my dogs. I could learn so much about my attitude to situations, circumstances and people, from observing them. We continued along the river. The roar of the Falls now overpowered everything, and seemed almost on top of me before they appeared eventually through the mist. Thinking of the falls in South America captured so dramatically in 'The Mission,' brought home to me the wonderful advances made by man in controlling his environment. So much inventiveness and creative communication, quite apart from all the cultural exchanges between different lands and nations. How was it that it all seemed to be going wrong, in the final years of the most extraordinarily inspiring century in the history of man.

When I returned to the camper van, I found David dressed, and the interior in functional order with breakfast underway. On my walk back, the slowly increasing warmth had begun to dispel the mist. The sky was now a uniform grey and the air humid. My mood had turned to one of nonchalance. Shortly after nine o'clock, I clenched my fists, smiled to myself, practiced a little German, and then entered the restaurant complex that was closed for service. I asked a woman washing the floor if I might speak to the proprietor. She disappeared and after a short time, during which I suppressed my feelings of nervousness, an immaculate man appeared and enquired "Ja, bitte schön." "Good morning", I began politely, "I am a professional dancer from England and I, with a colleague who is the director, are making a dance video recording."

His expression showed interest, and I felt that I had made a good start. Thus encouraged, I explained that I wanted his permission to put a dance floor in front of the restaurant, to play music a number of times over a period of four hours, and close the road for three minutes at various times during those four hours for each 'take.' I finished by saying that, unless the sun appeared, we wanted to start filming that afternoon at 1.00pm. No small request I thought, as I ended. However, he replied surprisingly "There is little hope of the sun shining today, Mein Herr. But yes, I think we can accommodate your wishes providing it does not detract from my business. First though, I must get agreement from my wife who is in charge of the shop, and also responsible for area in front of the restaurant that you want to use."

Together, we descended from the first floor restaurant terrace to street level and found his wife, an amicable lady. She listened to her husband's explanation of our request and, after reflecting, gave her agreement and continued "I'll give you a key to this garage where you can store your equipment. There are also extendable barriers in the garage, for when you need to stop the people from walking by. I hope it doesn't rain for you, but it certainly looks as though it might. Good luck."

Uplifted by my reception, I returned to the camper van through people who were now gathering by the riverside and the Falls. Although the Falls were not lit by bright sunlight, they were at least visible - all traces of mist having disappeared. David accepted my good news unemotionally. He got ready to leave with his camera, planning to capture the drama of the Falls in close-ups that would be used later as background material. In turn, I prepared to leave and take the dance floor and my costume to the garage. In so doing, I looked at the dull sky, distant Falls and regular departure of boats carrying the tourists. There were now thousands of people passing by where I would shortly be dancing. At least, I thought, I can be assured of a large audience, whether I liked it or not.

Unable to relax, I returned to the camper van and my dogs, intending to take them out for a walk. An activity that never fails in helping me put things into perspective. People who are not dog-owners, often remark how inconvenient it must be to have to exercise an animal twice a day, in all weathers. However, I believe that most dedicated dog-owners would agree that these walks are among the most rewarding of their daily routines. They are times for personal reflection, inter-active play and bonding, and for observation and learning. Had I had any children in my life, these would be times when they learnt about animals and were taught the need for tolerance and co-existence. In an age of 'farm factories,' where livestock are produced and raised remotely for our consumption, it is all too easy to 'switch off' to unnecessary suffering. We need to remind ourselves that all the animal species have rights, and that we have a moral obligation to uphold these rights, speaking out clearly and conscientiously whenever instances of unnecessary animal suffering arise.

A mile along the river, I heard the midday bells of a church in the far distance. As if in response, a shaft of bright sunlight appeared on the water. As I walked on, the clouds started to disappear and the warm sunshine caused me to stop and return to the Falls at a quicker pace. My heart quickened as everything around me reflected vibrant colour – the sun was still shining, and continued to shine. On reaching the agreed location, now busier than ever, I prayed that David had reacted with the same urgency and would join me soon. Waiting in anticipation, I changed into my costume and warmed-up my body by exercising vigorously. The Falls were transformed into myriad reflections of rainbow colours. The sun would be on the side of my face, the conditions perfect for recording. "Come on, David," I said to myself, "where are you. This is the opportunity, and we may not get another one."

I tried to draw him to the location with all my will-power. Tourists were flocking to the riverside drawn by the unexpected sunlight. But then, slowly and inevitably, the clouds returned and the sky became overcast again. At 1.00pm it began to rain and my despair returned. David approached half an hour later, soaked, his coat having been removed to protect the camera. I greeted him in silence and we returned to the camper van for shelter.

As I prepared a meagre lunch, David hazarded a friendly word which I ignored. I was in a childish mood, recalling my emotion of the morning. But then the rain suddenly stopped falling, and Puppy moved to the patch of sunlight that now shone through the windscreen onto the floor. I looked at David eating his pasta and went outside. He followed. A strong wind was blowing and an enormous blue hole had appeared in the grey sky above us. Clouds were being pushed aside and I shouted to David, "come on, this is it." I ran down the hill to the river. "Do you think the angle of the sun will be alright?" I called to him as he brought up the rear, clutching his camera, tripod and all accessories. "It looks perfect to me," David replied breathlessly. "It had better hang around for a bit this time," I said, my heart singing inside.

Three Dogs and a Dancer by Stephen Ward

The sun 'hung around' from 2.15pm until 5.00pm on that Monday afternoon, whereupon it was swallowed-up by the trees behind the restaurant. Shortly afterwards, the clouds returned and rain started again, and did not let-up until six days later – another miracle high up in the Alps. But at our location in front of the restaurant, I called to the proprietress in the shop that we would start recording immediately. "Did you order this sunshine beforehand?" she questioned, feigning a querulous manner. I smiled, unable to reply, already in another world.

David and I worked hard that afternoon, but the now perfect conditions brought other problems. The actions of laying the dance floor and setting-up a large video camera on its tripod, almost immediately attracted a large crowd of people. They gathered around us and only begrudgingly moved out of vision, having to be almost pushed while we re-positioned the barriers. Those wishing to cross between the floor and restaurant to get to the Falls, were obliged to pass in front of David as he prepared the camera for the first 'take.' However, a shout from myself induced curiosity and stillness for the three minutes that we needed during my dance.

David was unprepared for the rush in setting-up our equipment, and perhaps a little intimidated by the gathering crowd. He was taking time to organize himself and the camera, and there was an expectanct hush around us. I glanced behind me at the Falls and involuntarily took a huge breath. "It's unbelievable," I said to myself in a low and inaudible voice. I saw the Falls for the first time, as I had imagined it since arriving the night before. What was unbelievable was not the sensation of seeing the Falls and its spray in the bright sunlight, but knowing that we were about to capture this and my dance on video. All made possible by the transformation of a natural phenomena into a thing of awe and beauty, simply through the action of sunlight.

That afternoon, we completed twelve 'takes' with the camera either being hand-held or on the tripod. One 'take' included a passing cyclist who, with a warning from his bell, rode straight through our location oblivious to our efforts. Two other 'takes' included impatient people who insisted on their right to pass between the camera and myself while recording, despite attempts by others to restrain them. Another 'take' briefly showed a tourist boat mid-river, in the background. But these were not serious problems as plenty of material had been recorded, much of which would anyway be discarded during the editing. There were many stops and starts that afternoon, with a largely interested and sympathetic crowd around us, and by the end of it I felt my energy and intensity wilting. However, the sun remained with us and smiled on our efforts until it could do so no longer

When I returned the garage keys to the shop, thanking the lady for her help and cooperation, she said our activity had stimulated conversation on an otherwise monotonous afternoon. In my exhuberance I could not help but compare my life with her own, and perhaps millions like her. Undoubtedly she had taken some risks in her life, we all do. But how safe and controlled are our risks, and what stimulates them? What reasons lie behind them, and what profits are gained from them. The 'what if' syndrome is familiar in our society. What if it goes wrong, what if you lose everything, what if you have an accident. How strange, I think. The only time I had an accident in my life was all those years ago, when I was trying to live in an environment where 'what ifs' were taken to extremes. I paid a price for searching out a dance company that would offer me a good salary and security. It had all gone quickly wrong, and for the next two years I believed I had lost everything and had my accident. It marked the beginning in my life of taking risks, and closing my ears to 'what ifs' latent within my own head. However, also it set me on the road to a different life-philosophy, which now produces overwhelming feelings and sensations.

It began to rain heavily as I packed away the floor, and the mist came down over the distant Falls. Another different and equally magical effect, I thought. But a bubbling laughter welled up from deep inside of me, sweeping up my spine and through the pores of my skin to create 'goose bumps,' until I thrust my head back and spoke to the heavens. "Thank you. Thank you for my life. Thank you for the dance that teaches me about life. And thank you for the opportunities to express my gratitude for this beautiful natural world through my dance."

David had been correct when he said earlier that that the bridges, restaurants and viewing platforms would not be noticeable against the Falls, with my dance in the foreground. I reflected on how this and the other locations were chosen. Had I been a famous dancer and personality to whom impresarios and directors were attracted, effects would have been artificially created, and locations found and already transformed. The fact that none of these facilities were available, and no pre-conceived idea had been formulated beforehand by either David or myself on how we were to realise our intentions, demonstrated a huge leap of faith. I believed in my dance as a gift that could help and heal and, as such, it had a rightful place among nature's wonders. Everything necessary for recording "A Dancer's Journey' was therefore reliant on nature, and on its colours, its drama, and its lighting. There were so many factors not considered before embarking on the project, that only now did I realize that help seemed always on-hand to sort everything out. Not from lighting technicians or stage crew, but from natural sources both outside and within me.

The discovery of the location for my seventh and final dance, finally broke my doubts and signified there was an over-riding purpose in making the video.

Gournod's musical interpretation of the Latin prayer, Ave Maria, based on an original theme by Bach, needs no introduction. I added it to my repertoire of street-dance music three years earlier. Initially, I was warned that performing to Ave Maria in the street might offend some Catholics. While I am not a Catholic, nor indeed a Christian, I feel I have found a faith through my dancing that goes far beyond the limitations that man has set in his own beliefs. This faith is leading me higher up the ladder, day by day. I do not wish to expound on my faith, but believe it is a treasure that draws me gradually towards itself and, in my desire to know its wisdom, I must relate to it idiosyncratically since I have no terminology to describe it.

I had no clear idea of the setting I wanted for 'Ave Maria', knowing only that like 'Amazing Grace', 'Gabriel's Oboe' and 'Berenice', the location had to be inspiring and out-of-the-ordinary. Perhaps, because of its significance, more out-of-the-ordinary than anything else.

The all-important weather threatened any hopes by David and myself, that we would discover 'the perfect location' for the last dance. For six days, amid gales, torrential rain and freezing cold, neither we nor the dogs dared leave the shelter of the camper van for longer than was absolutely necessary. Once more, a challenging time for both of us. With only a few days left before David's departure, and also bearing in mind our need to complete the two previous, incomplete dances, I was struggling to hang-on to the faith that had so amply rewarded me earlier. But despite this we remained in good spirits, maintained a positive outlook on our project, and so avoided friction and temperament during this additional long confinement.

From the Rhine Falls, we travelled on to Lucerne, a place with which I was very familiar. I had previously lived and worked there following my return from Scotland, initially in professional dance and theatre, and later had passed through the town many times on my street-dancing tours. I had friends there whom it was always a pleasure to see again, and special places that only someone who had lived there could know. However, on this occasion I had little desire to renew old acquaintances, or show David places discovered in my youth. We arrived at a car park by the lake and, for five days, looked at the lake and mist through a rain-spattered windscreen. The howling gales unnerved us, invisibly shaking the van on its suspension.

On the sixth day, I suggested we drive through the twelve mile Gotthard road tunnel that connects the German-speaking region in the north with the Italian-speaking region in the south. Many times previously, I had left bad weather in the northern region only to find bright sunshine and blue skies when I emerged in the southern region, so successful were the Alps in creating an effective weather barrier. We stopped again in a car park, this time south of the Alps and near where the road to the Lukmanier pass leaves the motorway between Northern Europe and Southern Europe, wending its way up to that beautiful, natural garden.

But on this occasion, the storms on the south side of the Alps were even worse. Disillusioned, David and I sat and thought. The road to 'Berenice' beckoned us to follow it. We could ignore its enticing call and leave the recording of that dance incomplete. Or we could return to Tuscany, and hope the weather would be kinder there - particularly, I thought, for the 'water shots' for 'Syrinx'. I gave an involuntary shudder, imagining what our idyllic summer stream in the gorge might have now become. Perhaps we could simply film 'Ave Maria' on my terrace and cut out 'poor Charley.' Alternatively, we might try to do it at the marble quarry, recording in cloud from the opposite direction so that the lighting balance was not upset.

I was clutching at straws and I knew it. But, we had a decision to make, and we could not sit indefinitely in the rain trying to make it. However, I was unable to come up with a solution and therefore gave David the onus of making a decision. I said that wherever he asked me to drive would be all right with myself, and I would not question his decision, merely asking that he make the positive step forward that I felt unable to take. I knew that David's choice lay between moving on, which would preclude completing the recording of 'Berenice', or making the ascent back to the Lukmanier Pass, where we were unlikely to find anything resembling the conditions we enjoyed two weeks earlier. It seemed that our world had changed from Summer directly into Winter, without pausing for Autumn's moderating influence.

He thought long and hard, and in silence. I respected the silence and did not interrupt it. Afterwards, during my own contemplative thought, I wondered what factors weighed most in his mind, and how he reached his decision to go back up the pass. "What have we got to lose. Two hours will see us there and we might have another miracle. If not, we'll have to leave 'Berenice' and drive on. You told me there's a magnificent piazza in front of the cathedral in Milan. It's on our way and, if it's stopped raining by then, we can record 'Ave Maria' there. It makes no great difference if there's no sun. I know it's not a natural setting but perhaps, at this late stage, we have no other alternatives. What do you say." "I'm with you all the way, David," was my reply.

And so we were once more on our slow journey back up the pass. I knew David was sincere in his desire to come up with a best solution, at a stage where panic could easily have overridden rationality. At one thousand and five hundred metres, the rain and mist succumbed to heavy snow, and a 'whiteout' where nothing was visible beyond ten yards. I successfully blocked-out any negative thoughts and maintained a kind of 'mental void' that had earlier helped me to cope with David's decision. Reaching the point that marked the entrance of the valley leading to the pass, snow lay on the road making our progress treacherous. The wind had abated, and there was an eerie stillness as we edged our way slowly upwards.

I broke our silence. Softly I said "do you think, David, that there's much point in going on? If there's snow on the ground here, it may be quite thick a little higher up. Certainly 'Berenice' is out for keeps, and we might get stuck somewhere. My tyres, too, are not in such a brilliant condition. I can feel the back ones struggling to keep a grip on this incline." "I know. You're right, and I'm sorry, Stephen," David said, as if finally beaten into acknowledging defeat. "Pull into the next lay-by and we'll make a cup of coffee."

I let the dogs out into the snow and thick mist. There was little likelihood of fast cars, or indeed any cars, on the road beside us. Pulling on a coat and hat, I went outside the camper van myself. "How is it," I said to myself, "that we have come so far, so wonderfully, so inspiringly, only to reach a stalemate at perhaps the most important moment of these last six weeks? It must be," I continued to myself, resigned to accepting the gifts we had received to date, without yet holding in my hand the final pearl, "that we were not meant to complete 'Berenice' or record Gournod's beautiful music to a holy prayer. Maybe we'll just have to be content with Man's splendour." I bowed my bead and closed my eyes. "Father, its so hard to accept second best when you've given us, all along, of Your very best."

"Coffee's ready," David called half-heartedly, breaking into my thoughts. A wind was getting up, with the mist and snow swirling in playful scurries as far as I could see. I imagined how strange and different this beautiful valley would be when covered by thick snow.

Being closed to passage for six months of the year, it would hold onto its wonderful secret. I also thought it strange that police had not closed the road to traffic, in these extreme late-summer conditions. It had probably developed quite suddenly, although there was quite a lot of snow even at our lower level.

I went into the camper van and put the gas heater on. This was the first time I had used it since those cold, wet days in Bavaria when I struggled with two dogs and eight puppies who were close to driving me out of my mind. I had seen virtually no Spring, returning home to Tuscany in early May to the intense, dry heat that remained for four months. Then two weeks of mixed weather had brought us here, to severe Winter conditions. It was certainly cold, and the wind was really beginning to blow. The thought of dancing outside made me cringe.

"I think we should go back down as soon as coffee's over, David. I've just remembered that there's no antifreeze in the radiator, and I'll have to empty it if we get stuck. "Uh-huh," from David, then a pause. "You know, it's not a dead loss if we do 'Ave Maria' in Milan. It could be good to show the fruit of all else that we have, has its roots in such places. That's where it all started, isn't it, and continues for that matter. I'll work something out for 'Berenice', it'll be alright."

His words comforted me as I sipped my coffee, holding the cup in my palms, appreciative of its warmth. The windows in the camper van were steamed-up with condensation - nothing new over the last days. The wind blew more strongly. How fortunate were the dogs, who could simply lie down, close their eyes, and 'switch off' to everything.

Putting down my empty cup, and leaving David to secure various articles in places where they would not move, I made my way to the front of the camper van to start the engine. I took a cloth and wiped the windows, and switched on the windscreen wipers to clear the gathered snow. In the distance I saw a vague outline of white against grey. In the next instant I was outside, the dogs following in my wake as I unwittingly left the door open. A strong wind was blowing the mist down the valley. I rushed back to the camper van and collected my sunglasses, so intense was the light on the virgin white snow. David had also now left the camper van and was by my side.

The mist was gradually thinning, and blue was beginning to enter into the white and grey world. As if in the blinking of an eye, we were transported to a different planet. The mist simply swirled away, revealing not grey clouds, but a blinding blue sky over the pure white mountain landscape. I looked blankly at David, who returned my look. Puppy and Mossy chased each other madly in the snow, into which they would occasionally disappear from sight. Their tossing heads, bobbing up and down, made me laugh as I took in this metamorphosis - which made the hairs on the back of my neck rise.

"Come on, let's go, we've got to find a location somewhere," David said as he nudged me. Snow, under the strong sun, was already melting on the road. His watch said 2.30pm. I caught myself. Taking off my sunglasses and shielding my eyes from the intense glare, I said "David, how am I going to be able to dance with such strong light blinding me." "I don't know," he replied, calling the dogs to come back, "but you'll find a way, you'll see. We haven't got much time. Far less than we had at the Rhine Falls." As we drove onwards through the sunlit white valley, with blue skies above, I thought of secrets and their revelations. It seemed our world had become so small, and communications so instant, that amazing secrets which hitherto had been revealed to only a few, were now being sold to the masses. As a result, awe and respect disappeared as man sought to profit from his knowledge. Sometimes I wonder whether it would not be better for nature to hold on to its secrets.

Within minutes of the sun re-appearing, the road was clear of snow and I drove quickly to the top of the pass. As we passed the location used for 'Berenice,' I momentarily looked down to the place where the dance floor had been near the river. I did not recognize the place – as though it had been in a different world, at another time. We were now in a brand new world, saying new things, speaking new truths. "David, will you switch the heater off. I've forgotten I'd left it on and it's getting hot in here." The lake at the top of the pass, with thick snow down to its edge, had been transformed into a sparkling sapphire, set in white silver. The pylons, which prevented our recording there previously, had disappeared and merged into the white background. "What about here," said David. "Just pull up in that car park for a moment."

The car park had already been cleared of the snow, piled high at its edges, and contained a dozen cars of clients at the adjoining mountain hospice and restaurant. This was the highest point of the pass, commanding a view over the lake a hundred metres away, and thirty metres below us. Beyond and all around was a white wall of snow, reaching up towards an azure sky. Higher up, winds were blowing plumes of snow off mountain peaks and into the air - make-believe clouds. But down at our level, there was no wind at all, only hot sunshine and the sound of running water.

"At this rate, it looks like all the snow down here will be gone in a couple of hours," I shouted, as I ran to the hotel to ask permission for our recording. On returning, I found an empty coach parked at the place we intended for dance floor, where it awaited the return of its passengers from the restaurant. "You'd better ask him nicely," David whispered as I passed him, wide-eyed and expressionless.

Turning on a little of my theatrical charm, I asked in best German whether it would be possible for him to choose another place, as we were about to record a dance in the car park with this magnificent back-drop.

With an obliging smile, he started the engine without hesitation, and re-positioned the coach out of sight behind the building. I saw him enter the hospice, no doubt to alert his passengers where the coach was now situated and make them also aware of our activities. In due course, people gradually filtered from the restaurant in small groups to watch our work. Laying the dance floor on tarmac now covered with a film of melted snow, I battled to keep the upper surface of the floor dry. The smallest quantity of water could make it treacherous. Ten years of developing my dance had taught me to revere the marriage between the soles of my ballet shoes and the surface of the floor. I knew how far that relationship would allow me to abandon myself to dance, and still provide the essential safety margin. The slightest variation upsets the marriage, causing me to dance with less abandonment in the new margins, detracting from the intensity of my performance.

Strong, hot sunlight gives the surface of the floor a sticky feel. Very humid air creates a film of condensation, making it rather like an ice rink. When it has rained and my floor become wet, it is often impossible to dry it for the rest of the day, to the degree necessary. On a dry day following a wet one, I can often be seen on my hands and knees, in a somewhat undignified manner, drying the floor before my next performance. Sometimes I have been caught out in the middle of a dance by a sudden shower. Feeling unable to cut my dance short, I have continued on the wet floor until the end of the music, only to pay the cost in pulled back-muscles and leg-muscles. When conditions though are perfect for dancing, I discover the wonderful partnership between mind, body and floor, that gives me the sensation of flying, free as a bird.

With everything ready, and innumerable towels to cope with any seepage of melted snow onto my vinyl island, I put on a new pair of bone-dry ballet shoes, took off my sunglasses, and tried to acclimatise my sight to the light. "It's impossible, David. I can't open my eyes. Oh for a pair of polarizing contact lenses." Of course, I thought, the contact lenses I used in place of glasses since sixteen years of age, increased the glare. "I must take them out," I said to myself. I looked around me, took in the inspiration from the scenery I saw, and then forsook it as I removed my lenses. But the glare was still intense, painful and limiting. "Let's do one 'take' and see how it goes. You might find that you simply forget about the light?" How was it that David in his simple, matter-of-fact way, seemed to overcome all obstacles. We did a 'take,' and I forgot about the light.

But it was not a good 'take', as I was confused by my inability to focus clearly on the objects around me. David's camera angle was also incorrect. I put the lenses back into my eyes and covered my face until we were ready to film again, meditating on how to overcome the light intensity. Like everything else, it worked. During the afternoon, I discovered how to modify my movements so as to avoid looking directly at bright light, focusing instead on darker objects, such as cars, the hotel and lake - rather than the snow, sky and sun.

I considered our final dance to be a gift we had not anticipated, which had been meticulously prepared for us over six days of atrocious weather. It was also a gift that was ours for two hours only. What we had already learnt from experience was expertly put into practice, as one successful 'take' now followed another. Then a single cloud appeared in the west and, swallowing-up the sun, drew it ensnared behind the mountains, with others appearing as if from nowhere. David took advantage of the remaining pockets of sunlight, still high on mountains, to gain extra material for editing purposes. I retired to the camper van to pour out my heart, yet again. As I looked over the lake, the colour was starting to creep back into the landscape where snow had disappeared. Blueberry bushes returned their warm glow for the final hours before darkness arrived. I prayed that what was hidden secretly in David's camera was the visible proof of what we had just experienced. All our other locations, fabulous though each of them were, were not the 'one-off' that this location represented. They could be used individually again and again, whenever the sunlight prevailed. How, I pondered, could this final location ever be re-created, even with an endless time to wait.

"It's really gone very chilly outside again now," David said, as he returned to the van and set up the monitor to watch what he had recorded. I laughed, clapped him on the back, and left to pack-up the wet dance floor. When I returned, he proudly showed me the results of our work on the monitor. The proof, the evidence, was there for all to see. Was it a miracle, or just a co-incidence? But having entered into my 'Journey of a Dancer,' who can still remain either unmoved, unconvinced, or unsure.

There were ends to tie-up during the remaining three days of David's availability. We travelled to Milan that night, and the following morning we recorded 'Ave Maria' again in the piazza in front of the magnificent 'Duomo'. It was cloudy but not raining. David's concept was that my final dance would begin at the cathedral on the video, as a tribute to God, and then transition to the majesty of the mountains – God's covenant to man.

The next day we travelled on again, and returned to the location for 'Syrinx.' We found the water level had risen by a metre in the stream, and could no longer be described as such due to its now turbulent and frenzied movement. The Summer was definitely a memory. The gorge too was transformed, as was the third place where its narrow rocky confines gave way to a spreading, tree-filled valley and wide riverbed. Nevertheless, of the three places, only the last one gave any possibility of obtaining further recording material. I prepared myself for a 'take' where I would emerge from the freezing and fast-flowing waters of the streams.

David decided that the only camera angle he would use was one from mid-stream, where he had to perch his camera and tripod precariously in half a metre of rushing water. I wasn't able to believe that he was prepared to do this, and to risk losing a precious and possibly, for him, irreplaceable video camera until he was on his way to set up.

I braced myself and entered the water, barefoot and with only my green trouser costume covering me, then made my way to the centre of the stream. Hector suffers from acute hydrophobia and, while I have no fear of water, I do have an aversion to cold – and this water was cold, very cold. Within moments of entering the water, my feet were in pain from the temperature, and the situation was made worse by sharp and uneven stones on the bed of the stream. "Are you ready, David? I'm nearly there. I don't envisage staying more than about five minutes in this water, so you really had better be ready," I shouted above the sound of the water, now inches from my face, my numb hands steadying myself.

"I'm ready," his calm voice reached my ears, as though he were ready to go to sleep. I felt a slight surge of irritation rise in me at his serenity, as he stood there behind his camera, knee deep in water. I braced myself to go under the surface. "Here we go then, for better or for worse. Count quickly to three, once I've disappeared." It seemed an age as I counted, and the cold seeped into my bones, and I wondered how long I could keep this up. I

Three Dogs and a Dancer by Stephen Ward

emerged at last from the water. "Did you get it? You'd better have, or I'll kill you. Once more? OK! Same again."

Total immersion once more. My teeth started to chatter, and I surmised how pleasant it might be for my tormentor to lose his balance and experience the freezing temperatures of the water himself. These uncharitable fantasies helped me through the next six 'takes,' until I begged David to let me leave the water and seek warmth and comfort. It took two and a half hours to stop myself shivering once I had reached the camper van. Warm clothes were piled on my complaining body, all the heating was switched-on, and hot tea was poured down my throat. But the results of these efforts were only gradual, and David expressed his remorse when he saw the state to which I had been reduced. "Certainly was cold, the water. I think we've got it though." I was almost speechless, but managed "You'd better have. "I'm not doing it again, never."

Twelve hours before I took David to Pisa railway station, from where he would start his journey back to London, we sat in La Casetta and watched the highlights of six weeks of recording. Earlier in the day, we had travelled to Lucca to do some final 'takes' in Piazza San Michele, only to find every part of the square occupied by market stalls. It was Lucca's September market. Nevertheless, we found a vacant place but were promptly moved on by police as an obstruction - the only time this has happened in over eight years of dancing in this square.

In the cosiness of my house we relived the adventures and creativity, our moods and feelings, which were rich beyond measure for myself. After saying goodbye to David, I returned to my little terrace, underneath a pergola of grape vines, and watched the sunlight filtering through leaves onto the swollen fruit, hanging low. I reflected on the influence of that same light while David and I were recording our video project. Everything had appeared in the light and, by doing so, became visible to our eyes. Within myself, for me to begin to see with my inner eye, it had been necessary for the light to penetrate to my innermost being. It had burnt, it had stung. No doubt it will continue to burn and sting while it moulds my being into a different sort of dancer, where films, books, and even music, have no place.

I dream of a new 'dancers' journey.

Three Dogs and a Dancer by Stephen Ward

Chapter 16

A Letter, Dear Reader

April 1995

Dear Reader,

I thought that I would write you this letter, as there is a lot to tell you since I completed the video project. The book is almost complete too, and it's gone a bit deep for me. Sometimes, when I read what I have written, I wonder at my motivation, but it has been great fun doing it. It has made me think about myself, and as a result I have watched much less television in the process. Suddenly I find that I have more time to do things that I have been meaning to do for ages. I can really recommend that everyone writes a book, just think of a title and then go for it.

By now you will have realised that I am besotted with my dogs, and I must tell you about old Hector. I went through a terrible time after he was shot, and felt very guilty that I had neglected him. After the shooting, poor Hector had an awful time getting used to life without the use of his eyes. I could not help but feel for him, and it brought home to me what it must be like to lose one's sight. Or lose anything for that matter, one's hearing, voice, arm or leg. How terrible it must be to be handicapped.

I met someone the other day, who was introduced to me by two friends three years ago. This person was driving along a road one day with his wife by his side, and his family at the back. Another driver, high on drugs, smashes into his car and kills his wife and family, leaving him not only a cripple but also with a nightmare of a memory. So it can really happen to anyone.

But Hector was luckier. After six weeks of floundering about, trying to adjust to his new world, he suddenly starts to see once more. Not by very much, but it certainly uplifted my spirits. Although one eye is still blind, and will probably remain so now, his sight in the other eye has recovered to the extent that he can see reasonably well — although by no means perfectly.

Mossy and Puppy are full of life, and continue to be rather a pain for Hector. In their playfulness, and because of his limited eyesight, he is always on the receiving end of some bumps and bangs when they become over-exuberant. So I have to keep my eye on him all the time. Mealtimes are also difficult as I almost have to hand-feed Hector or he does not get anything. I think the other two are gradually coming around to the idea that there has to be some 'give and take,' as otherwise it can sometimes be bedlam.

At least I do not have to take Hector everywhere on a lead now. Previously, if I did not keep him on a short lead, he would keep hitting anything in his way and, if he did not have black fur coat, he would have been black and blue all over. Something stirred within me when I saw how dependent he was on myself, as Hector had always been a very independent spirit up to that time. It brought home to me how vulnerable we all are, and particularly when one thinks of the man who lost his wife and family. How does one live with something like that, I do not really know myself.

While I was very pleased with the video project undertaken by David and myself, I was not so pleased at the delay in producing the final video-tape. The problem was in the editing of all the material, which requires the use of an editing suite. A costly facility, which I was unable to finance at the time. So I started writing my book in the interim. It's great fun and I am really enjoying it – everyone should write at least one book in their life. I know it will not become a 'best seller', and doubt that I will ever make any money from it, but I did it. Just like I realised eventually my ambition to be a street dancer, even though it was not easy.

Mum is nearly eighty now, and my father is eighty-six. He has been through a rough time recently. When I was in England a while back, my mother told me about a television programme that she had seen, where scientists have reasonable proof that intelligent life exists in other worlds within the universe. "Makes you think about God," she said. Well I think that is what it is all about, really. A lot of things have happened to me in my life, that I could not seem to explain. Sometimes I just gave up, and took the easy way out by watching mundane television, drinking, and not trying to analyse the things that were in my head.

The book has helped me get things clearer about my life and myself. It's not much to write about for, after all, who really wants to know about a street dancer. Although, having said this, some of those whom I have met on the streets - playing their music and performing their 'magic' - are extraordinary people. In my time, I have learnt a lot from them. They have a lifestyle very much like my own.

Going back to the video project, and our inability to finance its editing, a small miracle happened last September. Since I last saw them in their home on the coastal boat in Amsterdam, the Kelly Family have become very successful. When they moved with the boat to Germany, they did not give me their new address and consequently I lost touch with them. So you can imagine my surprise when a telegram arrived in my mailbox, asking that I telephone and go and visit them.

Initially, I was unsure whether I should go. It was four years since we last met and in the meantime the Kelly Family had become famous, which meant that the circumstances of our previous relationship would be changed. But, as you probably will have guessed, I decided to go anyway. When I arrived, they showed me around their new home and the warehouse they were renting. I was amazed to see that there was a computer-editing suite in the middle of the warehouse. It was not long before I told the Family the whole story of our video project, and my unrealised dream of making the video-tape. "We haven't changed really," they said, "the music's changed, but not us. We're just the same." But I am not so sure, because I feel as though I have moved on, and learnt more in my life. But the Kelly Family just said to me "take the editing suite and use it to complete your video." I cannot help but think that God was somewhere behind this opportunity.

We are still working on the editing of the video, which is not yet complete, and I am still writing my book. If you ask me why I am writing it, then it is not to make money. It is simply to tell a story about myself, my emotions and modest ambitions, and how I have travelled life's road in search of my goals.

> "I am a far, far richer man now, for the thought, than I was before the idea of thinking was conceived within me."

All my best wishes,

Stephen.

Three Dogs and a Dancer by Stephen Ward

Chapter 17

Conclusion?

or the Next Rung of the Ladder

To draw to the end of something that has reached a definitive conclusion is, in my opinion, a sad and limiting moment, especially when that something has brought joy and understanding in its conception. Reaching the end of something that, in fact, marks the beginning of something else, due to passing through a door that was never noticed but always open, is revelation, is new birth, in which a new and greater joy and a more poignant definition of understanding is revealed. I have striven, in the pages of this book, to stress the importance of being able to recognize joy and beauty on a level of understanding beyond that which the senses can communicate with us. For it seems to me that we become consumed with the negative forces all around, to the degree that we conform and, in so doing, lose our humanity and the way to the doors that have freely been left open for our entry.

A need to conform to what is fashionable is not necessarily negative, providing thought and decision have accompanied conformity. What is dangerous is when our logic fails in its function, and we step blindly with the crowd into a position where we are manipulated in a game of power.

Three Dogs and a Dancer by Stephen Ward

There used to be a time when young people revered their elders, and respected them for their wisdom based on life's experience. But our world gears its most profitable and marketable products almost exclusively towards the young, who so desire to be fashionable that they conform and accept what is offered them without question. It becomes unfashionable not to be young; and youth becomes exclusive to the cost of all else. Who can therefore blame young people when they reject values and morals set by those who clearly have made no precedent. However, when the same older generation also conform by revering its younger generation, we should appreciate just how far we travelled along the path that leads to a closed door.

In a hard world where pride and 'saving face' are of primary importance, integrity is given a false definition; and corruption, deceit and falseness become a means to status. In this situation, where is the joy, the beauty, the understanding that is realised by those who choose simplicity, honesty and deep-searching experiences in their lives? Have joy and beauty become unfashionable? Has it become unacceptable now to strive towards enlightenment, and seek to find ourselves - without the hindrance of props, profit or prejudice?

How do we pass on to future generations the wealth, treasure and beauty, that is within each of us, if we do not know of its existence? How can we hope to gain the respect of the younger generation when we seek to profit from them using the never-ending conveyor belt of conformity. Those who find true integrity, acquire wisdom and strive to follow their personal beliefs, who found the door open and the light welcoming, are surely non-conformists. Establishing a precedent worthy of consideration by others is a noble action, providing it stimulates individuality and does not command conformity. Man is, by nature, a thinking and rationalising being.

As a dog robbed of its freedom becomes fearful and vicious, so a man becomes angry, frustrated and irrational when robbed of the ability to put his life into perspective within his own environment. Who is the thief, the profiteer in such circumstances.

The influences in our modern world that create unrest and despair, in their subtle ability to produce conformity, are all around us. Profitability and control: no entry, private property, access forbidden, authorised persons only, keep out, stop. A world in which all the doors are closed is indeed a fearful place.

It is natural to 'want' in a world of material values, and to retain it once acquired, thereby causing envy, greed and fear of loss. In a world geared to the spiritual values in all of us, it is also natural to share discoveries about ourselves and our discovered joys. It is natural to give and receive wisdoms without misunderstandings, and seek approval from others for our actions. In so doing we know that we have passed through one door towards another, stepped-up one rung to a higher level where the air is fresh, the view more expansive, the final truth a little bit closer.

During my dance on the streets, I have learnt that some people find my performance and solicitation to be too direct, and are uncomfortable. They react with a behaviour that I initially found to be threatening and intimidating, until I realised there is no danger in standing my ground, providing my message was strong and carried conviction. Nevertheless, it is hard to put oneself in a position of receiving ridicule and, in moments of weakness, to feel the problem is with oneself - paving the way for greater ridicule and eventually moral defeat.

At first, whenever this occurred, I simply stopped dancing, packed-up and left. In so doing, I felt anger, bore a grudge on all youth, and wondered what was happening to our world when culture and communication are made objects of fun. Gradually I was shown another way, to soften and melt, to succumb. Not to ridicule, but to the power within me, that made me understand why my dance provoked affront in certain people, and gave me the will-power to overcome their insults. From then onwards, it surprised me that those ridiculing me, who were invariably isolated by other members of the audience, were loath to depart and wanted to pursue the confrontation to a conclusion. But, given patience, I discovered also they would often quieten down and eventually watch and accept my performance - sometimes even coming forward to make a contribution into my collection box. I would know then that I had reached them spiritually.

After a few years, I became conscious of the infiltration of a deeper message in my street dancing, and a mental tug-of-war developed within myself. I became increasingly aware that my collecting box, with its ability to attract people to place money in it, was starting to be distasteful to me. I needed money to survive, but loathed having to need it. I questioned my priorities, was it the dance and its message, or what went into the collection box? Previously, I had measured the quality of my performances by the amount in the box, and my success was therefore related to money. Now, I started thinking on what I could give in my performance, rather than what I would receive. Yet another rung up the ladder. I began to gauge the quality of my dance by what I received in terms of my own well-being: the power in my movements, conviction in my message, encouragement and applause. These I readily understood, and they quickly overcame the importance of what was placed in the collection box.

I realised the income I derived was merely the 'icing on the cake.' It had finally ceased to be my motivation. I toyed with the idea of occasionally removing the collecting box, and dancing simply for the sheer joy and pleasure that I received from my dance. But I never did so. This was because I felt my dance was more than just a performance designed to amuse or titivate an audience. Lacking the possibility of a two-way communication, the audience might then interpret my dance as a sort of preaching, which was an impression that I did not wish to convey. However, neither did I wish to give the impression that I was clever and so deserved to be rewarded. With so many issues in my mind, I bordered on confusion until it was taken out of my hands by another entity within me - whom I shall call God.

Once this questioning within me was accomplished, I found myself able to react calmly to most situations, and to one that I could no longer shirk. I had always believed that I am here for a purpose, and would have to 'bear my cross' accordingly. But it was a particular experience that showed me, symbolically, that I do indeed receive poignant and relevant messages in return for the message that I impart through my dance.

It was Good Friday in 1996, and I was setting-off for an Easter-weekend tour of Tuscan towns. Starting in Lucca, at my familiar home ground in the Piazza San Michele, I found my usual site occupied by a stall selling plants in support of victims of the AIDS virus. In the world of the dance theatre, I had inevitably seen a number of my friends and colleagues afflicted with this disease, and many had died. Setting-up my dance floor twenty metres in front of the stall, I became aware that my performance had made people turn their backs to the stall, which made me reflect on the miracle of health and strength.

Without these attributes, one's life is severely restricted as indeed my own dance would be. During my performance, I thought of my departed friends and their passion for the dance. I wondered whether they had stepped through another open door, in the final analysis of their life on this earth. I thought of times when I had been physically weak in my life. They had been moments of self-interrogation, of questioning and realizing, of moving forward. While also moments of restriction, they enticed me to doors that were open, waiting patiently for me to step through and into the light.

Inevitably, I thought of the symbolic meaning of Good Friday. Suffering as a means to enlightenment, to awareness, to open doors, to higher rungs - to God. Perhaps for the first time in my life, I saw what Christ had been trying to say to us, and why his message has lived in the hearts of so many for almost two thousand years. At the end of my performance, I felt impelled to offer the contents of my collection box to the stall opposite, for a cause that was both higher and nobler than my own. I did not feel any gratification or enlightenment. Only remorse at my own failings.

The following day I travelled from Lucca to another nearby town. There, among a typical Saturday evening crowd, I laid out my floor, positioned my collection box, put on my ballet shoes, and then commenced my performance. I knew beforehand what might happen, but the over-powering message of the previous day helped focus my thoughts, and equipped me for the situation that later arose. A group of hardened young people surrounded me, and did their utmost to humiliate, degrade and embarrass me during my performance. In despair I thought of Christ on the Cross, and the degradation and humiliation he suffered, which thousands before and since have borne for the sake of ultimate truth and enlightenment. And so, in the eyes of my tormentors, I was made to suffer. But in truth I was some place else. Where I could not be reached by these young people, but only by the one person who approached to give me a note at the end of my performance. Looking into my eyes, he said "thank you, for them."

The next day I moved to another town on Easter Sunday. I

reflected on the last two days, and felt a gladness within me for what I was being shown. The atmosphere within the town was little different from the day before, but there was no mockery or confrontation during my performance from the crowd that gathered round me. Many images crowded into my mind while I danced and I became lost in what I was doing, lost in what I was saying. My emotions of joy, wonder, despair and longing seemed to be on a different plane, in a different dimension. The crowd dispersed at the end of my performance and, as I was rolling up the floor, a group of five teenagers approached and offered to buy me a drink. At first, I declined politely on the grounds that it was hot, and three dogs were still in the camper van. However, eventually I compromised, and accepted their offer being intrigued why they should want to buy me a drink.

The group consisted of four boys and a girl, all from Sicily. They told me they were a rock band, which had just won the quarter final of a national competition to discover new talent. One of the boys told me they had watched my dance, and believed they understood the message I was conveying. It had moved them into speaking to me, to find whether the message they received was the same as I was attempting to give. It was one of the nicest gin and tonic ever offered to me, and I became reconciled with the younger generation. During a long conversation, the group gave me their addresses in Sicily, and told me I would be welcome to visit them anytime. As I pondered over my experiences of the last three days, I thought how rich is life, how very rich, and perhaps there is more to Christ's message than I have hitherto given credence.

As we draw near the end of this final chapter, I would like to share a last thought. This is the first book that I have ever written, the first birth that I have experienced. I have bared my soul in words. If you have been able to enter the world I have described, then you will know that its beauty is without comparison, its revelations unlimited, and its joys unfathomable. Please join me in its discovery. Please share with me its delights and dance with me in its freedom. It is there for all of us. It is calling us. It is us.

So I sit again under a pergola of vines. Three dogs look at me with expectancy in their eyes, and the grass needs cutting to generate some hot water. It is April and buds are swelling. It is a time of anticipation. As one door closes for myself, as I finish this book, so another opens to realise a new beginning. It was always so, and so it will always be. In three years we shall move into a new age in time, and no doubt it has great significance for those who are ruled by time. It has little significance, I feel, for those for whom time is but a step from one place to another within themselves, within their minds. Those who see it as leading to a greater knowledge, accompanied by wisdom, awareness, compassion, fulfillment and understanding. We may be filled with feelings of unity and hope by the arrival of the Millennium, but unless these are also accompanied by enlightenment, I fear they may be short-lived and ultimately meaningless.

In having written this book I have turned a page in my own life. I have been forced to think, analyse, and draw conclusions about issues that were always there, but by which I had never before been confronted. Distractions, which always encircle us, can entice us away from clear thought. In trying to put away these distractions, I have come to know myself better, and find that I am immeasurably richer in knowledge as a result.

Who will join me on my journey? Who will join me in the dance? Who will walk by my side towards the light, that burns, that builds, that molds, that melts, and unites us with God?

Epilogue

It was deeply significant to have met Stephen Ward for the first time on the Day of Liberation, 25th of April 2012. I had parked my car in front of the clock tower of Fiano, discovering the valley from San Martino di Freddana onwards, and was looking for a suitable walk with my dogs. Having caught sight of a man working in the garden with a dog beside him, I thought he might know a nice way nearby. I asked him in Italian and he answered that I should drive up to the cemetery, from where a nice walk into the woods began. I had a second question, if he would allow me to take a picture of the irises in front of his garden door. The gardener agreed and added that there would be more irises in his garden and if I would like to enter. He offered me a cup of tea or a glass of wine, but I refused and told him that my dogs were really waiting eagerly for their walk. *Dogs? How many do you have? May I see them and accompany you to the car?* The gardener took his own dog with him and was very pleased to get to know my three Golden Retrievers named Giacomo, Stella and Étoile. Strangely enough we could not stop talking for another half an hour and I kept in mind that the gardeners' name was Stephen, that he was an artist and ill with cancer, although looking full of energy. When I finally drove up to the cemetery he wanted me to stop at his house to give me something to have his address - it was his dance-DVD. During the walk, which was gorgeous, I reflected on this last half an hour and felt a special freedom and lightness in myself.

We met again after a few days at La Casetta, talking from midday until evening about the deep questions of life and sensing an incredible relationship of both our souls. Now I knew Stephen was a dancer, a profession that often attracts people, although I felt drawn towards him because of his personage and his simple way of living. We both felt deep similarities on the spiritual level, in music, adventures in nature, the joy of writing, collecting and eating "wild food", rising to challenges, not owning a TV-set - and of course our passionate affection for dogs.

For much of the year I live in Salzburg, Austria, but whenever it is possible I love to be in my tiny, modest little house in a mountain-village above Camaiore, Italy, about half an hour-drive north of Fiano. Before leaving for Salzburg again, Stephen came to my little village, bringing a big bunch of his irises in his arms – what a gift! He had told me about the fire in his cabin some months ago, which had burnt down most of his personal belongings and this gave me the idea to give him as a present my CD of Mahler's 2nd Symphony. Obviously I had not the slightest idea what that music meant to Stephen. Back in Austria I got a letter with the most precious words I had ever received: *It has been my* **tremendous** *joy, yesterday evening and* **again** *this morning, to be privileged to relive creative days in my 20's through listening once again to Mahler's 2nd Symphony. There have been certain pieces of music which have arrived and then accompanied me along a sublime stretch of life's' pathway.* **This** *is one of them. I cannot express fully to you in words how I have been transported back to an* **unbelievable** *time, an awakening, in my 20's, to an inner voice. If I die to this life* **tomorrow,** *I will die a happy man, for I know now that all is as it is* **meant to be.** *You gave me so* **very much** *of your beautiful soul...*

I lead the association KIBELLO in Salzburg, where therapy-dog-teams help children in hospital through interventions with dogs, and this work meant I had to organize and work a lot before going back to Tuscany three weeks later. At that time Stephen's illness did not distract him much, so at the end of May we were able to enjoy special parts of Tuscany, the natural wonders in the Apuane Alps, climbing together, but also working in the garden of La Casetta. We felt we were being blessed, and were thankful for it!

A special excursion brought us to Montefegatesi, a village in the Apuane Alps, with a little piazza on top, crowned by a monument of Dante Alighieri. The scenery of the sunset behind the chain of the high mountains without anyone else but Stephen, me and the dogs was a special gift. I felt the wish to dance and asked Stephen to make music. He started to sing Beethoven's' "Ode an die Freude" from the 9th symphony.

In summer 2012 I travelled a lot between Tuscany and Austria. I remember so well an evening in July; Belgian friends had come to visit Stephen, and I invited them all to my little house at Greppolungo. One of them played the accordion at the piazza there and some little girls of the village, one being a ballet-pupil, started to dance, integrating also our dogs by touching them now and then. Some adult inhabitants of Greppolungo came to watch too and it was a most pleasant atmosphere. Stephen and I were sitting on the warm stones on the edge of the piazza, chuckling with joy!

Stephen showed me lovely places in nature and I remember an unforgettable trip, where he guided me in the direction of Passo di Abetone. Dark-green water flowing in a deep canyon was an amazing sight, but when Stephen took out the DVD-recorder and started his dance-DVD I realized that we stood on the same place this scene of his film had been taken. *Just here on this rock Antonio played Debussy,* Stephen explained *and over there is the place where I performed my dance in the water.* I really was overwhelmed. Together we crossed rivers and climbed up rocky areas. I still was some metres above him when he said I should jump into his arms. Not hesitating a second I jumped, being full of trust. Stephen caught me safely, laughed and said: *In former times I often caught dancers, but you are now the first one for many years jumping into my arms.* And he added: *I have shown*

this place to some who are younger than you, but none of them managed all the obstacles as you did —congratulations! You are looking like an excited child.
Stephen spoilt me often by cooking nice food and as he had several eating- places in his garden, we enjoyed the change. I remember a special warm meal long after midnight, feeling so free, so similar to students' times. We always celebrated our meals and enjoyed eating very slowly, finishing sometimes after hours. And now and then Stephen took me out to a nice restaurant, where he never allowed me to pay.

My crazy dancer was not only fond of Migie, his own dog, but also of my gang. His favorite one was Giacomo, who is sometimes a bit a rascal. All our four dogs were born in the same year, 2004 and accept each other very well.

When I left Tuscany again at the end of August, Stephen lifted me up with his arms, proving that he still had strength in his body. For the next weeks we could stay in contact only through writing letters, as Stephen had no mobile phone. In the last September-days I got the message through friends that Stephens' condition had changed for the worse. He needed morphine and after a short stay in Lucca Hospital had been brought to Hospice San Cataldo. It seemed an incredible challenge for me not to go to Tuscany immediately, but Stephen did not want me to come before a special event at Salzburg on San Francis Day (4th of October) had taken place – it was the annual divine service with a lot of children together with all the KIBELLO-dogs in San Francis-church and Stephen knew I would be needed there. Meeting again on October 5 at Hospice San Cataldo near Lucca brought more tears of joy than sadness to both of us. From that day on Stephen's dog Migie was staying with me and my "la banda" , so I could bring her into Stephen's room daily and whenever he felt a bit better, we made little trips to the seaside, to Lago di Massaciúccoli or just into a bar for a glass of wine.

On October 6 a stage was built up in front of the Hospice for an autumn-festival. What a surprise for me to watch Stephen dancing for the first time in my life! Edward Elgar's Nimrod from the Enigma-Variations he had chosen for the music and he gathered all his strength. Being a patient of the Hospice with a cannula in his right arm, he touched not only me, but everybody watching. His special language in the expression of his dance seemed to be on a divine level and I was so thankful to Stephen and our Guide for it! Lots of friends from many countries came to visit Stephen in October and he enjoyed it. When his 62nd birthday approached, we both decided to organize a little party at Chris Redsell's house, a very close friend of Stephen for decades. This celebration brought hours of delight in a circle of wonderful people. Tears of joy in Stephens' eyes when my dog Stella brought the dance-booklet in her mouth which I had created together with a friend from the pictures of the autumn-festival at San Cataldo.

After a talk with his doctor at the Hospice Stephen longed to have a try going back to La Casetta with the help of a nurse once a week and a woman who came daily for one hour for cleaning and other necessities. For some more days I joined him at his home and we both felt that we had become very close. At the beginning of November I had to go back to Salzburg to organize important work for KIBELLO, but it tore my heart apart to leave Stephen. This farewell had been a heartbreakingly sad one; both not knowing what might happen in the next ten days. I handed over all our fears into God's hands and prayed He might protect and guide Stephen.

When I returned on November 14 Stephen had been brought to Hospice San Cataldo again. I found him sitting in the rose-garden. Seeing and feeling each other again caused an enormous stream of tears, our hugging was nearly endless und our joy of being together overwhelming. When I asked him if he could imagine coming to Salzburg with me, there was suddenly a light in his eyes and he wanted to know if we could go immediately. After a few telephone calls with the oncological department at the hospital in Salzburg I told Stephen that it needed just two days to organize everything and to collect his personal things from La Casetta. We arranged to leave San Cataldo on Saturday, 9.00 a.m. – at 7.00 I got an SMS from Stephen *"I am ready when you are"*. My car was packed up to the top and I had tried to make it as comfortable as possible for Stephen lying on the bench of the VW-bus, but there were four big dogs on board too and quite some luggage. Gianluca, a good friend, wanted to come with us, but there was absolutely no space left. Stephen was in such a good mood, although we both knew it would be a long journey of about ten hours. We got enough medication for the trip from the Hospice, I had cooked a warm soup for provisions and equipped with our confidence in God we left Tuscany.

Arriving at Salzburg, late evening, Stephen was more than exhausted. Together, step by step, we managed to reach the first floor of my house with a lot of thankfulness in our hearts. On the next day Stephen was welcomed at Salzburg hospital in a most friendly way and he seemed much relieved. Some examinations had to be done to gain more information about the parts where metastasis had grown and to find the right painkiller. He laughed and waved watching the KIBELLO-teams with the little patients of the psychosomatic ward just in front of his hospital-window on the following day. As often as possible I accompanied him to examinations; the different departments of the hospital worked together in a wonderful way and Stephen fully agreed to start with the first chemotherapy.

I sent out emails dictated by Stephen to his family and his friends and visited him daily, mostly with Migie. On our walks in the park of the hospital we must have given the impression of a most fortune and crazy couple – Stephen sitting in a wheelchair being pushed by me, holding Migie's leash in his hand, smiling, laughing.

I remember a man asking if he might take a picture of the three of us – what did we radiate?

Stephen and I tried to live the **present moment fully** and nothing around us was important any more. At the end of November Stephen came home with effective painkillers against his back pains and some more medication. He walked around the house, cooked his breakfast himself, we visited the training of the Salzburg wheelchair-dancers and went up the snow-covered mountains in the car to enjoy the loveliest view on the Austrian Alps. Friends of mine and my sister Elizabeth came to make music with guitar and transverse flute, we all sang together and Stephen joined in. And some days later he started to dance again and I took pictures. Despite his illness there was an expression on his face and a tension in his body that showed his incredible joy of dancing! Outside there was a lot of snow and icy temperatures, but in the house a great warmth. And an intense atmosphere of love and trust. Maria, the nurse from the Mobile Hospice Team and Ute, the doctor, said they had known many patients in their lives, but never had felt such a special loving atmosphere.

The next appointment in hospital mid-December was for laying a port to make it easier for infusions or medications to enter the body. Although there had been some little complications after this operation, the second part of the chemotherapy was planned. Shortly before Christmas Stephen decided not to continue the chemotherapy. It was a very sudden decision. I tried to listen to my heart which told me not to persuade but accept, for it was Stephens' decision over his life. We went home with the intension to make the best out of what was coming towards us.

One last time we went up the snowy mountains again and Stephen watched the dogs playing and rolling in lots of snow. Then Christmas approached. When Stephen had talked in October that it would be wonderful spending Christmas together, I not even had dared to dream about it. What richness in our simple way of celebrating our Christmas Eve! There was a deep inner peace and the amazement of God's miracle, as well as the consciousness that it would be our first and our last Christmas in common on this earth. Just a natural pine tree with real red candles, no electric lights and the beautiful Händel-aria on CD from Rinaldo "Lascia ch'io pianga" sung by Renate Frank-Reinecke, a friend and opera-singer from Berlin. No one else but Stephen and me and our four dogs, being blessed by our Lord. Each of us had written a letter to the other one as a Christmas gift – our last letters. Our confidence was imperturbable, without limits, there was no fear whatever would come. Stephens' illness stayed in the background. What counted was our deep, wonderful love.

When Stephen could not get up any more from his bed, he motivated me to dance for him and I chose the music from Giacomo Puccinis Preludio Sinfonico. I still hear him applauding after my dance and he asked me to dance for him every evening. While dancing I sometimes took his arms and integrated this wonderful dancer into my non-professional dance. And Stephen smiled his special smile. In his last weeks his face had an expression of an intense inner beauty. A strong similarity to the expression of Jesus' face when nailed to the cross. The day before his death on January 27, 2013, his left arm was still in dance-movements. **Dance** had been his **life.**

We often prayed together, free prayers out of our hearts, and also in these last weeks of Stephen's life there was a lot of thankfulness. Father Alexander, a Franciscan priest and spiritual friend of mine came to pray with us, to bless us, to anoint Stephen. Since having left Tuscany Stephen wore my little Franciscan wooden cross around his neck. Five days before his death he took it off and put it around my neck again: *May HE bless you – always.*

My last gift for Stephen was giving him the possibility to die at home in peace. Stephens' last written words are: *I am so grateful to God that he brought us together in* **unconditional love**.

Now, more than a year after Stephen's death, I still feel connected to him on a higher level of consciousness, and I am never surprised when he enters my dreams. I am dancing often, daily, sometimes with tears in my eyes, often filled with great joy. My dance seems a reaching-out of my hands, my body and my innermost feelings towards Stephen's spirit and Stephen's soul. God has written the same melody into our hearts and it is a melody of joy and inner peace.

The intensity of these nine months together granted to us is still very present; it has not changed since Stephens' body has left. Now and then I sense a sign from Stephen, as he always has been also an artist of surprises. One is his little red rose-tree from La Casetta, growing now on my terrace in Salzburg. It has stayed in bloom since Gianluca gave it to me in spring 2013. And this bloom continued all summer, autumn and even winter, outside in cold temperatures and snow. Now spring approaches and it continues unchanged, being in full bloom. Stephen's deep red roses.

Nannerl Wenger, March, 2014

Three Dogs and a Dancer by Stephen Ward

Migie and the roses

Three Dogs and a Dancer by Stephen Ward

Three Dogs and a Dancer by Stephen Ward

Printed in Great Britain
by Amazon